CENSORSHIP

LIBRARY IN A BOOK

CENSORSHIP

Gail Blasser Riley

Facts On File, Inc.

To my children, Rachel, Jillian, and James,
who are the summers and springs of my life.

"You can muffle the drum, and you can loosen the strings of the lyre,
but who shall command the skylark not to sing?"
—Albert Camus

CENSORSHIP

Facts On File, Inc.
11 Penn Plaza
New York NY 10001

Library of Congress Cataloging-in-Publication Data

Riley, Gail Blasser.
  Censorship / Gail Blasser Riley.
    p.   cm.—(Library in a book)
  Includes bibliographical references (p.) and index.
  ISBN 0-8160-3373-0
  1. Censorship—United States. I. Title. II. Series.
Z658.U5R55 1997
363.3'1—dc 21   97-8382

Facts On File books are available at special discounts when purchased in bulk quantities for businesses, associations, institutions or sales promotions. Please call our Special Sales Department in New York at 212/967-8800 or 800/322-8755.

You can find Facts On File on the World Wide Web at http://www.factsonfile.com

Text design by Ron Monteleone
Cover design by Nadia Furlan Lorbek

Printed in the United States of America

MP FOF 10 9 8 7 6 5 4 3 2 1

This book is printed on acid-free paper.

CONTENTS

PART I

OVERVIEW OF THE TOPIC

CHAPTER 1

THE HISTORY OF CENSORSHIP

In 1977, a Nazi group planned a demonstration in Skokie, Illinois, a town of primarily Jewish population. The citizens of Skokie attempted to stop the demonstration; they formulated an intricate application process the Nazis would be required to follow in order to obtain a license to demonstrate. The legal ruling came down in favor of the Nazis; the demonstration was allowed.

In 1990, musical rap group 2 Live Crew released As Nasty as They Wanna Be, *a sexually explicit album which many found vile and offensive. A Florida prosecutor filed obscenity charges; members of the group were arrested for obscenity during a performance. Shop owners across the country pulled the music from their shelves.*

In 1994, in a suburb of Houston, Texas, a school board candidate distributed brochures stating her platform. If elected, she promised to remove from the district's schools those books that mentioned sexuality, AIDS, and other topics she felt were not appropriate for junior and senior high school students. She won the election.

Censorship, the restriction of expression, is at the heart of each of these cases. Many think censorship issues revolve only around freedom of speech; however, censorship encompasses a much wider range. Forms of expression addressed in censorship issues include spoken and printed words, photographs, paintings, and other types of visual art, as well as symbolic speech, such as armbands and flag burning.

While some feel that freedom of expression should be absolute, others believe that absolute freedom of expression can infringe upon protection of the individual or the government. Ongoing debates over censorship issues rage daily. For example, some claim that if the government is allowed to choose when to censor, people will never be truly free; that people will be oppressed because they will be unable to express themselves without fear of reprisal. Some liken this atmosphere to one in which victims' rights are stressed and criminals' rights are stripped.

Conversely, those who believe that absolute freedom of expression can infringe upon protection of the individual or the government claim that absolute freedom of expression can require the government to disclose information regarding critical weapons strategies—or that individuals can become targets of hate speech when freedom of expression is absolute.

Censorship has existed for centuries. Today's censorship debates are generally grounded in the First Amendment to the United States Constitution: "Congress shall make no law . . . abridging the freedom of speech, or of the press . . ." In cases dealing with the First Amendment, the United States Supreme Court has ruled that censorship is permissible only in certain limited situations, generally when such censorship is intended to protect individuals or national security.

Ancient Greece has gone down in the annals of history as a progressive, freedom-loving society; however, the philosopher Socrates put Greek principles of freedom to a resolute test around 400 B.C.E. Socrates questioned many things, including the government, religion, and his society at large. Powerless to censor Socrates for questioning and criticizing, Athenians charged him with corrupting the children and offending the gods. Such charges have incited public ire and been successfully prosecuted throughout history.

Socrates defended himself, saying that he had never meant to offend gods or corrupt youths, that his ultimate goal was only to seek the truth. Socrates' defense fell on deaf ears, and he was sentenced to death. Though he might have been able to escape, Socrates held firm in his conviction to die for the right of free speech, and in 399 B.C.E., after drinking hemlock, a poison, at the hands of his executioners, he gave his life for his principles.

As centuries progressed, censorship continued to be a viable, powerful force. It created a veil of silence that permitted political and religious leaders to exercise an unyielding freedom. As their freedom increased, the freedom of expression for others diminished.

In 213 B.C.E., at the beginning of the Qin dynasty, new Chinese Emperor Shi Huang Ti established a central government and did away with local states. He ordered the construction of the Great Wall of China to halt enemies. Additionally, he ordered the destruction of virtually all books. Only those works dealing with agriculture and other similar practical matters, such as medicine, were to be spared. The emperor wanted to record a new history for his country commencing with his rule. Though an air of compliance prevailed, many of the books ordered destroyed were secreted away and were pulled from their hiding places during later dynasties.

Among the many accomplishments of the philosopher Confucius (circa 500 B.C.E.) were the moral principles he advanced. A great deal of Confucius' work was burned following Shi Huang Ti's orders. Following Shi Huang Ti's rule, however, the Han Dynasty (202 B.C.E. to 220 C.E.) adopted Confucianism as the philosophical foundation for governing the people. Toward the end of the Han dynasty, Buddhism set down strong roots. The arts and education began to flourish in China.

Around the world, freedom of expression was increasingly restricted. Around the time of Socrates, in 387 B.C.E., Homer's *The Odyssey* fell victim to the censors in Greece. *The Odyssey*, an epic poem, established the foundation for Greek culture and education for the duration of the classical age; Plato advised that the work be edited and purged for younger readers. By 35 C.E., Emperor Caligula in Rome worked to ban the poem because it contradicted the philosophies of autocratic Roman rule.

In 8 C.E. Ovid was banished to Tomi, a Greek town, by Roman Emperor Augustus for having written "Ars Amatoria" ("The Art of Love") and other offenses. This was only the beginning of censorship of Ovid's work, which continued to be banned through the Middle Ages and beyond.

In Europe, in 321, Arius, the presbyter of Alexandria, was excommunicated. His "Thaleia" was celebrated through song by workers and travelers. This poetic verse advanced a new philosophical approach to the New Testament; the work characterized Christ as a secondary deity, a perfect creature on the earth. In 325, Arius was exiled, and "Thaleia" became the first writing that the Catholic church banned.

Certainly, the Bible comes to the forefront as one of the most frequently banned or expurgated works in the world. For example, in 553 in Italy, Emperor Justinian ordered that only the Greek and Latin versions of the Bible be used, and banned the *Midrash*. (He still allowed the Hebrew Old Testament.)

In 1059, in Europe, the Christian Church banned and began burning the works of Peter Abelard. Abelard, a theologist, examined and worked to reconcile the Bible, the works of Aristotle—and reason—with faith.

By the thirteenth century, the prefered form of government was a monarchy, and tyrannical governments were common. And though the fight for freedom of expression had met with opposition at virtually every turn, it had certainly not died, especially in England, where some of the earliest laws protecting minor freedoms of speech were developed.

In 1215, King John of England was under attack by his people, particularly the nobility. King John had abused his power, and the nobility brought pressure to bear in order to right these abuses. A rebellion was imminent. In order to quell the growing rebellion, King John signed the Magna Carta, a document that acknowledged the rights of nobility and stated that a king did not have the power to proceed without regard for these rights. Still, many actions and much speech remained crimes. Criticizing the royal family or having the audacity to "imagine" the death of the king could result in serious punishment.

In 1352, the British Parliament passed a new law dealing with treason. This law limited the acts that would qualify as treason, thereby eliminating a number of crimes. The Magna Carta and the antitreason law of 1352 were tiny steps toward freedom of expression in Great Britain.

But the road ahead was a long one. In 1579, a British citizen, John Stubbs, publicly opposed the impending marriage of Queen Elizabeth I to a Frenchman. Stubbs paid for this crime with his right hand, which was promptly severed by British officials. Not only was Stubbs convicted of a crime; his attorney was jailed for exercising the boldness to defend Stubbs in court.

In 1593, Queen Elizabeth I forbade debate on the floor of Parliament, proclaiming that privilege of speech existed, " . . . but that your privilege is Aye or No." The Queen permitted the right to vote, but would not allow debate. King James I continued the prohibition against debate—on the floor of Parliament, in homes, and on the streets. During King James's rule, citizens were ordered to report others who spoke about public affairs. Anyone neglecting to report according to the law was also guilty of a crime.

Members of Parliament pressed forward vigorously to gain the right to debate on the Parliament floor and in 1689, this right was granted. The right to discuss public issues extended only to members of Parliament, however, and not to other citizens, a policy which, ironically, Parliament endorsed.

While members of Parliament pressed for freedom in Britain, in Italy Galileo was denied his intellectual freedom rights. In 1632, Galileo printed his scientific findings, against the admonition of the Church, that the earth is not the center of the universe. He stated that the earth, and other planets, revolve around the sun. Galileo was arrested and threatened with torture if he did not disavow his findings. Before a large crowd, he kneeled and stated that his findings were erroneous and foolish.

In 1636, censorship remained powerful. When William Prynne published a book that criticized the theater, he landed in jail with a life sentence—and no ears! His ears were cut off as part of his punishment. King Charles I liked the theater and the queen was an amateur actress, thus Prynne's book was considered an assault on the royal couple.

By the beginning of the sixteenth century, the movable-type printing press was in wide use. Foreseeing the potential problems from wide dissemination of the printed word, government and church officials promulgated a prior restraint law, which required people to obtain a license before printing any material. Church and state officials issued the licenses and scrutinized material to be published. This ensured that no literature critical of government or religion was dispersed.

During the sixteenth and seventeenth centuries, those arrested for printing material in England without a license found themselves before the Star Chamber. The Star Chamber was a quasi-judicial body prone to forceful interrogation; its membership was made up of advisers to the king. Those who appeared before the Chamber were not permitted the benefit of a jury. And the right against self-incrimination (which later became law in the Fifth Amendment to the United States Constitution) was virtually unheard of, until John Lilburne came before the Chamber and asserted his right not to incriminate himself. (Lilburne was held in prison for four years until the English government declared his treatment illegal.)

But for most who appeared before the Chamber, punishment was swift and harsh. Many writers, printers, and publishers felt the Chamber's wrath until it was abolished in 1641.

But the spirit of Socrates lived on; the human spirit would not be oppressed. Many people published their own pamphlets without licenses. By the seventeenth century, these unlicensed pamphlets filled Great Britain. Pamphlets encouraged spirited discussions and reading became an important skill to acquire because citizens wanted to be able to take part in the debates and discussions.

The poet John Milton is one of the best-known authors of unlicensed pamphlets. Milton was strongly opposed to the licensing system. Through his "Aeropagitica" (1644) and other works, he advocated freedom of the press—in direct opposition to licensing and other stringent censorship methods by Parliament. Milton presented the idea that people tend to be comfortable with that which is known and uncomfortable with that which is unknown—thus they deem new ideas false and reject them. People should be allowed to hear both true and false information, Milton reasoned, so they can form their own opinions. Milton held that new ideas were not to be feared. In "Aeropagitica," Milton wrote, "Where there is much desire to learn there of necessity will be much arguing, much writing, many opinions; for opinion in good men is but knowledge in the making." Though citizens flocked to read and discuss Milton's pamphlets and ideas, his position had little impact on Great Britain's policies. The licensing practice remained until the middle of the seventeenth century.

Across the Atlantic, in the British colonies in America, political debate grew heated. In 1721 James Franklin was the publisher of the *New-England Courant*. In the *Courant*, James mocked public officials and often satirized the statements of Puritan religious leaders. In one article, he asserted that the government had failed to respond firmly to a pirate raid. James Franklin was forced to appear before the Royal Council. He was held in contempt and incarcerated, and was finally freed from prison when he promised to stop publishing pamphlets and newspapers. Upon his release, he turned his newspaper over to his younger brother, Benjamin.

Benjamin Franklin invited journalist Thomas Paine to come to Philadelphia from England. By the mid-1770s, pamphleteers who called for freedom and independence had become quite active, and Thomas Paine was one of the best-known. Paine was among the first who publicly advocated a declaration of independence from England by the colonies.

In his "Common Sense" pamphlet, Paine advanced the cause of independence, writing, "Until an independence is declared, the continent will feel itself like a man who continues putting off some unpleasant business from day to day, yet knows it must be done." The pamphlet was enormously popular and was instrumental in starting the American Revolution.

In 1783, the American Revolution came to an end—and a new country, promising new rights, was born. Though some colonists sought only freedoms identical to those of the British, others wanted a good deal more. James Madison abhorred the British system that silenced government criticism. Madison and his colleague Thomas Jefferson had definite goals in mind: the new country should permit the exchange of ideas without governmental interference, and citizens should be free to express opinions about their leaders and the laws these leaders promulgated. It was in such an atmosphere that the Declaration of Independence was born.

Jefferson directed the committee that readied the Declaration of Independence, and served as its primary author. He once stated, "The people are the only censors of their government." Madison had worked with the Virginia Independence Committee. Both Jefferson and Madison had been influenced by the Enlightenment, an eighteenth century intellectual movement that promoted nonspiritual views based on human understanding, natural rights, and reason.

In 1787, the Constitutional Convention upheld the ideal of freedom of thought and exchange of ideas. It eliminated most of the acts considered treason under British law. Because a number of states felt that the Constitution did not adequately define the protections afforded to citizens under the law, however, not all states ratified the Constitution. This was one reason why Congress drafted the Bill of Rights, the first ten amendments to the Constitution. Another was the viewpoint espoused by Thomas Jefferson in a 1787 letter to James Madison. Jefferson detailed his support of religious freedom; he also discussed his concern over freedom of speech and of the press. Madison was not as enthusiastic about these freedoms as Jefferson. Of the dozens of amendments proposed, twelve were presented for addition to the Constitution. Of these twelve, only ten were approved.

The History of Censorship

The First Amendment to the United States Constitution created a framework for free speech that would become a cornerstone of liberty in the United States of America. It stated, "Congress shall make no law . . . abridging the freedom of speech, or of the press."

When the First Amendment was enacted, many felt that its purpose and intent were quite clear. As is often the case with statutes, however, citizens learned that the First Amendment was open to interpretation.

A prime challenge lay in the John Peter Zenger case. Zenger was a German immigrant who published the *New-York Weekly Journal*. He was arrested for seditious libel and jailed for several months awaiting trial after printing a criticism of New York Governor Cosby. Neither the editor nor the writer was placed on trial.

When Zenger was tried in 1735, the jury was asked to find only whether he had printed the material in question. Jurors were told that it was then up to the judge to decide whether libel existed. (The judge had been chosen by Governor Cosby.)

Truth had not yet been legally established as a defense to libel. Although the jurors had been told to disregard the question of whether the material was true and to consider only whether Zenger had printed the material, Andrew Hamilton, Zenger's lawyer, still chose to plead the truth of the criticism as a defense; Zenger was acquitted. Historically, some view Zenger's acquittal as a major victory against prior restraint. Other historians, however, believe that Zenger's acquittal arose out of the jurors' sympathetic loathing of the governor, rather than out of any great legal epiphany.

Within a decade of its having been adopted, the First Amendment again faced a major challenge, one that arose from the political climate at the time. The two major political parties, the Federalists and the Republicans, had very different ideas about the way the United States should be run. Because the electoral procedure required that the claimant of the second-highest number of votes in the presidential election become vice president, a Federalist, John Adams, became president and a Republican, Thomas Jefferson, became vice president.

The difference in party affiliation led to predictable problems. Adams and Jefferson held divergent views on government matters, and when the country became involved in an undeclared war against France in 1798, political accusations ran rampant. The Federalists charged that the Republicans were taking up the cause of the French. With an eye toward the upcoming election of 1800, Jefferson's supporters began stringent verbal and written attacks against the Federalists. In evaluating the First Amendment and keeping their own preservation in mind, Federalists concluded that the Amendment did not permit the right to promulgate lies about government leaders.

Censorship

In the late 1700s, President John Adams feared the views of French revolutionaries, as well as the views of their supporters in the United States. The country was plagued by political unrest and seemed destined for war with France. Adams wished to silence his political opposition. Hence, the Sedition Act of 1798 was born—only seven years after the Bill of Rights had become part of the Constitution. The Federalists claimed that foreign agents had tipped them off to a conspiracy against the United States. Using this claim as the basis of their argument, the Federalists influenced Congress to pass four statutes. Three of the laws centered on foreigners and provided for their confinement or deportation in the event of war; however, the fourth provision gave the government the right to fine and jail those who made malicious statements in writing or speech about the government "with intent to defame" or with intent to "excite against the government the hatred of the people." Federalists reasoned that the Sedition Act did not violate First Amendment rights as it did not prevent "reasonable" speech, but only false, malicious statements. Federalists stressed that in contrast to licensing the Sedition Act did not involve any prior restraint and did not require prior approval of speech by the government.

Opponents of the Sedition Act found these arguments unpersuasive. They concerned themselves with who would judge "false" and "malicious" speech. Since the government that sought to protect itself would decide what was false and malicious, it was not difficult to predict the outcome of any charges brought under the Sedition Act. Citizens would be jailed or fined merely for exercising their First Amendment rights.

The Sedition Act passed over strong opposition, and under its provisions many Americans were fined or jailed for expressing their opinions freely. Among them were twenty-four editors of a pro-Republican newspaper, as well as Republican Congressman Matthew Lyon. Lyon was jailed for four months and fined $1,000 for having criticized the government for its "ridiculous pomp, foolish adulation and selfish avarice . . ."

In 1801, the Sedition Act lapsed. By that time, Thomas Jefferson had been elected president of the United States. Given his passion for First Amendment rights, Jefferson's decision not to renew the Sedition Act came as no surprise, nor did his decision to pardon all those convicted of offenses under it.

Divisiveness between the Federalists and Republicans was further illustrated when Federalist Supreme Court Justice Samuel Chase was charged in 1804 with asserting seditious, libelous claims against the Jefferson administration. Subsequent to impeachment, the Senate tried and acquitted Chase.

James Madison followed Jefferson as president. His steadfast belief in the First Amendment right of free speech was seriously challenged during the War of 1812, when political enemies criticized his wartime actions. Disregarding advice from others, as well as merciless personal attacks, Madison did not waver in his support of the First Amendment.

During the 1800s, many Europeans were growing increasingly dissatisfied with the repression under which they lived. Not only were many born into poverty, but their governments dictated what they could read and say. Many thousands fled to the freedom and opportunity of the United States. By 1833, the number of newspapers in the United States had grown to more than 1,200 and the freedom of the press was once again in the spotlight. It was then that Benjamin Day set about publishing the first penny newspaper, the *New York Sun*. The *Sun* sold for only a cent and reported on current events, politics, and police activities, which had never before been covered on a regular basis by a newspaper in the United States. The *Sun*'s success spawned competitors, and the penny newspaper began to thrive.

Other newspapers included the *New York Herald*, the *New York Tribune*, founded by Horace Greeley, and the *New York Times*. By the late nineteenth century, industrialization had led to the growth of bustling metropolitan centers. Scores of daily newspapers rose to meet the demand for news.

So many papers appeared on the competitive news scene that "yellow journalism," a form of sensational reporting designed to capture readers' attention, spread through the newspaper industry. This irresponsible reporting provided gossip, detailed horrific crime, and spewed spicy scandal. Yellow journalism gained its moniker from the yellow ink used in the comic sections of the *New York Journal* and the *New York World* as part of the papers' pointed rivalry. The battle reached its pinnacle in the 1890s just prior to the Spanish-American War, when *New York Journal* and *New York World* editors learned that reports of unconscionable acts by the Spanish military in Cuba garnered readership.

Yellow journalism clearly indicated the freedom of expression permitted to the press. Ultimately, it was newspaper publishers themselves who, in recognition of the importance of truth and responsibility in reporting, changed the face of journalism. Now newspapers gained their funds through quality stories and competitive pricing. Adolph S. Ochs became the *New York Times* publisher and showed his dedication to clean journalism through the slogan "All the news that's fit to print." By the mid-twentieth century, yellow journalism had significantly diminished.

In 1925—in response to yellow journalism—the Minnesota legislature passed the Public Nuisance Abatement Law, which came to be known as the Minnesota Gag Law. This law allowed a judge, without benefit of a jury, to halt newspaper publication upon a decision that newspaper material was "malicious, scandalous, and defamatory." The Gag Law was applied in the case of *Near v. State of Minnesota*. The *Near* case focused on a Minneapolis newspaper that often published heavily anti-Semitic articles. One stated,

Censorship

"Practically every vendor of vile hooch, every owner of a moonshine still, every snake-faced gangster and embryonic egg in the Twin Cities is a JEW . . . Whereupon I have withdrawn all allegiance to anything with a hook nose that eats herring . . . it was . . . a Jew who boasted that he held the chief of police of Minneapolis in his hand—had bought and paid for him."

The defendant in the case did not try to justify his articles. He stated that the Gag Law was unconstitutional because it allowed prior restraint, that is, the right to review material before it was printed. The lower court ruled against the defendant; however, the Supreme Court reversed the decision, stating that such prior restraint was unacceptable, that remedies existed to address the issue after the wrongdoing.

Few freedom of speech debates arose for a century after James Madison's presidency. But the onset of World War I caused a dramatic change in the government's laissez-faire free speech policies. Officials grew concerned that citizens' growing opposition to the government's draft policies, which was sometimes supported from outside of the United States, could weaken the armed services to the point of collapse. Hence, it was feared that the United States would not be able to fight the war effectively.

In response to this concern, Congress enacted the Espionage Act of 1917. The act assessed criminal penalties for making or conveying false reports with the intention of interfering with the operation or success of the military or naval forces of the United States and for promoting the cause of enemies of the United States. Criminal sanctions were also mandated for displaying disloyalty or disobedience to the armed forces and for obstructing recruiting. Any written material that violated the act was barred from the mails. Additionally, the act set out penalties for obtaining or communicating national defense information.

Subsequent to the Espionage Act becoming law, Charles Schenk supervised the printing and mailing of more than 15,000 leaflets that encouraged those registered with draft boards not to submit to the draft. In "impassioned language," the leaflets advised Americans of the "wrongs" of the draft, and stated that anyone refusing to recognize the right to oppose the draft was guilty of violating the United States Constitution. Federal agents arrested Schenk; he was convicted in the lower court and appealed his case to the Supreme Court of the United States, stating that his First Amendment rights had been violated. Schenk's case was the first major censorship case to come before the Supreme Court. In a unanimous decision, the justices upheld the Espionage Act of 1917.

Justice Oliver Wendell Holmes enunciated the now-famous "clear and present danger test." He drew a distinction between wartime and peacetime, stating that the speech in Schenk's pamphlet would have been constitutionally protected during "ordinary times." He stated: "When a nation is at war many things that might be said in time of peace are such a hindrance to its effort that their utterance will not be endured so long as men fight . . . no Court could regard them as protected by any constitutional right."

He went on to state, "The question in every case is whether the words used are used in such circumstances and are of such a nature as to create a clear and present danger that they will bring about the substantive evils that Congress has a right to prevent." Holmes went on to explain that it was not necessary to prove that the pamphlet had, in fact, deterred men from joining the armed forces. It was enough to show a conspiracy to obstruct existed. Holmes stated that freedom of speech does not give anyone the right to stand in a crowded theater and yell, "Fire!"

A debate began to brew across the country. While some opposed the Espionage Act, many others felt that it did not go far enough. They wanted a wider range of crimes designated, as well as more stringent penalties. They promoted this position cloaked in the guise of patriotism.

In response to the cry for more stringent measures against any antiwar sentiment, Congress enacted the Sedition Act of 1918. Reminiscent of its 1798 counterpart, this act stated that it was crime to communicate disloyal or profane comments—about the government, flag, or uniforms—through speech, print, or publication. Displaying any support for a country at war with the United States was also a crime.

Under the Sedition Act of 1918, thousands of Americans were sentenced by their peers, whose passionate, misguided patriotism ran like a train out of control. Americans found themselves imprisoned for making such idle comments as suggesting that the United States raise taxes rather than sell war bonds, and those who merely discussed their opinions about the war in public places could find themselves in a courtroom. One man even landed in jail for expressing his own opinion in his own home—he was arrested on the strength of an affidavit sworn out by fellow Americans who had stopped by his farmhouse when they ran out of gas!

As the runaway train claimed the civil liberties of more and more Americans, free speech issues again began to rise to the forefront. By 1919, the United States was caught in the grip of the "red scare," when the fear of communism stole reason from many. People were arrested because they "looked" like Communists or because they made casual comments about Russia. When a man was shot because he refused to stand for the "Star-Spangled Banner," people cheered for the murderer. In response to all this, the American Civil Liberties Union (ACLU) was founded in 1925. Its members represented many of those accused during the red scare.

Another scare arose in the late 1940s and early 1950s, when it was feared that Communists had found their way into positions of influence across the country. Some Americans were terrified. The House Un-American Activities

Committee (HUAC) investigated musicians, actors, politicians, academicians—anyone in an influential position. People were afraid to speak, not knowing how their comments might be interpreted. Many lost their jobs, their lives destroyed in the wake of innocent comments—or no comments at all.

Since the 1950s, many more censorship issues have arrived at the United States Supreme Court. Myriad others have not been heard in the judicial forum but have been catalysts to decades of debate and activism. This chapter provides an overview of censorship. The following sections examine specific censorship issues and their backgrounds.

UNPROTECTED SPEECH

The First Amendment provides for freedom of speech and press; however, the United States Supreme Court has determined that not all types of expression are protected under the First Amendment. Obscenity, discussed in detail later in this chapter, is not a protected form of expression. "Fighting words," those words that incite imminent hostile reaction, are also unprotected. For example, in a riot setting where an activist used abusive language to a police officer (*Chaplinsky v. New Hampshire*), the words were considered "fighting words" and so were not protected. Libel, the defamation of another, is also an unprotected form of expression. Truth is an absolute defense to libel.

The Supreme Court has heard decades of cases and has ruled, fine-tuned, and elaborated on a wide variety of censorship issues. A representative sampling of cases is included in chapter 3.

OBSCENITY AND PORNOGRAPHY

Content regarding sexual activity—whether presented through the medium of speech, print, television, film, or radio—has always created cavernous divides between people. Moral and religious issues loom large in debates; equally represented are civil liberties issues.

In legal terms, obscenity and pornography are not synonymous. That which is obscene is not protected under the First Amendment. That which is pornographic is generally thought of as lewd or erotic. *Pornography* has a broader meaning than *obscenity*, and not all pornography is obscene.

One of the earliest obscenity cases, *Roth v. United States*, in 1957, gave rise to the oft-cited words of Justice Brennan—"utterly without redeeming social importance." The *Roth* case focused on the actions of Samuel Roth, considered by some to be a leading American pornographer during the 1950s. Roth was convicted of advertising and mailing obscene materials. The Supreme Court enunciated the following test to determine whether material was obscene: "whether to the average person, applying contemporary community standards, the dominant theme of the material taken as a whole appeals to prurient interest." The court decided that Roth's work was obscene. This decision was met with great disapproval on many fronts. Many felt that the test was much too vague, making it impossible to determine what was obscene. Still, it remained the law from 1957 to 1973.

The case that changed the law arose in California when a restaurateur and his mother opened unsolicited advertisements they had received; the two were greeted by obscenity. The advertisements offered books for sale with titles such as such as *Intercourse* and *Sex Orgies Illustrated*. Many explicit drawings and pictures of groups of people engaging in sex acts were splattered across the brochures. In its ruling, the Supreme Court enunciated the now-famous three-prong test to be used in obscenity cases: "(a) an average person, applying contemporary community standards, would find that the work, taken as a whole appeals to the prurient interest; (b) the work depicts or describes, in a patently offensive way, sexual conduct specifically defined by the applicable state law; and (c) the work, taken as a whole, lacks serious literary, artistic, political, or scientific value." The Court ruled that the brochures were obscene.

Many criticized the outcome of *Miller* case, stating that the ruling meant that a work could be found obscene in one community and not in another, and therefore citizens could be deprived of the work in certain locations. Others stated that the test was still vague and needed greater clarification. Still, the case remained the standard for determining obscenity.

Radio

In the late 1970s, radio broadcasting and censorship issues came into play in the well-known *FCC v. Pacifica* case. George Carlin, comedian and satirist, had recorded his monologue "Filthy Words" before a live audience. The twelve-minute piece, which focused on the seven words that could "never" be said over the public airwaves, was broadcast over a New York radio station one afternoon. A father and his young son who were out driving at the time heard the broadcast, and the father registered a complaint with the Federal Communications Commission (FCC). The complaint stated, "[I can understand the] record's being sold for private use. I certainly cannot understand the broadcast of same over the air that, supposedly, you control."

Pacifica, the owner of the radio station, replied that the monologue had been included in a program on "contemporary society's attitude toward language," and that immediately prior to the broadcast, an advisory stating

" . . . sensitive language which might be regarded as offensive to some . . ." had been aired. Pacifica referred to Carlin as a "significant social satirist" and compared him to the likes of Mark Twain and Mort Sahl, stating that, "Carlin is not mouthing obscenities, he is merely using words to satirize as harmless and essentially silly our attitudes towards these words."

The FCC issued an order granting the complaint, but did not impose sanctions. Rather, the FCC said that the complaint would be held in the station's file and if further complaints arose, the FCC would choose whether to impose sanctions. The Supreme Court upheld the FCC's action, though it never declared the monologue obscene. Cases that have arisen since the *Pacifica* case have eroded this decision.

The Motion Picture Industry

Film censorship has been controversial since the inception of the motion picture industry. Silent films were criticized for depicting too much kissing in closeups. In 1922, the motion picture industry recognized that federal censorship was imminent and imposed self-censorship through the establishment of the Motion Picture Producers and Distributors of America (MPPA) in preference to federal regulation. The MPPA set up a Production Code, and, over the years, has liberalized this code.

In the mid-1940s, the MPPA became the Motion Picture Association of America (MPAA). In 1968, along with the National Association of Theater Owners (NATO) and the International Film Importers and Distributors of America (IFIDA), the MPAA established a rating system. Government played virtually no role in film censorship because the industry had elected to police itself.

The initial ratings category, as detailed by Jack Valenti, president of the MPAA, were: "G for general audiences, all ages admitted; M for mature audiences—parental guidance suggested, but all ages admitted; R for Restricted, children under 16 would not be admitted without an accompanying parent or adult guardian (later raised to under 17 years of age [and varies in some jurisdictions]); X for no one under 17 admitted."

Through the ratings, the industry claimed to carry out its " . . . primary task as giving advance cautionary warnings to parents so that parents could make the decision about the movie going of their young children." Because parents seemed to perceive the M rating as stronger than the R, M was changed to GP (general audiences, parental guidance suggested.) Within one year, GP was changed to PG: parental guidance suggested.

In 1984, the PG rating was divided into PG and PG-13, with a PG-13 film being of greater intensity than a PG. By 1990, the Rating Board chose to provide more guidance regarding the content of R-rated flms by adding such cautions as "violence" and "nudity." The X category was changed to NC-17: no one under 17 admitted. All of the current ratings are federally registered certification marks so that only films submitted to the Rating Board may utilize the ratings. Criteria considered by the Rating Board include theme, violence, language, sensuality, and nudity. Though producers and distributors are not required to submit their films for rating, the majority do so.

As co-founders of the rating system, cinema owners voluntarily enforce the guidelines. If there are no local laws, enforcement is solely in their hands, and no penalties are enforced by the government for failure to follow rating guidelines.

Funding for the Arts

The National Endowment for the Arts (NEA) is an agency that utilizes federal funds, and hence taxpayers' money, to support the arts. In 1989, the NEA fell under close scrutiny by members of Congress, as well as by members of the community at large. Waves of disapproval rocked the nation when exhibitions by artists such as Robert Mapplethorpe and Andres Serrano were funded by the NEA.

Work such as Mapplethorpe's homoerotic photographs, including males engaging in sex acts with each other and an anus being penetrated by the handle of a bullwhip, and "Piss Christ," Andres Serrano's portrayal of a crucifix submerged in a bottle of Serrano's urine, were among the projects condemned by legislators.

In 1994, the Walker Art Center in Minneapolis hosted "Four Scenes in a Harsh Life," a production by an HIV-positive actor-playwright. During the performance, which was sexually explicit, a scalpel was used to carve patterns into an actor's back. Paper towels were used to blot the blood; the towels were then hung to dry on a line stretched across the stage and partially into the audience area; and the dried paper towels were sold at the end of the show.

Journalist Jeff Jacoby stated that the Walker Center had received more than $100,000 in funding from the NEA. He called for major adjustments to the funding guidelines, dependent on the content of the work. He further supported his position by pointing to a poem, published in "The Portable Lower East Side," which "exalts the attackers who raped and slashed a Central Park jogger nearly to the point of death." "The Portable Lower East Side," Jacoby explained, "acknowledges 'generous support' from the NEA."

Senator Jesse Helms introduced an amendment to the NEA's Fiscal Year '95 Amendment Bill to restrict federal arts funding. Helms' amendment would have barred funding for works that "involve human mutilation or invasive bodily procedures on human beings dead or alive; or the drawing or letting of blood."

Opponents charged that the Helms amendment was too broad and that it would proscribe NEA funding for a great deal of War depiction and crucifixion scenes. The amendment was tabled, but the controversy raged on.

In 1996, a law that imposed content restrictions on the NEA was examined in a federal appeals court. The statute, 20 S.C. S954–959, required that an NEA grant of funding "take into consideration general standards of decency and respect for the diverse beliefs and values of the American public." It was passed in response to public pressure resulting from the work of artists such as Mapplethorpe and Serrano. In *Finley v. National Endowment for the Arts*, four performance artists and the National Association of Artists' Organizations (NAAO) filed a lawsuit against the NEA. The Court held that the plaintiff's due process rights and First Amendment rights had been violated because the statute was vague, and its requirements were unclear. Those who could not determine what the standards were certainly could not be held to live up to those standards.

Arts funding is clearly an issue that divides opinion. Many feel that art and politics should not mix. Others believe the two to be indivisible. The controversy is sure to continue into the twenty-first century.

Feminism and Pornography

Feminists hold divergent views regarding pornography. Some believe that it is a woman's fundamental right to portray herself in any way she chooses. Others believe that pornography diminishes and otherwise victimizes women.

Both viewpoints came to the fore during a 1996 art exhibit at the University of Michigan Law School. The exhibition, *Picturing Prostitutes*, drew both praise and fire. It was ultimately called "threatening" and was dismantled. A lawsuit ensued. The result was a small monetary award to the artists and an agreement to exhibit the art the following year, as well as to feature a program on art, feminism, and censorship.

Michigan law professor Catharine MacKinnon and author Andrea Dworkin have been at the forefront of the feminist pornography debate. Working together since the 1980s, the two have authored city ordinances and state bills throughout the country that resemble their 1983 Minneapolis and Indianapolis Dworkin-MacKinnon laws. The premise on which these laws are built is the assertion that pornography is a form of sexual discrimination. As such, providing sanctions against pornography and those who purvey it is not censorship, but rather a furtherance of women's rights.

The Minneapolis ordinance was vetoed by the mayor; the Indianapolis law was passed, but it faced a number of court challenges. The Minneapolis law defined pornography as "the sexually explicit subordination of women, graphically depicted whether in pictures or in words . . . [in which] "(1) women are presented as dehumanized sexual objects, things or commodities; or (2) women are presented as sexual objects who enjoy pain and humiliation; or (3) women are presented as sexual objects who experience sexual pleasure in being raped; or (4) women are presented as sexual objects tied up or cut up or mutilated or bruised or physically hurt; or (5) women are presented in postures of sexual submission; or (6) women's body parts—including but not limited to vaginas, breasts, and buttocks—are exhibited, such that women are reduced to those parts; or (7) women are presented as whores by nature; or (8) women are presented as being penetrated by objects or animals; or (9) women are presented in scenarios of degradation, injury, abasement, torture, shown as filthy or inferior, bleeding, bruised, or hurt in a context that makes these conditions sexual."

If the content of material met the above requirements, the material's owner or exhibitor could be charged with a variety of actions, including production, sale, or exhibition of the material, or with assault by someone who had read or viewed the pornography.

"Pornography currently has more protection than women do," MacKinnon has stated. In support of the Dworkin-MacKinnon laws, witnesses have testified that they have been sexually abused by spouses and boyfriends who admitted having been influenced by pornographic material. One witness testified that her boyfriend assaulted her and demanded that she reenact scenes from pornographic films. "If he had seen a snuff film, I wouldn't be here," she charged.

Opponents of the Dworkin-MacKinnon bills and philosophy, such as Marilyn Fitterman of the National Organization for Women (NOW) and Nancy Ryan of the Cambridge Women's Commission, claim that men who perform such heinous acts would do so regardless of the influence of pornography. Burt Neuborne, who has served as national legal director of the ACLU, has stated that it's not enough to show that pornography causes harm, that in order to censor such expression, "you have to show, in addition to the harm, that there is no other societal way of dealing with a problem than censorship." He charges that the Dworkin-MacKinnon laws do not pass muster on that point.

ACLU president Nadine Strossen is the author of *Defending Pornography: Free Speech, Sex, and the Fight for Women's Rights*. She holds that "this view of sexuality as inherently dangerous does profound damage to human rights in general, and to women's rights in particular," and advocates that " . . . on the history of obscenity laws, . . . censorship has long been—and continues to be—used as a tool to repress information vital to women's equality, health, and reproductive autonomy."

The dichotomy of viewpoints was readily apparent in 1992 when the United States Senate debated §1521. The bill provided that sex crime victims could sue producers, distributors, and vendors of obscene material and child pornography upon proving that the material was a "substantial cause" of their injuries. Section 1521 took on the nickname "the Bundy bill," so dubbed because serial killer Ted Bundy stated, just before his execution, that pornography had been catalyst to "his violent fantasies." Section 1521 never became law; however, the feminist pornography debate is certain to continue as new legislation is proposed around the country.

Music Censorship

The recording industry has always come under tight public scrutiny. During the rock'n'roll era of the 1950s, music was routinely censored. Organizations sprang up to advocate censorship of records, warning of the dangers to children from the gyrating, hip-swinging impact of this art form.

In 1985, wives of Cabinet officials, members of Congress, senators, and Washington, D.C. businesspeople formed the Parents' Music Resource Center (PMRC). At the forefront of the group were Tipper Gore (the vice president's wife), B. A. Bentsen, and Susan Baker. Baker stated, "Some of these lyrics reinforce all the wrong kinds of values for children at a very tender age." This group successfully originated congressional hearings (dubbed the "Washington Wives hearings") on recording industry regulation. The group's purpose was not to seek legislation, but rather to focus public attention on the issue.

Following the congressional hearings, the Recording Industry Association of America (RIAA) elected a course of self-regulation. Though not required, most members of the association agreed to include lyric inserts or place "parental advisory-explicit language" stickers on recordings whose lyrics involved violence, sex, or drug or alcohol abuse. Though many within and outside the recording industry balked at this, stressing the importance of First Amendment rights and freedoms, the RIAA stated that the measures were intended to respond sensitively to the concerns of parents of younger children to achieve a fair balance with the essential rights and freedoms of creators, performers, and adult purchasers of recorded music."

Though no enforcement is required by law (unless a local law has been enacted), many stores require that a consumer be sixteen or older to purchase a recording bearing the warning; photo identification is often required. Some stores point out the warning to adult consumers at the time of purchase.

In 1993, Wal-Mart stores placed a ban on the Nirvana album *In Utero*. The album included the song "Rape Me," and the cover art portrayed pink fetuses in a field of flowers. Geffen records ultimately made alterations in order to garner Wal-Mart's business. Because "family-oriented" stores such as Wal-Mart and Target make up approximately one-fourth of all recording sales, the recording industry is often anxious to temper its products to make them salable at these stores.

By the late 1980s and early 1990s, rap music had become tremendously popular, and censorship continued to be a critical issue. When the rap group 2 Live Crew recorded an album entitled *As Nasty As They Wanna Be*, including cuts such as "Me So Horny," many objected to its sexual content, "dirty" words, and promotion of violence toward women.

In 1990, a federal district court judge in Florida found *As Nasty As They Wanna Be* obscene. Pursuant to this finding, shop owners who sold the recording could be placed in jail, fined, and saddled with a criminal record. Many pulled the album from their shelves; others refused.

Several days after the album was ruled obscene, members of the rap group were arrested during a performance and charged with obscenity. A great hue and cry arose from the American public. Many were pleased and felt vindicated that music of this nature had landed the rappers exactly where they belonged. Others were outraged; they felt that the group's First Amendment rights had been violated.

Ultimately, the group members were found not guilty on the charge of obscenity. The verdict embittered the already heated discussion of the rap genre, which had been going on for several years.

LIBEL

Libel is an unprotected form of expression. Though the First Amendment grants freedom of speech, such freedom does not extend to the right to defame (make damaging untrue statements about) others.

Early on, it was greatly feared that laws against libel could repress free expression in the political arena. Because libel suits were brought and won so easily through the early 1960s, and because judgments typically came in so outlandishly high, some feared that journalists would be unwilling to print the news for fear of a libel action against them.

It was in that climate that the 1964 *New York Times v. Sullivan* case was decided by the U.S. Supreme Court. In this case, a Montgomery, Alabama, commissioner sued four African-American clergymen and the *New York Times* for libel. The commissioner's action was in response to a full-page advertisement that profiled the civil rights movement and solicited donations for the movement.

In court it was proven that several of the statements in the advertisement were incorrect, and hence, libelous. For the first time, however, the Court decided that in order to recover, the commissioner had to show, by clear and convincing evidence, actual malice on the part of the clergymen and the newspaper. This meant that the statements must have been made with "reckless disregard" for the truth.

From that time forward public figures were required to show actual malice against them in order to recover in a libel case. The theory behind the decision in the *Sullivan* case was to avoid a chilling effect that would curtail public discussions of a political nature. The decision was extended to public figures other than politicians because they too place themselves in the public eye. Some charge that public figures should not be able to win libel suits, even with a showing of malice, because they have thrust themselves in the public eye and must accept the consequences. The courts do not agree.

In 1981, it was once again proved that public figures are offered protection from libel under the law. The *National Enquirer* printed an article linking actress Carol Burnett romantically with a prominent politician. Additionally, the article spoke of Burnett's behavior at a local restaurant in such a way as to suggest that she had been intoxicated. The statements in the *National Enquirer* were false.

Because Burnett had lost relatives to alcoholism and because she campaigned zealously against the disease, the article was poignantly damaging to her reputation. A jury, incensed at the *National Enquirer*'s reckless disregard for the truth, did something very unusual. It awarded Burnett more than the amount requested in the lawsuit—$1.6 million! The amount was later reduced, but the principle had been upheld. Burnett contributed the award to charity.

The law on libel remained clear.

SYMBOLIC SPEECH

Acts such as flag desecration, draft card destruction, and the wearing of armbands are types of conduct that have been tested on First Amendment grounds as symbolic speech. In principle, the United States Supreme Court has held that the First Amendment does protect nonverbal expression; however, the legal evaluation works to balance the protection of nonverbal communication against the protection of safety and legitimate government interest.

For example, flag desecration has generally been held not to impinge on government interests, and therefore has been protected. One of the best-known flag desecration cases (*Texas v. Johnson*) came about in 1989 after Gregory Johnson participated in a march and rally to protest Reagan administration policies. Approximately 100 demonstrators participated in the march, which ended in front of Dallas City Hall. There, Johnson doused a flag with kerosene and set it ablaze, chanting with the other protesters, "America, the red, white and blue, we spit on you."

At no time during the march or flag-burning incident was there injury or threat of injury. Johnson was the only protester arrested. He was charged under a Texas law with "desecration of a venerable object." The United States Supreme Court struck down the Texas statute, finding that Johnson's conviction violated his First Amendment rights. Supreme Court Justice William Brennan stated, "We do not consecrate the flag by punishing its desecration, for in doing so we dilute the freedom that this cherished emblem represents."

Before the end of year, however, the United States Congress enacted the Flag Protection Act, which prescribed criminal sanctions for flag desecration. This statute was struck down as unconstitutional in the 1990 case of *United States v. Eichman*.

In response, the Citizens Flag Alliance, a coalition of groups across the country, formed to promote a new U.S. constitutional amendment—the Flag Desecration Amendment—in 1995. The amendment was never enacted into law, or ratified.

By early 1997, another, similar statute stood ready to be introduced to Congress. This issue can be anticipated to run through the annals of U.S. history.

The wearing of armbands, as discussed below, has generally been supported as a form of free expression. However, as in the 1968 case *O'Brien v. United States* when protesters have mutilated draft cards, the Supreme Court has held that such expression does impinge on a viable government interest. The draft cards were held to have been part of an important government regulation and registration process.

RIGHTS OF PUBLIC SCHOOL STUDENTS

Powerful censorship issues have historically come to the forefront with respect to students' rights. These issues include symbolic speech, press freedom, and the banning or removal of books from libraries and classrooms.

One of the most significant symbolic speech cases was decided during the Vietnam War era when protests against the war raged across the country. In Des Moines, Iowa, a group of families, including the Tinker family, met and decided to protest peacefully by wearing black armbands throughout the December holiday season. When area school principals learned of the plan, they immediately promulgated a policy providing for the suspension of students who refused to remove their armbands.

When the Tinker children went to school, they were told to remove their armbands. They refused to comply and were suspended. The Supreme Court held in their favor, ruling that their conduct was not disruptive to others and was clearly within parameters protected by the First Amendment. In its decision, the Court stated: " . . . state-operated schools may not be regarded as closed-circuit recipients of only that which the State chooses to communicate."

It is important to note that the students won the case because their armbands were a peaceful, nonintrusive type of expression. Vulgar and offensive speech does not fall into that category and is not a form of protected expression in the public school setting.

Though the decision was in favor of the students in the *Tinker* case, another case, one dealing with school press freedom, was decided against students. In *Hazelwood School District v. Kuhlmeier*, a 1988 case, a school newspaper in Missouri was censored. The issue was slated for publication at the end of the school year. Three days before the publication date, the newspaper was presented to the principal, as it always had been, for approval. The principal objected to two of the articles in the paper. One focused on student pregnancies at the school. The other discussed the impact of divorce. The article regarding teen pregnancy did not use students' real names. Nonetheless, the principal expressed concern that the girls might still be identifiable. Additional concern was expressed over the information in the article about sexual activity and birth control and whether this material might be inappropriate for younger students.

In the divorce article, a student identified by name made allegations against a parent. The principal believed that there was not enough time to contact the parent and allow the parent sufficient time to respond before the publication date.

As a result, the principal removed pages containing the two controversial articles and allowed the paper to go to press as a four-page issue rather than the intended six.

The students sued. The Supreme Court ruled on behalf of the school district. It stated: "First Amendment rights of students in the public schools are not automatically coextensive with the rights of adults in other settings, and must be applied in light of the special characteristics of the school environment. A school need not tolerate student speech that is inconsistent with its basic educational mission, even though the government could not censor similar speech outside the school."

This case made it clear that freedom of expression rights inside the schoolhouse gate are not the same as those afforded to the public outside a school setting.

Another issue of great debate in the education arena is censorship through the removal of books from school libraries and classrooms. Organizations and individuals across the country address this issue, and local school board elections often turn on it. The question has been whether the removal of books is constitutional.

In 1982 in *Board of Education v. Pico*, the Supreme Court decided that school officials do have the right to remove books for good faith or educational reasons. If, however, the books are being removed in an effort to advance a particular way of thinking or a particular religion, such removal is not constitutional.

CAMPUS SPEECH CODES

During the 1950s, when fear of communism was running rampant through the United States, universities felt the shock waves. Assigned books, lectures by professors, and guest speakers came under close scrutiny. The HUAC seized book lists from a number of campuses to examine them for evidence of subversive activity. Some professors changed the content of classroom materials and removed books from their reading lists because they feared reprisal from the university or the HUAC. Some universities demanded that professors take a loyalty oath to show their allegiance to the United States.

Though this oppression dissolved in later years, a new form of free expression limitation arose—the campus speech code. During the 1980s, hate speech had taken root at campuses throughout the country. Racist groups had sprung up like weeds, and epithets against minorities flew across campuses.

Universities faced with a dilemma that required them to balance their obligations to minority students with those of all students under the First Amendment. Many campuses initiated speech codes that required a higher standard of care in on-campus speech than the standard required of the public at large.

Though these codes have generally been upheld, their critics speak out vehemently, contending that verbal purity is not tantamount to social change. The solution is to confront problems such as racism and homophobia head-on, rather than dealing with the words that arise as a result, they claim. Those in favor of speech codes believe that it is unconscionable to allow such hatred to spew freely across campuses, and that some form of discipline must be initiated to protect potential victims. Many believe that hate speech is a precursor of and catalyst to physical violence.

In the 1940s, the Supreme Court held that an in-your-face style of verbal confrontation was tantamount to "fighting words," and that if these words acted as catalyst to immediate illegal action, they were unprotected speech under the First Amendment.

It is important to draw a distinction between verbal and symbolic hate expression. Symbolic expressions, such as a swastika, displayed publicly, are

25

protected under the First Amendment; however, once the symbols are used to deface another's property, the expression is no longer protected.

Great controversy over this issue continues. The morality dimension is important because universities try to protect the rights of all students.

NATIONAL SECURITY

NATIONAL SECURITY IN WARTIME

As discussed earlier, the Espionage Act and the Sedition Act illustrate the power of the United States government to limit freedom of expression during wartime. Additionally, the government is allowed wide latitude with respect to freedom of the press during times of war.

Partly because the press had been given such great freedom in covering the Vietnam War, when the United States invaded Grenada in 1983, the press was barred from the scene. The government held that press coverage of the Vietnam War had caused negative public reaction, and it did not want problems caused by stories about the Grenada invasion.

During the Persian Gulf War, limitations were again placed on reporters. Censors read stories before they could be submitted for print, and the censor's word, with rare exception, was the law.

Moral and ethical issues abound in the discussion of national security and censorship. Most feel that full freedom of expression during wartime would seriously jeopardize national security. Others believe that the government should not restrict freedom of expression at all.

Though the government does have strong power over freedom of expression during wartime, this is not absolute. During the Vietnam War, Secretary of Defense Robert McNamara, at the request of President Johnson, researched and wrote the *Pentagon Papers*. This document, thousands of pages long, was deemed classified by the government, meaning its distribution was highly restricted. Its pages revealed incident after incident that exemplified the trickery and clandestine activities, especially in the Executive Branch, which led to the military action in Vietnam.

Daniel Ellsberg, former deputy secretary of defense, leaked the *Pentagon Papers* to the press. On June 13, 1971, the first installment appeared in the *New York Times*. At that point, Nixon had become president. At first, he considered that the *Pentagon Papers* might reflect negatively only on prior administrations and that publication of the document would not be harmful to him. In the end, however, he considered the impact on the Executive Branch, as well as the potential for future problems in maintaining the status of classified documents.

He pursued an injunction to prohibit further publication of the document. The government stated that national security in this set of circumstances overrode previous cases holding against prior restraint. A temporary injunction was granted.

When the case arrived at the Supreme Court, the Court emphatically denied the injunction, stating that the Executive Branch seemed "to have forgotten the essential purpose and history of the First Amendment." The Court praised the action of the newspaper in printing the story and stated that journalists had done "precisely that which the Founders hoped and trusted they would do."

NATIONAL SECURITY IN PEACETIME

One of the best-known cases in the area of peacetime national security is *Snepp v. United States*. In this case, a former CIA director published a book about CIA activities in Vietnam. The problem arose because Snepp had signed an agreement stating that he would not publish any information on CIA activities without "specific prior approval" by the CIA. Snepp had failed to obtain such approval before publishing his book.

The government sued Snepp and won. The Court considered the fiduciary relationship (relationship of utmost trust) between Snepp and the government and held that the government could enforce its requirement that an employee submit writings to prior review, even if the material to be published was not classified.

Other peacetime national security issues include the classification system for U.S. government documents, begun in the mid-1940s. Documents were classified at different levels of access, and citizens without government clearance were not permitted to see them. Classifications included: confidential, secret, top secret, special intelligence, and for official use only.

FREEDOM OF INFORMATION ACT

In response to mounting public pressure to allow access to government records, President Lyndon Johnson signed the Freedom of Information Act (FOIA) in 1966. Though the act required the release of many types of documents, nine classes of information were exempt. These included documents relating to national security, trade secrets, financial institution regulations, criminal investigations, an individual's right to privacy, and other areas the government deemed highly sensitive. The law provided for sanctions if the government illegally withheld documents.

The Privacy Act of 1974 further addressed the issue by mandating that federal agencies release documents to individuals about whom information appeared in government files. Many people obtained records relating to World War II. For example, a stamp collector and vendor was shocked when he heard that an FBI file about him might exist. When he requested documents, he was told that he had not been the subject of an investigation, but that his name did appear as a reference in an FBI file "only due to your prominence in the philatelic field." The FBI refused to release the information, stating that doing so would constitute "an unwarranted invasion of personal privacy, disclose the identification of a confidential source, and disclose investigative techniques and procedures."

On appeal, the FBI file was released, and the philatelist learned that his name had been included because he had received a stamp price list from a Bolivian who was suspected of being a Nazi spy. As it was not uncommon for those with stamp businesses to receive price lists from around the world, the philatelist did not have any independent recollection of the event. As it turned out, all who had received price lists from the Bolivian suspect had been investigated by the FBI. It was through the FOIA that the individuals were able to learn the details of investigations that had proceeded against them many years before.

By 1995, Senator Patrick Leahy and Representative Randy Tate worked to bring FOIA standards into the computer age. Tate stated, "We're trying to move it into the 1990s—if not into the next century. The federal government needs to be more user-friendly." "Long delays can mean no access at all," Leahy charged.

Leahy had already tried, without success, to pass legislation to update FOIA provisions; however, his 1995 attempt did succeed and resulted in the Electronic Improvement of Information Act (EFOIA) of 1996. The EFOIA created provisions to take advantage of modern technology, including procedures to speed up the processing of FOIA requests, as delays had been a continuing problem.

In 1966, when the FOIA was promulgated, the government had approximately thirty computers. Within thirty years, that number had soared to more than 35,000. By 1996, FOIA requests numbered approximately 600,000.

Many people, including Pulitzer Prize–winning journalist Eileen Welsom, claimed that it was critical for the government to come of age and begin responding more rapidly to FOIA requests. When commenting on the FOIA, Welsom said, "I think of it primarily as a tool for the 'little guy,' a law that helps reporters, public-interest groups and taxpayers without subpoena power or influence to obtain documents about the actions of our government."

Welsom had become particularly frustrated while working on an award-winning series on radiation in the 1990s. Her work examined cases in which more than a dozen people had been injected with plutonium, and her research took her to the Department of Energy (DOE). Because of a substantial backlog, Welsom did not receive the requested information for more than three years. She testified before Congress in support of the EFOIA, and the law was passed in 1996.

TELEVISION

With the advent of television, a whole new set of censorship concerns sprang up. Television has made it more difficult for parents to control the images their children were viewing. Violence seems to permeate the airwaves. A technological solution called the v-chip (antiviolence chip) was developed to address this concern. The v-chip is installed in new televisions, and can be programmed to deny access to programs that rise above a level of violence predetermined by the viewer. President Clinton signed the Telecommunications Act of 1996, which mandated installation of the v-chip in new televisions. Additionally, the bill mandated that within one year the television industry must create a rating system to advise viewers about violence and "other objectionable content." Further, the bill stated that if the industry failed to establish such a system, the federal government could create its own ratings system.

A variety of reactions arose to the chip. Some expressed relief that broadcast technology seemed to have caught up with the level of violence. Others believed that the v-chip represented a form of censorship and impinged on First Amendment rights.

Television violence has caused contention for decades. Some sources estimate that, by age eighteen, a child is likely to have seen thousands of murders on television. The question on the lips of many is whether or not such violence affects long-term behavior. Data exist to support both positive and negative responses to this question.

Ultimately, the television industry elected to regulate itself through a ratings system initiated in 1997. Viewers can use these ratings to program the v-chip.

INTERNET

During 1995, violence on television and the v-chip were certainly not the only technologically based concerns; the worldwide network of computer users and computers known as the Internet was growing exponentially. Debate over content became a key issue. A sampling of material readily available on the net in 1995 follows.

- **A student conjures up a story of sexual torture and gives the name of an actual person to the victim. The story includes horrific acts of violence. A detailed, systematic step-by-step description of the torture leaves no holds barred.** Internet stories—explicitly detailing torture, rape, and murder—written by Abraham Jacob Alkhabaz (also known as Jake Baker), a Michigan University student, were determined by the Sixth Circuit Court to be constitutionally protected speech. Baker served as the test case; he was the first person to be criminally charged for such Internet communication. He was subject to a maximum imprisonment of five years if convicted. Baker's Internet stories received international attention when he authored his most infamous story—in which he himself was the predator and the tortured victim was named after a female University of Michigan student who actually existed. The court deemed the story a fantasy rather than a threat.

- **An on-line manual provides step-by-step bomb-making instructions.** By the mid-1990s, information was readily available via the Internet on constructing pipe bombs and similar explosives. Materials were specified, and step-by-step instructions were provided. Debate over such Internet content rose to fever pitch after the April 19, 1995, Oklahoma City bombing of a federal building and the 1996 Atlanta Olympics explosion. The government responded by sponsoring an antiterrorism bill and by attempting to bring back a formerly failed proposition that would provide for criminal sanctions (twenty years in prison and/or a $250,000 fine) for dissemination of information on bomb-making via print, radio, television, or the Internet.

- **A site offers instructions on how to commit a murder.** A net site also offered vivid, clear, and matter-of-fact descriptions of committing a murder. Those opposed to regulation of such content argued that such information was readily available through a variety of sources, including popular novels.

- **Child pornography became available on a large number of sites.** Explicit photos were available, and certain newsgroups encouraged sexually graphic on-line "chat." The U.S. government handled such content staunchly through strong legislation. Actual transcripts of legislative hearings on this issue can be found in chapter 6.

Moral, ethical, and legal questions of regulation have been closely scrutinized by those of a panoply of beliefs and philosophies. Regulation of Internet content promised to be rife with the potential for litigation and legislation. Many "netizens" believed that the Internet should remain wide open for the free exchange of ideas, that there should be no censorship. They felt that control should remain with individuals. If parents did not want their children to access particular sites, they reasoned, the parents should take advantage of software available to restrict access. For those who advocated censorship of the net, the question of who should be held culpable had to be addressed.

One argument advanced the belief that whoever places the information on the Internet should be solely liable. Others believed that any service providing access to the sites should be held responsible. The need for a clearer definition of the Internet became obvious. If it was a broadcaster, it would liable for the content of the broadcasts. On the other hand, if it was more like a telephone service, then it would not be liable for the content of conversations it carried. The question was not easily settled.

In 1995, the German government advised the on-line service CompuServe that it would hold the company criminally responsible if it failed to remove certain obscene newsgroups from the Internet. CompuServe complied. Because CompuServe did not have the technology to offer a batch of newsgroups to only a portion of its subscribers, it was forced to restrict the access of all users to these newsgroups. Cries of censorship and lack of intellectual freedom rang out around the globe. CompuServe ultimately developed the technology to restore the newsgroups to subscribers outside of Germany.

In 1995 and 1996, a variety of legislation involving broadcasting and the Internet came before the U.S. Congress. Most addressed the interest of minors and were designed to protect them from pornography. Two of the most important were the Telecommunications Act of 1996 and the Communications Decency Act of 1996 (which amended the Telecommunications Act).

The Communications Decency Act of 1996 (CDA) addressed four areas relating to transmission via interactive computer services. The first provision criminalized the use of interactive computer services and telecommunications services to send harassing communications or to display "indecent" material to minors. Another section made it a crime to use a facility to coerce or entice minors to engage in criminal sexual activity.

The CDA, strongly promoted by Senator James Exon, Jr., met with sharp criticism from liberals and conservatives. The act provided criminal penalties for displaying "indecent" material to minors, but critics charged that the Act was vague, that there was no way to determine the meaning of "indecent." For example, would sex education materials sent over the Internet be considered indecent?

When the CDA passed on February 1, 1996, many on the Internet dubbed that day Black Thursday, and thousands of websites turned their backgrounds black in protest. On the same day, the ACLU filed a lawsuit in United States District Court for a temporary restraining order against the "indecent" and "patently offensive" provisions of the CDA. (See appendix E for full text of the CDA.) The American Library Association (ALA) joined in the action. A temporary injunction was granted. The Court determined that the statute was too broad, and hence unconstitutional. The case was immediately appealed to the U.S. Supreme Court. The Supreme Court agreed with the lower court and, on June 26, 1997, declared the CDA unconstitutional.

Perhaps these actions can be compared to early Supreme Court decisions regarding obscenity. In the late 1990s, Internet censorship issues are only in their infancy. Legislators and the courts have yet to formulate standards and tests to afford First Amendment rights and protect the public in general, and children in particular.

STATE INTERNET LEGISLATION

By 1996, seventeen states had either enacted or promulgated Internet regulation statutes. Many of the statutes focused on content accessible to juveniles; others focused on "explosive materials" and "terrorist acts." Chapter 2 includes a detailed discussion of state statutes.

The Georgia and New York statutes were two of the first to be challenged in court. Both trials included an "online tour" before the judge. A similar tour had been granted to the federal judge in the *Reno* Communication Decency Act case. A new age in courtroom procedure had arrived.

FOREIGN CENSORSHIP

Historically, foreign censorship has been rampant. Countries around the world have exercised censorship on a regular basis. Revolutionary changes have occurred in some; others remain virtually unchanged. Volumes have been written on the topic. The following is a brief survey of foreign censorship and offers representative examples.

IRAN

One of the most explosive and best-known examples of foreign censorship comes out of Iran. When Salman Rushdie wrote the novel *The Satanic Verses*, Iran's religious and political leader, the Ayatollah Khomeini, not only denounced the work as blasphemous to Islam and banned it, but also called for Rushdie's death. Rushdie was forced into hiding in 1989. The impact of the Ayatollah's edict rippled around the world.

Many stores refused to carry the book, as they had been threatened with bombing if the novel was found on their shelves. Though many of the booksellers felt morally that the book should be sold, practicality and self-preservation often outweighed support of free speech.

SOVIET UNION

In the Communist USSR, censorship was a part of life until President Mikhail Gorbachev came to power in 1988. Propaganda against the Western free press abounded; Soviet leaders claimed it was not free at all, but rather constantly bowing to the dictates of advertisers and factory owners. Foreign broadcasts were "jammed" to keep uncontrolled information from the Soviet public.

Under Stalin, intellectual freedom was virtually nonexistent. Those who attempted to exercise such freedom were routinely tortured and jailed. Those who did not support party policy were excised from official history books. Gorbachev's *glasnost*, or policy of openness, however, revealed the culture and history of the Soviet Union to its own population, as well as to those abroad who had never before had access to such information.

Glasnost, however, did not always go smoothly. In 1988, a Soviet journalist was accused of "professional incompetence" and demoted when he wrote a piece that included a public-opinion poll on *perestroika*, Gorbachev's plan to restructure the economy. The poll revealed that 30 percent of the population was for *perestroika*, 50 percent undecided, and 20 percent against. Though there were allegations that the reporting was indeed based on false or inaccurate information, it is unclear whether such allegations were founded or unfounded.

SOUTH AFRICA

South Africa has perhaps one of the most notorious records regarding censorship. Throughout history, the country has been burdened with myriad acts focusing on censorship, including the Suppression of Communism Act, the Entertainment Act, the Publications Act, and the Newspaper and Imprint Registration Act. Basically, the government banned any mention of opposition to apartheid, its policy of separating races by law. Speech and all printed material were censored, in order to quell any expression against apartheid. During a discussion of freedom of expression and the media, an official stated that censorship did not exist, that what existed was "merely a control effort that limits what newspapers could print."

It appears in this circumstance that the distinction is in the eye of the beholder. Historically, South Africa has been the target of many attacks regarding censorship.

DENMARK

At the other end of the spectrum is Denmark. Its 1953 Constitution prohibits censorship—in printing, in writing, and in speech. Freedom of print has long been a tenet of Danish government and, except in rare circumstances, journalists have not been obliged to reveal their sources.

Obscenity laws relating to print in Denmark were abolished in 1967; in 1969, obscenity laws relating to films, photos, and other visual art for adults were also abolished. A board was established to determine suitability of films for children, and serves a censorship function in that regard.

After the Danish obscenity laws were abandoned, pornography circulation plummeted by nearly 50 percent.

RECENT INCIDENTS OF CENSORSHIP IN FOREIGN COUNTRIES

- In 1994, Palestinian police outlawed distribution in the Gaza Strip of *An-Nahar*, a pro-Jordan newspaper. This was the first known incidence of censorship under Palestinian rule. The banned newspaper had failed to mention P.L.O. Chairman Yasser Arafat's protestations to the "special role" of Jordan in administering Islamic holy sites located in Jerusalem.

- In 1994, director Steven Spielberg would not allow the film *Schindler's List* to open in the Philippines because censors cut several scenes, including one in which bare breasts were exposed as women marched to their deaths in the gas chamber. Manuel Morato, who was then president of the Censorship Board stated, "If we allow ourselves to be cowed by an American Jew . . . that is the worst case of American imperialism."

- In 1995, four prominent journalists, Ben Charles Obi, Kunle Ajibade, Chris Anyawu, and George Mbah, were sentenced to life imprisonment (later reduced to fifteen years) in Nigeria for being "accessories after the fact of treason." It was widely believed that the four were imprisoned because of stories they had written about an alleged coup attempt. Kunle Ajibade's story, "No-one guilty: the Commission of Inquiry presents an empty file regarding suspects of the coup," prompted officials to demand sources; the story depicted the attempted coup as a government-engineered attempt to delay the transition to civilian rule.

- In 1995, *The Emigrant*, a film by director Youssef Chahine, was banned in Egypt because it ran afoul of the Islamic depiction ban. Al-Azhar, a learning institute and source of religious guidance, had proclaimed in 1983 that no television, film, or theater productions would be permitted to depict prophets. It was alleged that Chahine's film violated the ban by portraying the Biblical story of Joseph.

- In early 1996, approximately thirty comedians, singers, and musicians were imprisoned in Somalia, Mogadishu because they did not offer their material to the Islamic court for censorship prior to performance. The audience was also detained for a short period.

- In May 1997, in Cambodia, one death and two serious injuries were reported when seven masked people fired on Television Kampuchea (TVK) studios, a state-run local station. A number of media workers had recently been murdered in similar attacks. Information Minister Ieng Mouly cautioned, "Government-controlled media should prepare to face further political intimidation." The attacks occurred in the midst of rivalry between two major factions of Cambodia's coalition government.

ON THE HORIZON

By the mid-1990s, research had begun in a new censorship area. A law professor and a sociology professor had begun to document what they dubbed "SLAPPs—strategic lawsuits against public participation." In their book, *SLAPPS: Getting Sued for Speaking Out*, George Pring and Penelope Canan examined lawsuits filed by teachers, police, corporations, real estate developers, politicians, and civil rights opponents against those who exercised their right of free speech.

They discussed many cases, such as one in which a student was sued for libel after complaining about water quality. Pring and Canan found that retaliatory lawsuits against those exercising First Amendment rights were gaining steam.

Arguments concerning SLAPPs in the late twentieth century were very similar to arguments in the eighteenth and nineteenth centuries that focused on the "chilling effect" of action against free speech. An acute concern began to grow that people might come to fear expensive lawsuits, and hence be silenced in areas that should give full vent to free speech.

Linda Tanner, a private Missouri citizen, wrote a letter to express her anger regarding "the operation of an infectious waste incinerator by Bunker Resource, Recycling and Reclamation, Inc.—a subsidiary of the Canadian firm DECOM Medical Waste Systems, Inc."

Though Tanner's letter was not published, an editor placed it in the hands of the town's mayor, who was alleged to have an economic interest in the plant. DECOM filed a SLAPP against Tanner (who filed a countersuit), and it is alleged that DECOM "led a smear campaign against Tanner." Tanner lost her job as a result. She was awarded $86 million in damages by a jury, including a $10 million award against the owner of DECOM for his role in Tanner's firing.

A similar type of incident found its way into the United States legislature. In 1997, House conservatives attempted to bring impeachment proceedings against federal judges they "view[ed] as activists." Supreme Court Justice Antonin Scalia, disapproving of the move, stated, "I think we have enough respect for our courts, enough understanding in the country that if you let the legislature intrude too much on the judiciary, we'll be in trouble."

Another phenomenon of the late 1990s was the computer wave that swept through gang activity. Pagers had been considered an ultimate status symbol for gang members; computers soon rose to that level of prominence. Street gang websites in 1997 offered details on hiding a gun in a hollowed-out notebook and the best floor plan for a crack house.

David Gonzales, head of the Phoenix, Arizona Gang Enforcement Unit, feared that gang leaders would come together via Internet sites and form stronger national groups. He cautioned, "It's a lot like what happened with the Mafia back in the Prohibition days. Only now, they're using the Internet to do it."

The Chicago and Boston Mafia of that time had roots in neighborhood gangs, and though fueled by Prohibition, the Mafia organized and prospered through contemporary technological advances, the automobile and a coast-to-coast phone system.

Though fewer than 1 percent of the nation's estimated 147,000 gang members were online in 1997, seeds of nationally linked gang activity were scattering across cyberspace. Ironically, the first known gang website originated as a prank through the efforts of a middle-class teenager in suburban Michigan. It grew to host obituaries of gang members, gang enemy lists, and details of assaults committed. Unless they show an "explicit intent to commit a criminal act," those who post on the gang sites are generally protected under the First Amendment.

SLAPPs, Internet censorship, control over access to television broadcasts with violent and sexual content, Supreme Court rulings, Internet gang presence—these are some of the issues whose full dimension will be explored in the twenty-first century.

CHAPTER 2

THE LAW OF CENSORSHIP

UNITED STATES LEGISLATION

Thousands of pieces of legislation relating to freedom of expression have come before the U.S. Congress and the congresses of the states. This section details some of the best-known and most important.

ALIEN AND SEDITION ACTS

Espionage Act of 1917 and Sedition Act of 1918

The Espionage Act of 1917 and Sedition Act of 1918 made it a crime "willfully to utter, print, write, or publish any disloyal, profane, scurrilous or abusive language about the form of government of the United States or the Constitution . . ." The law also provided for criminal penalties for those who made or delivered false reports with the intention of interfering with the armed services, promoting insubordination, or influencing others not to submit to the draft. Alleged traitors were prosecuted under these statutes. These laws were promulgated to address the nation's ills subsequent to its entry into World War I.

Eugene Debs was one of the best-known historical figures to be prosecuted under the Espionage Act of 1917. Debs, who lost his U.S. citizenship, was arrested in 1918 after speaking out in Ohio against the Espionage Act. He was released in 1921 after being pardoned by President Warren Harding.

Aliens Registration Act of 1940

The Aliens Registration Act of 1940, also known as the *Smith Act*, provided criminal penalties for advocating (through words or writing) the forcible or violent overthrow of the government. Prosecutions were conducted under this law for almost twenty years, and though the law still exists, in 1957 the

Supreme Court (in *Yale v. United States*) overturned the convictions of fourteen communists. It held that advocacy alone was not enough to uphold a conviction. No prosecutions have been launched under this statute since the late 1950s.

BROADCAST FAIRNESS

The Federal Communications Act (1934), also known as the *Fairness Doctrine*, provides equal access time to the airwaves for politicians, as well as mandates that all sides in a matter of public concern be given equal time to present their views.

CIVIL SERVANTS AND THE MILITARY

Hatch Act

The Hatch Act, Title 5 U.S.C., §7324ff. details the political activities in which U.S. civil servants employed by the federal government are permitted to engage. The act states that civil servants may not run for office, may not campaign for a candidate or assist in any way with a political campaign, and may not serve in an office in a political party—essentially, the act states that civil servants may not take part in partisan politics except to cast personal votes. The act has come under scrutiny, as some advocate that it violates First Amendment rights. Many states have laws similar to the Hatch Act.

Civil Service Reform Act

The Civil Service Reform Act, also known as the "Whistleblowers" Act (1978), was promulgated in an effort to protect civil service workers who revealed wrongdoing within the government; that is, those who revealed what they reasonably believed to constitute "a violation of any law, rule or regulation, mismanagement, a gross waste of funds, an abuse of authority, or a substantial and specific danger to public health or safety." Civil servants lose this protective shield if they contravene an executive order, a statute, or reveal information essential to national security.

Military Honor and Decency Act

The Military Honor and Decency Act, an amendment to an American Defense Authorization, was offered in mid-1996 in the House National Security Committee on a defense appropriations bill. It proposed to proscribe the rental or sale on any United States military base of any magazine, video, or compact disc that "depicts or describes nudity in a lascivious way." The representative who introduced the bill stated, "Uncle Sam has no business subsidizing smut." The ACLU Legislative Counsel Daniel Katz stated, "This legislation sends an extremely disturbing message to soldiers who are risking their lives to uphold the Constitution. Although soldiers are willing to fight for the freedoms that Americans enjoy, Congress does not believe that the freedom of the First Amendment should apply to US soldiers or their families." The Military Honor and Decency Act passed but faced challenges in the judicial system.

FREEDOM OF INFORMATION

The Freedom of Information Act

The Freedom of Information Act was signed into law in 1966 in response to mounting public pressure to obtain government documents. The act requires the release of many types of government documents, while exempting nine classifications, including documents relating to national security, trade secrets, financial institution regulation, criminal investigations, an individual's right to privacy, and other areas the government deemed damaging if released. A very detailed procedure was established to request documents, and sanctions were laid down for governmental failure to release documents under the act.

The Privacy Act of 1974

The Privacy Act of 1974 mandated that the government release documents to individuals whose names appeared in a government file. An appeals policy was promulgated in the event that access was denied.

The Electronic Freedom of Information Act

The Electronic Freedom of Information Act (EFOIA—see Appendix F for full text) amended the Freedom of Information Act (FOIA) by providing standards to bring the FOIA into the computer age. When the FOIA was enacted, the government had approximately thirty computers; that number rose to more than 35,000 within forty years. The EFOIA provisions set out procedures for the more expeditious release of information and detailed means of electronic access.

NATIONAL SECURITY

Comprehensive Antiterrorism Act of 1995

The Comprehensive Antiterrorism Act of 1995 (§735, Public Law 104–132, enacted April 24, 1996) was introduced shortly after the 1995 bombing of a federal building in Oklahoma City. The act provides for heavy penalties for terrorist acts and restitution to victims. Opponents voiced strong opposition to the act, claiming that the definition of terrorism was too broad and could give rise to a "red scare" type of mentality through which political groups would be labeled as terrorists. Opponents further stated that immigration clauses included in the bill were biased and irrelevant to combating terrorism, and that state governments already had statutes in place to deal with the types of activities proscribed by the bill, making federal legislation unnecessary. In the late 1990s, no cases had yet come before the judicial system to challenge the constitutionality of the statute.

OBSCENITY AND PORNOGRAPHY

Obscene Publications Law of 1865

The Obscene Publications Law of 1865 was the first law passed in the United States dealing with obscenity sent through the mails. It was inspired by a plethora of complaints regarding material mailed to U.S. Civil War soldiers. Punishment included a fine up to $500, imprisonment for twelve months, or both. This law was replaced by the Comstock Act (see below).

Federal Anti-Pornography Act

The Federal Anti-Pornography Act, (Title 18 U.S.C. §1461, enacted in 1873), also known as the Comstock Act, made it a crime to send through the mails "every obscene, lewd, lascivious or filthy book, pamphlet, picture, paper, letter writing, print or other publication of an indecent character." Anthony Comstock, one of the country's best-known anti-pornography crusaders and head of the Society for the Suppression of Vice, promulgated and lobbied strongly for this bill. He was appointed a special agent for the U.S. Postal Service and regularly engaged in raids. Comstock claimed that he destroyed more than 194,000 "questionable pictures" and 134,000 pounds of books of "improper character" in the first year the act was enforced. The Comstock Act was repealed in 1915.

Federal Communications Commission Regulations on Indecency and Censorship

The Federal Communications Commission Regulations on Indecency and Censorship, (Title 18 U.S.C., §1464) state "Indecency: Whoever utters any obscene, indecent or profane language by means of radio communication shall be fined not more than $10,000 or imprisoned not more than two years, or both."

Title 18 U.S.C., §1465 deals with the transportation of obscene material and states, "Whoever knowingly transports in interstate or foreign commerce for the purpose of sale or distribution any obscene, lewd, lascivious, or filthy book, pamphlet, picture, film, paper, letter, writing, print, silhouette, drawing, figure, image, cast, phonograph recording, electrical transcription . . . or other article capable of producing sound or any other matter of indecent or immoral character, shall be fined not more than $5,000 or imprisoned not more than five years, or both." Other Title 18 sections include: §1460, possession with intent to sell, and sale of obscene matter on federal property; §1461, mailing obscene or crime-inciting matter; §1462, importation or transportation of obscene matters; §1463, mailing indecent matter on wrappers or envelopes; §1464, broadcasting obscene language; §1466, engaging in the business of selling or transferring obscene matter; §1467, criminal forfeiture, under which property may be forfeited to the government; and §1468, distributing obscene material by cable or subscription television.

Title 47 U.S.C., §223 deals with telephone regulations and provides for protection against obscene and harassing telephone calls. This statute was strengthened by a 1983 law passed in response to a proliferation of phone sex businesses. The law is enforced by the United States Attorney General's Office. In addition, most states have their own statues dealing with harassing telephone calls. These statutes are generally enforced by the District or County Attorney's Office and often involve recording telephone calls and placing a "trap" through the local telephone company to track the calls.

Communications Decency Act

The Communications Decency Act, §314, was the focus of tremendous controversy in the mid-1990s, as Congress worked to formulate the Telecommunications Act of 1996. The Communications Decency Act (see appendix E), also known as the CDA, mandated criminal penalties (a fine of $100,000 or two years in prison) for anyone who "makes, transmits, or otherwise makes available any comment, request, suggestion, proposal, image, or other communication" that is "obscene, lewd, lascivious, filthy, or indecent" while utilizing a "telecommunication device." The bill expanded obscenity and harassment laws that formerly dealt with only telephone communications to include communications by "any telecommunications device." Identical to a 1995 measure that failed with the Senate Telecommunications reform bill (§1822), the CDA was introduced by Senator James Exon and was said to have been designed to protect minors from access to sexually explicit material in interactive media, including the Internet, electronic bulletin board services, and online services. The act was attacked for many reasons, particularly overbreadth and vagueness. Opponents charged that there would be no way to determine the meaning of "indecent." Even sex education materials, they contended, could be deemed "indecent" under the statute.

The CDA passed on February 1, 1996. The Internet community called the day "Black Thursday," and thousands of websites turned their backgrounds black in protest. The same day, the American Civil Liberties Union filed a lawsuit seeking a temporary restraining order against enforcement of the CDA. The order was granted. Attorney General Janet Reno agreed not to "initiate any investigations or prosecutions" under the challenged provisions of the CDA until the district court had heard the case. The district court upheld the injunction and the case was appealed to the United States Supreme Court, where an opinion was awaited in mid-1997.

SYMBOLIC SPEECH—FLAG DESECRATION

Flag Protection Act of 1989

The Flag Protection Act of 1989, 18 U.S.C. §700 included a section of a flag protection act promulgated in 1968. The act (which followed a Supreme Court decision overturning a Texas flag protection statute—*Texas v. Johnson*) proscribed physical desecration of the United States flag and provided for criminal penalties of a fine and/or imprisonment for up to one year. The Flag Protection Act of 1989 (see appendix D) was struck down by the United States Supreme Court as a contravention of the First Amendment in *U.S. v. Eichman* (1990).

In 1995, the Citizens Flag Alliance, a coalition of groups across the country, promoted a new flag desecration amendment which came before the House of Representatives as H.J. Res. 79 (see appendix D). The bill was not passed. By 1997, another flag desecration bill (H.J. Res. 54) had made its way to Congress and stood ready for a vote (see appendix D).

STATE AND LOCAL STATUTES AND RULES

Federal law addresses transportation of obscenity through the mails and otherwise across state lines. Additionally, federal legislation such as the CDA covers cyberspace censorship. Most states have statutes that deal with non-Internet obscenity. These statutes are constantly challenged on First Amendment grounds but generally pass constitutional muster. The laws apply to a wide array of people, including those who sell in stores or otherwise distribute obscene material, as well as projectionists in theaters who exhibit obscene material. Thousands of people are prosecuted annually under these state statutes.

Additionally, many states have their own cyberspace censorship statutes. By the late 1900s, such legislation existed in the following states:

California
Assembly Bill 295 enacted September 1996: expanded child pornography and obscenity statues to include a prohibition against transmission of images via computer.

Connecticut
House Bill 6883 enacted June 1995: criminalized transmission of an online message "with intent to harass, annoy or alarm another person."

Florida
Senate Bill 156 enacted May 1996: holds owners or operators of computer online services liable for illegal actions of subscribers. (This bill amended child pornography law.)

Georgia
House Bill 1630 enacted April 1996: proscribes unauthorized web links with trade names or logos and dealts with criminalization of Internet pseudonyms.
House Bill 76 enacted March of 1995: proscribes the cyberspace use of obscene or vulgar speech to minors, "fighting words," and material dealing with terrorist acts and specific weapons.

Hawaii
House Bill 2665 pending in 1997: amends existing statute to include electronic transmission of child pornography.

Illinois
Senate Bill 747 enacted July 1995: criminalized the use of computer for the purpose of sexual solicitation of minors.
House Bill 362 pending in 1997: added "threat by computer" to existing criminal statute.

Kansas
House Bill 2223 enacted May 1995: amended child pornography laws to include computer-generated images.

Maryland
House Bill 305/Senate Bill 133 enacted May 1996: added online communication, as a method of committing an offense, to existing child pornography laws.

House Bill 619 pending in 1997: proscribes annoyance, abuse, or embarrassment by e-mail.

Senate Bill 163 pending in 1997: amended existing "harmful to minors" law to include computer transmission.

Montana

House Bill 0161 enacted March of 1995: amended existing child pornography laws to include possession of computer-generated images displaying child pornography and computer transmission of child pornography.

New York

Senate Bill 210E passed July 1996: proscribes the transmittal of "indecent material" to minors.

Assembly Bill 8509 pending in 1997: amends existing harassment law to include harassment via computer.

North Carolina

House Bill 207 enacted June 1996: amended existing law to include computer-generated sexual solicitation of minors.

Oklahoma

House Bill 1048 enacted April 1995: proscribed computer transmission of that which is "harmful to minors."

House Concurrent Resolution 1097 passed May 1996: mandated that all state agencies, including educational institutions, purge their computer systems of all illegal obscene material.

Virginia

House Bill 7 enacted March 1996: proscribes the use of Virginia-owned computers by government state workers, including university professors, to access sexually explicit content.

Senate Bill 1067 enacted May 1995: criminalized electronic transmission of child pornography (amended existing law).

House Bill 9 pending in 1997: mandated labeling of "sexually explicit content" by online service providers.

Judicial challenges began as soon as these statutes were enacted, and the future promises to be rife with litigation in this area.

Other state statutes and policies of note include the following:

The Law of Censorship

- In the mid-1990s, Rhode Island had a statute that banned advertisement of retail liquor prices at any location other than where the liquor was sold. The law was challenged on First Amendment grounds by 44 Liquormart, Inc., whose case went to the United States Supreme Court. The Supreme Court found that this regulation of commercial speech was unconstitutional.

- In 1997, the American Civil Liberties Union filed a petition for writ of certiorari to the United States Supreme Court regarding an injunction granted in a San Jose, California case, *People ex rel Gallo v. Acuna*. The case was based on a public nuisance law that allowed the city to identify certain individuals as gang members. The law did not require a showing of prior criminal activity, nor did it require a showing of a proclivity to engage in future criminal activity. The law allowed the city to petition for an injunction to prohibit gang members from a variety of activities, including associating with other "known" gang members.

  More than thirty young Latinos were "identified" under the law, and the city obtained an injunction prohibiting them not only from associating with each other, but also stripping them of many rights, including the right to a jury trial, a showing of guilt beyond reasonable doubt, and the right to an appointed attorney. The Latinos were faced with the possibility of six months imprisonment and a $1,000 fine if they violated the injunction.

- In February of 1997, Oregon Department of Corrections officials implemented new rules regarding witness observation and reporting of executions. The rules prohibited witnesses from viewing the first thirty minutes of preparation for an execution and from viewing the condemned entering the execution chamber and undergoing intravenous tube insertion. A further provision required that witnesses sign a stipulation that they would not disclose any information that might identify corrections officials carrying out death sentences. Opponents charged that the law allowed "public officials [to] carry out most of the execution process in secret" and that the rule relating to identification of corrections officials constituted prior restraint. Many among the media were outraged. Judicial challenges began almost immediately.

Statutes relating to freedom of expression issues exist across the country. The future promises to be filled with litigation in regard to intellectual freedom issues. The following section details cases that have already come before the courts.

COURT CASES

A tremendous amount of litigation has arisen over censorship issues. This chapter plucks representative cases from among the numerous United States court decisions. These cases include issues such as prior restraint, students and symbolic speech, censorship of films and public school newspapers, obscenity, and national security.

SCHENCK V. UNITED STATES, 249 U.S. 47 (1919)

Background

The Espionage Act of 1917 was passed during a time of dire national concern over spies and foreign agents' subversive activities. The act addressed a wide array of issues, including military recruitment. The act made it a crime to "obstruct the recruiting or enlistment service . . ."

On August 18, 1917, federal agents arrested Charles Schenk for violation of the Espionage Act. Schenk was general secretary of the Socialist party. He had supervised the printing and mailing of more than 15,000 leaflets that encouraged American men who were registered with draft boards not to submit to the draft. The leaflets, "in impassioned language," proffered the argument that conscription was "despotism in its worst form and a monstrous wrong against humanity in the interest of Wall Street's chosen few." The pamphlets went on to state that anyone refusing to recognize the right to oppose the draft was guilty of violating the United States Constitution.

Legal Issues

Schenk was convicted in the lower court. He based his appeal to the Supreme Court on an attack of the Espionage Act, stating that the act was unconstitutional and violated the First Amendment. Schenk's lawyers examined the differences between the language of Schenk's pamphlets, which they asserted only expressed honest opinion, and language that is likely to act as a catalyst to illegal action. The prosecution asserted that the First Amendment was not an issue in this case, that the issue involved was one of congressional draft policy.

Decision

In an unanimous decision, the Court upheld the Espionage Act of 1917. In enunciating his now-famous "clear and present danger test," Justice Oliver Wendell Holmes drew a distinction between wartime and peacetime, stating that the speech in the pamphlet would have been constitutionally protected during "ordinary times." Holmes stated: "The question is every case is whether the words used are used in such circumstances and are of such a nature as to create a clear and present danger that they will bring about the substantive evils that Congress has a right to prevent."

Holmes went on to state that it was not necessary to prove that Schenk's pamphlet had, in fact, deterred men from joining the military. It was enough, under the act, to show a conspiracy to obstruct the draft.

Impact

Interpretation of the First Amendment was new ground for the Supreme Court. As Justice Holmes pioneered the way, he worked toward distinguishing between protected and unprotected speech. A number of cases followed in this area.

Schenk dealt powerfully with prior restraint and the issue of wartime censorship. The Court stated: "When a nation is at war many things that might be said in time of peace are such a hindrance to its effort that their utterance will not be endured so long as men fight and that no Court could regard them as protected by any constitutional right."

NEAR V. STATE OF MINNESOTA, 283 U.S. 697 (1931)

Background

By the early 1900s, yellow journalism had found its niche in the American landscape. In an attempt to limit this type of journalism, a variety of states passed legislation. The Minnesota Gag Law, formally known as the Public Nuisance Abatement Law of 1925, was at the forefront of such laws. It was widely touted across the country as a miracle cure for the sensationalism that ailed the nation's front pages.

The Gag Law provided an injunction as relief against any who participated in the business of producing, circulating, selling, or giving away: "(a) an obscene, lewd and lascivious newspaper, magazine, or other periodical, or (b) a malicious, scandalous and defamatory newspaper, magazine or other periodical." The injunction ordered the defendant to immediately stop producing or circulating the periodical or magazine. A fine and imprisonment could be levied against those who disobeyed the injunction. Even if the statements were true, if they were made maliciously, they were punishable under this law.

The Gag Law was used for the first time in an action against the *Saturday Press*, a Minneapolis weekly newspaper. The *Saturday Press* explored and exposed its view of public corruption and racketeering, attacking officials such as the chief of police and the mayor. The newspaper often published heavily anti-Semitic pieces. Articles contained content such as: "Practically every vendor of vile hooch, every owner of a moonshine still, every snake-faced gangster and embryonic egg in the Twin Cities is a JEW . . . Whereupon I have withdrawn all allegiance to anything with a hook nose that eats herring. I have adopted the sparrow as my national bird until Davis, law enforcement league or the K.K.K. hammers the eagle's beak out straight . . . It was Mose Barnett, a Jew, who boasted that he held the chief of police of Minneapolis in his hand—had bought and paid for him."

An action for an injunction was brought against J. M. Near, the publisher of the *Saturday Press*.

Legal Issues

Near did not attempt to justify his articles. He claimed that the Gag Law was unconstitutional. The lower court found against Near, issuing an injunction and ordering that Near stop producing and distributing any publication "which is a malicious, scandalous or defamatory newspaper. . . ."

Near appealed his case to the Supreme Court. The major issue was that of prior restraint. Near stated that he was entitled to due process of law under the Fourteenth Amendment. The Fourteenth Amendment provides that no person shall be deprived of life, liberty, or property without due process of law. Near argued that prior restraint violated his Fourteenth Amendment rights, depriving him of his liberty and property.

Decision

The Court found for Near, declaring the Gag Law unconstitutional in a 5–4 decision. The Court looked to the issue of suppression of the newspaper and stated, "This statute is . . . unusual, if not unique, and raises questions of grave importance transcending the local interests involved in the particular action." The Court went on to state that it had been firmly established that freedom of press and speech fall within the purview of the Fourteenth Amendment. The Court also emphasized that those who thought they had been defamed had other remedies. This could sue for libel.

The Court examined a sort of censorship see-saw, looking at the balance between liberty of the press and protection of the public. The decision stated, "Some degree of abuse is inseparable from the proper use of everything, and in no instance is this more true than in that of the press. . . . it is better to leave a few of its noxious branches to their luxuriant growth, than, by pruning them away, to injure the vigour of those yielding the proper fruits.

"The fact that the liberty of the press may be abused by miscreant purveyors of scandal does not make any the less necessary the immunity of the press from the previous restraint in dealing with official misconduct. Subsequent punishment for such abuses as may exist is the appropriate remedy, consistent with constitutional privilege."

The Court emphasized that to allow the government to control the freedom of the press through prior restraint would be equivalent to the government shielding itself. "And it would be but a step to a complete system of censorship."

Impact

Near was the precursor to a long line of cases that struck down prior restraint. The decision was well received across the country. Freedom of the press and freedom of thought were established as permanent U.S. rights. Government officials were served a warning that they would no longer be able to exercise prior restraint to interfere with the public's right to know by using legislation such as The Gag Law.

CHAPLINSKY V. STATE OF NEW HAMPSHIRE, 315 U.S. 568 (1942)

Background

During the 1940s, the state of New Hampshire had a law that stated, "No person shall address any offensive, derisive or annoying word to any other person who is lawfully in any street or other public place, nor call him by any offensive or derisive name, nor make any noise or exclamation in his presence and hearing with intent to deride, offend or annoy him, or to prevent him from pursuing his lawful business or occupation."

Chaplinsky, a Jehovah's witness, was disseminating religious literature on public streets in Rochester, New Hampshire. Local citizens complained to City Marshal Bowering "that Chaplinsky was denouncing all religion as a 'racket'." The city marshal advised the citizens that Chaplinsky's acts were legal "and then warned Chaplinsky that the crowd was getting restless."

Later, following a disturbance at an intersection, a traffic officer headed for the police station with Chaplinsky; however, he did not advise Chaplinsky that he was under arrest or that he would be arrested. On the way to the station, Chaplinsky and the traffic officer passed Marshal Bowering, who was racing to the intersection, having been told that a riot had begun there.

Bowering again warned Chaplinsky, and Chaplinsky's reply was made the basis of a criminal complaint. Chaplinsky, it was charged, called Bowering a racketeer and "a damned Fascist" and stated that "the whole government of Rochester are Fascists or agents of Fascists." It was charged in the complaint that Chaplinsky's statement constituted "offensive, derisive and annoying words and names" and thus were actionable under the law.

Legal Issues

Chaplinsky was convicted in the municipal (city) court. In a trial de novo (a new trial in which the lower court trial is not considered for any purpose) before a Superior Court jury, he was again convicted.

On appeal to the United States Supreme Court, Chaplinsky raised the issue that the Rochester law was invalid under the Fourteenth Amendment because "it placed an unreasonable restraint on freedom of speech, freedom of the press, and freedom of worship, and because it was vague and indefinite."

Decision

The Supreme Court opinion stated that only Chaplinsky's "attack on the basis of free speech is warranted," that only the spoken word was involved, and that it could not conceive that "cursing a public officer is the exercise of religion in any sense of the term."

The Court examined the statute, citing prior rulings, and stated, " . . . it is well understood that the right of free speech is not absolute at all times and under all circumstances . . . there are certain well-defined and narrowly limited classes of speech, the prevention and punishment of which has never been thought to raise any Constitutional problem." The Court went on to specify, "the lewd and obscene, the profane, the libelous, and the insulting or 'fighting' words—those which by their very utterance inflict injury or tend to incite an immediate breach of the peace."

In looking to the reasoning behind the designation of punishable classes of speech, the Court looked to prior cases and stated, "It has been well observed that such utterances are no essential part of any exposition of ideas, and are of such slight social value as a step to truth that any benefit that may be derived from them is clearly outweighed by the social interest in order and morality."

The Court ruled against Chaplinsky. It looked to the purpose of the statute, that being to "preserve the public peace" and to prohibit only those words that "have a direct tendency to cause act of violence by the person to whom, individually, the remark is addressed." In examining what a particular addressee thinks when certain words are uttered, the Court stated, "The word 'offensive' is not to be defined in terms of what a particular addressee thinks . . . The test is what men of common intelligence would understand would be words likely to cause an average addressee to fight."

The opinion stated that the Rochester statute was constitutional and "does no more than prohibit the face-to-face words plainly likely to cause a breach of the peace by the addressee, words whose speaking constitute a breach of the peace by the speaker—including 'classical fighting words,' words in current use less 'classical' but equally likely to cause violence . . ."

Impact

Chaplinsky validated statutes all over the country. Still, Supreme Court opinions later chipped away at the *Chaplinsky* ruling. From the date of the *Chaplinsky* decision to the 1990s, no other Supreme Court has upheld a conviction solely on the basis of "fighting words" addressed to public officials.

Brandenburg v. Ohio, decided in 1969, tempered the *Chaplinsky* fighting words decision. It held that advocating illegal action would be punishable only if "such advocacy is directed to inciting or producing imminent lawless action and is likely to incite or produce such action."

In the 1971 case *Cohen v. California*, Cohen wore a jacket bearing the slogan "Fuck the Draft" into a courthouse. He was arrested (and subsequently convicted in the lower court) for disturbing the peace. The Supreme Court overturned his conviction, stating that a hostile reaction to the words on the jacket was not imminent. Subsequent decisions in this area have strongly supported the *Cohen* opinion.

ROTH V. UNITED STATES, 354 U.S. 476 (1957)
(Companion case to [decided with] *Alberts v. California*)

Background

A variety of cases that touched on censorship issues came before the Supreme Court in the 1940s and 1950s; however, the Court truly took obscenity to task in the *Roth* case.

Samuel Roth, regarded by some as a leading American pornographer of the 1950s, advertised, published, and sold books, magazines, and photographs in New York. Roth was convicted of "mailing obscene circulars and advertising, and an obscene book, in violation of the federal obscenity statute." The relevant provision of the statute stated, "Every obscene, lewd, lascivious, or filthy book, pamphlet, picture, paper, letter, writing, print, or other publication of an indecent character; and . . . Every written or printed card, letter, circular, book, pamphlet, advertisement, or notice of any kind giving information, directly or indirectly, where, or how, or from whom, or by what means any of such mentioned matters, articles, or things may be obtained or made, . . . whether sealed or unsealed . . . Is declared to be nonmailable matter and shall not be conveyed in the mails or delivered from any post office or by any letter carrier . . . Whoever knowingly deposits for mailing or delivery, anything declared by this section to be nonmailable, or knowingly takes the same from the mails for the purpose of circulating or disposing thereof, or of aiding in the circulation or disposition thereof, shall be fined not more than $5,000 or imprisoned not more than five years, or both."

Legal Issues

Roth claimed that the federal statute was unconstitutional, and that it was vague and ambiguous. The Court rejected this argument, stating, "lack of precision is not itself offensive to the requirements of due process . . . That there may be marginal cases in which it is difficult to determine the side of the line on which a particular fact situation falls is no sufficient reason to hold the language too ambiguous to define a criminal offense . . ."

Roth further argued that the federal obscenity statute unconstitutionally encroached upon the powers reserved by the Ninth and Tenth Amendments to the States. The Court rejected this argument, stating that obscenity was not a form of protected expression, and hence no such encroachment could exist.

Decision

The Court ruled against Roth, holding that the statute was neither vague nor unconstitutional, and that because obscenity fell into the category of conduct rather than speech, it was not necessary to show harm. The Court held that, though the First Amendment provides protection to all ideas, even those of the most minimal social importance, obscenity is not protected because it is "utterly without redeeming social importance."

The Court further rejected the test based on the 1868 English case *Regina v. Hicklin* that permitted convictions based on mere excerpt from material and the excerpt's proclivity to "deprave and corrupt." Instead, Justice Brennan's opinion enunciated the test for obscenity: "whether to the average person, applying contemporary community standards, the dominant theme of the material taken as a whole appeals to the prurient interest." The opinion defined prurient interest as "having a tendency to excite lustful thoughts" or a "shameful and morbid interest in sex."

Impact

The *Roth* case solidified the position of obscenity as a nonprotected form of expression under the First Amendment. It further established the requirement that a work must be considered as a whole and must appeal to the prurient interest of the average person. No longer would a simple excerpt that might be considered obscene to a child be the standard for obscenity.

Still, courts and the public in general grappled with the definition of "prurient interest" as set forth in the opinion. Many cases followed. In the 1973 *Miller v. California* decision (included in this chapter), the Court enunciated a test that would clarify the grounds for obscenity convictions.

BANTAM BOOKS, INC. V. SULLIVAN, 372 U.S. 58 et al. (1963)

Background

In the 1950s, Rhode Island passed legislation that created the Commission to Encourage Morality in Youth. One of the duties given to the commission was "to educate the public concerning any book, picture, pamphlet, ballad, printed paper or other thing containing obscene, indecent or impure language, or manifestly tending to the corruption of the youth as defined [in the general laws] and to investigate and recommend the prosecution of all violations of said sections . . ."

Upon finding magazines or books objectionable, the commission would send notices advising distributors and police officers that they should be removed from stores.

The *Bantam v. Sullivan* case was based on a commission edict issued to distributor Max Silverstein & Sons advising that specific books should no longer be distributed by their company. By the time the *Bantam* lawsuit was filed, Silverstein had received no fewer than thirty-five such notices regarding a variety of books and magazines, including such titles as *Playboy*, *Frolic*, and *Rogue*.

In this case, the commission notified Silverstein that books by such publishers as Dell and Bantam should no longer be distributed. Among the books were *Peyton Place* (Dell) and *The Bramble Bush* (Bantam). The commission's notice, as usual, advised Silverstein that the commission had a duty to "recommend to the Attorney General prosecution of purveyors of obscenity." The notice went on to inform Silverstein that it planned to hand over titles of objectionable publications to the local police. The commission thanked Silverstein in advance for his cooperation.

As was his usual course of action upon receipt of such notices, Silverstein removed the objectionable titles from his sales list and stopped providing copies to his customers. He further directed his employees to go out to his customers' places of business to gather all unsold copies. Silverstein returned these to the publishers.

Silverstein testified in court that he complied with the commission's directives "rather than face the possibility of some sort of a court action against ourselves, as well as the people we supply." Shortly after taking action on the commission's notices, Silverstein would usually receive a visit from a local police officer, whereupon he would advise of the number of titles being returned to the publishers.

Bantam Books and the other publishers filed this case "(1) to declare the law creating the Commission in violation of the First and Fourteenth Amendments, and (2) to declare unconstitutional and enjoin the acts and practices of the appellees thereunder."

Legal Issues

Lawyers for the publishers argued that the commission's activities constituted a "scheme of government censorship" and failed to "provide safeguards for state regulation of obscenity." Because of this, they argued, the publishers' First and Fourteenth Amendment rights had been violated.

The commission's lawyers argued that Silverstein was under no obligation to observe the notices and that, had he refused to comply, he would have broken no laws. The commission itself did not have the power to file criminal charges. The lawyers further argued that the commission had not regulated or suppressed obscenity, but had merely advised booksellers of their "legal rights."

Decision

"This is censorship in the raw," the Supreme Court declared upon finding for the publishers. The Court held that Silverstein's action was not voluntary. "People do not disregard public officers' thinly veiled threats to institute criminal proceedings against them if they do not come around," the decision stated.

The Court held that the commission's actions created a sort of double-edged sword. Because it did not have the power to prosecute, the commission could not impose criminal sanctions for obscenity. Thus, the commission felt that it did not have to provide safeguards such as notice and hearing, as required by the Constitution.

It was true that the commission did not provide notice and hearing; however, because of the color under which it acted, the Court held its actions to constitute prior restraint. It was not tenable for the commission to state that it could not imposed criminal sanctions and so did not have to provide notice and hearing. "Any system of prior restraints of expression comes to the Court bearing a heavy presumption against its constitutional validity," stated the Court.

Impact

At a time when the atmosphere in the country allowed individuals and groups to make unconstitutional decisions about what was "objectionable," this case emphasized that legal credibility would not be granted to such efforts.

FREEDMAN V. MARYLAND, 380 U.S. 51 (1965)

Background

In the 1960s, the state of Maryland required by law that all films be submitted to the State Board of Censors before being screened in public. Those who failed to submit to this prior restraint law were subject to criminal sanctions.

Freedman failed to submit the film *Revenge at Daybreak* to the board prior to showing it in a public theater. He was arrested and convicted under the Maryland statute. His arrest came about at a time when the country was testing First Amendment rights and many individuals were exercising intellectual freedom.

Legal Issues

Though the state of Maryland admitted that it would not have found the film in violation of board standards, it held that this was immaterial, as the infraction was based upon a failure to submit the film prior to screening rather than a finding that the film violated standards. Further, the state asserted that the Supreme Court had found prior restraint constitutional in some earlier cases, and that the Court should follow its line of reasoning in those opinions.

Decision

The Court agreed that prior restraint was "not necessarily unconstitutional under all circumstances;" however, the opinion also stated, "It is true of motion pictures, as well as other forms of expression, that any system of prior restraint comes to court bearing heavy presumption against its constitutional validity."

The Court was concerned with procedural safeguards under the Maryland statute and stated, "the burden of proving that film is unprotected expression must rest on the censor."

The Court found for Freedman, declaring the Maryland statute unconstitutional. The Court found that the law failed to provide adequate safeguards "against undue inhibition of protected expression" because, if the censor determined that a film violated standards, the burden was on the exhibitor to begin legal proceedings to prove "that the film was protected expression."

And once the legal action had commenced, the exhibitor was prohibited from showing the film until legal proceedings, no matter how lengthy, had come to a close.

The opinion stated, "Apparatus of censorship is always fraught with danger and is viewed with suspicion."

Impact

This decision clarified censorship issues regarding film. Its strong stance against prior restraint rang through the film industry, which ultimately decided to regulate itself. This case should not be confused with obscenity cases, as it focuses on prior restraint, rather than on film content.

TINKER V. DES MOINES INDEPENDENT COMMUNITY SCHOOL DISTRICT, 393 U.S. 503 (1969)

Background

In December 1965, children and adults held a meeting in a private home and decided to publicize their objections to the Vietnam War by wearing black armbands during the holiday season. The Tinker family attended the meeting.

When the principals of the Des Moines schools learned of the plan, they met and formulated a policy stating that any student who wore an armband to school would be asked to remove it and that refusal would result in suspension until the student returned without the armband.

After the policy was adopted, students wore their black armbands to school. They were suspended and told not to return to school until they removed their armbands. After the holidays the students returned to school without the armbands.

This case was filed by the fathers of the students who had been suspended for wearing the armbands. It asked that school officials be restrained from disciplining the students and requested nominal damages.

Legal Issues

A lower court ruled against the students. "It upheld the constitutionality of the school authorities' action on the ground that it was reasonable in order to prevent disturbance of school discipline." Upon appeal to a court of appeals, the case was affirmed. Before the Supreme Court, as before, the students advocated that their First Amendment rights had been violated. The school district advanced the position that the school had the right to control disturbances in the school and to maintain school discipline.

Decision

The Supreme Court held for the students, noting that they were quiet and passive while wearing the armbands, that their conduct did not intrude upon others, and that their actions were clearly within the parameters of speech protected by the First Amendment.

The Court held that students and teachers did not "shed their constitutional rights to freedom of speech or expression at the schoolhouse gate." The Court also referred to other political symbols that had been worn by students in Des Moines schools without school censorship. The Court stated, "state-operated schools may not be regarded as closed-circuit recipients of only that which the State chooses to communicate."

Impact

This case holds a position of almost singular significance in constitutional law regarding the rights of students. It was decided at a time when the country was in turmoil and the rights of citizens were greatly at issue.

Focusing on the First Amendment, this case determined that students have the right to exercise certain freedoms in public schools. A later case, *Hazelwood*, decided in 1988, focused on rights that students may *not* exercise in public schools.

NEW YORK TIMES CO. V. UNITED STATES, 403 U.S. 713 (1971)

Background

During the Vietnam War, Secretary of Defense Robert McNamara, at the direction of President Lyndon Johnson, researched and wrote the *Pentagon Papers*. This document, thousands of pages long, was classified by the government. It revealed a chain of trickery and clandestine activities that led to U.S. military action in Vietnam. Daniel Ellsberg, former deputy secretary of defense, leaked the *Pentagon Papers* to the press, and on June 13, 1971, the first installment was published in the *New York Times*.

By this time, Richard Nixon was president. He held mixed ideas regarding the publication of the *Papers*. Perhaps he thought that they could injure only earlier administrations, and they might serve as a valuable political weapon. Ultimately, however, Nixon opposed the publication of the classified document, noting its potential impact on his own and future administrations, as well as on the power of the Executive Branch to maintain classified communication.

Within two days, the government sought, and received, an injunction against the publication of further installments of the *Pentagon Papers*; however, this was only temporary. The government filed for a permanent injunction, which was denied. Upon appeal to a higher court, the government won an injunction that remained effective until the Supreme Court ruled on the matter.

Legal Issues

The government contended that "in spite of the First Amendment, [t]he authority of the Executive Department to protect the nation against publication of information whose disclosure would endanger the national security stems from the two interrelated sources: the constitutional power of the president over the conduct of foreign affairs and his authority as Commander-in-Chief." National security should override First Amendment protections in a case such as this, the government argued.

The main issue in this case was that of prior restraint and whether national security issues in this set of circumstances overrode numerous cases holding against prior restraint.

Decision

In a 6–3 decision, the Court emphatically denied the injunction, citing such cases as *Bantam Books v. Sullivan* and *Near v. Minnesota*. Justice Black wrote of the history of the First Amendment, stating, "For the first time since in the 182 years since the founding of the Republic, the federal courts are asked to hold that the First Amendment does not mean what it says, but rather means that the Government can halt the publication of current news of vital importance to the people of this country . . . the Executive Branch seems to have forgotten the essential purpose and history of the First Amendment."

In discussing the government's argument that the powers of the Constitution should be limited in this situation, Justice Black wrote, "I can imagine no greater perversion of history." The Court went on to praise the courage of newspapers such as the *New York Times* and the *Washington Post* for exposing the workings of government and for doing "precisely that which the Founders hoped and trusted they would do."

Impact

During this period the press and the administration had been careening headlong into a powerful collision. This case was the result. After this decision was handed down, Nixon's relationship with the press certainly never improved; in fact, its deterioration provided a backdrop for some of the most startling events in the country's history, including his resignation.

Daniel Ellsberg, who had leaked the *Pentagon Papers* faced criminal charges. His case resulted in a mistrial.

MILLER V. CALIFORNIA, 413 U.S. 15 (1973)

Background

Miller mailed unsolicited advertising brochures to a California restaurant that were opened by the manager and his mother. Though a small amount of text appeared on each page advertising such items as books entitled *Intercourse* and *Sex Orgies Illustrated*, the brochure was primarily filled with very explicit "pictures and drawings that depicted men and women in groups of two or more engaging in a variety of sexual activities, with genitals often prominently displayed."

Legal Issues

In 1973, the state of California had an obscenity statute that provided for criminal penalties. This case revolved around the application of the state obscenity statute to Miller's actions in mailing the brochures. Miller's lawyers argued that the obscenity test was vague and that it was impossible to determine what was, or was not obscene under the statute, hence the statute was unconstitutional.

Decision

The Court ruled against Miller in a 5–4 decision, restating its position that obscenity is not protected by the First Amendment. *Miller* was critically important in the history of obscenity because it further clarified the Court's position in this area. In an earlier case, *Roth v. U.S.*, decided in 1957, (included in this chapter) the Court had outlined its test for determining obscenity as that work which, "taken as a whole," appealed to the "prurient interest" of the "average person." In *Roth*, the Court stated that obscenity was unprotected because it was "utterly without redeeming social importance."

In *Miller*, the Court went on to enunciate the now-famous three-pronged test to determine obscenity. The Court held that material is obscene if "(a) the average person, applying contemporary community standards, would find that the work, taken as a whole, applies to the prurient interest; (b) the work depicts or describes, in a patently offensive way, sexual conduct specifically defined by the applicable state law; and (c) the work, taken as a whole, lacks serious literary, artistic, political, or scientific value." For the first time, the Court applied a geographic test, and stated that the "community" standard was to be applied.

Impact

The *Miller* decision was met with a range of reactions. Some felt that it would be difficult for a jury to determine what an "average" person would believe. The matter gave rise to further controversy due to concern that a particular book or film might be considered obscene in one area and not in another, thereby restricting the right of some to see the material.

FEDERAL COMMUNICATIONS COMMISSION V. PACIFICA FOUNDATION, 438 U.S. 726 (1978)

Background

George Carlin, a comedian and satirist, recorded a twelve-minute monologue entitled "Filthy Words" before a live audience in California. The monologue discussed the seven words that could "never be broadcast over the public airwaves."

Later, while a father and young son were out driving one afternoon, they heard the broadcast. The father filed a complaint with the Federal Communications Commission (FCC), stating, "[I can understand the] record's being sold for private use. I certainly cannot understand the broadcast of same over the air that, supposedly, you control."

Pacifica, the owner of the radio station, responded by stating that the monologue had been included as part of a program regarding "contemporary society's attitude toward language," and that Carlin's monologue was not designed to spew obscenities, but rather to examine and satirize society's attitudes toward certain words.

The FCC issued an order granting the complaint, but did not apply any sanctions. It did, however, inform Pacifica that the complaint would be retained in the radio station's file, and that if further complaints arose, they could be examined as a whole to determine whether the station's license should be revoked or other sanctions should be imposed. Additionally, the commission stated that it planned to "clarify the standards" taken into consideration in evaluating the increasing number of complaints about "indecent speech on the airwaves."

The commission found that the language, which referred to sexual and excretory activities, was "patently offensive."

Legal Issues

The Court considered a variety of issues, including whether the commission had the power to "impose sanctions on licensees who engage in obscene, indecent, or profane broadcasting." The Court also examined whether the broadcast was indecent "within the meaning" of the statute.

Decision

The Court found that the FCC did have the right to cite the radio station; however, the Court did not find the monologue obscene. The Court looked to previous interpretations of the statute and the power of the FCC in rendering its opinion.

Impact

Though this decision had a somewhat chilling impact in its time, it has been substantially eroded over the years. It is interesting to note that a decency standard was at issue in this case, just as it was in the *ACLU v. Reno* case of 1996. The *Reno* case (detailed later in this chapter) dealt with the Internet and expounded at length upon the decency standard.

FRANK W. SNEPP, III V. UNITED STATES, 444 U.S. 507 (1980)

Background

Frank Snepp, a former CIA agent, published a book detailing CIA activities in South Vietnam. Upon accepting employment with the CIA, Snepp had signed an agreement in which he promised that he would "not . . . publish . . . any information or material relating to the Agency, its activities or intelligence activities generally, either during or after the term of [his] employment . . . without specific prior approval by the Agency."

Snepp failed to request the required prior approval before publication of his book. The government filed this lawsuit and asked three remedies of the Court: 1) to declare that Snepp had breached the contract, 2) to issue an injunction requiring Snepp to submit future writings for "prepublication review," and 3) to "impose a constructive trust" on behalf of the government so that the government could take profits from the book. Snepp had received approximately $60,000 in advance funds and was to receive royalties and additional future profits from the publisher in connection with his book.

Legal Issues

Snepp's position was that he had divulged no classified information and therefore had not harmed the government in any way. The Court looked to the fiduciary relationship (relationship of utmost trust) between Snepp and the CIA, as well as the agreement itself.

Decision

The lower court ruled for the government, agreeing that Snepp's duty was one of utmost trust. The Supreme Court agreed with the lower court, stating, "a former intelligence agent's publication of unreviewed material relating to intelligence activities can be detrimental to vital national interests even if the published information is unclassified."

Impact

The *Snepp* case made it clear that the prior restraint so condemned in regard to the general public was not to be treated in the same fashion in the military sector. The distinction was clearly drawn. Whereas prior restraint had been struck down time and again in cases not involving governmental security, the Court staunchly upheld the government's right to enforce its prior review contracts in this case.

HAZELWOOD SCHOOL DISTRICT V. KUHLMEIER, 484 U.S. 260 (1988)

Background

During an era when students had truly begun to explore their independence and vigorously pursue their constitutional rights, students at a Missouri high school newspaper included two controversial stories in their May 13 edition. As was school procedure, the principal received page proofs of the *Spectrum* for his approval. He received the proofs on May 10, three days before the newspaper was to have been printed.

The principal objected to the controversial articles. One detailed experiences of pregnant teen students attending the school. The other explored the impact of divorce on students at the school. Although the pregnancy article did not use the students' real names, the principal indicated his fear that students might, nonetheless, divine the identity of these students. He also expressed concern that information referencing sexual activity and birth control might not be appropriate for younger students.

As to the article on divorce, the principal was concerned that the allegations of a student (whose real name was used in the story) against one of her parents should be taken to the parent, and the parent given an opportunity to respond, before the issue went to press.

Because this issue was the last of the year and because the principal felt it would be impossible to make necessary changes before the newspaper was scheduled to appear, he decided that the two pages with the controversial pieces must be excised, making the final newspaper of the year four, rather than six, pages long.

The school newspaper was printed with funds allocated from the Board of Education. Additional funds for printing were obtained from newspaper sales.

Legal Issues

A court refused to grant injunctive relief to the students. The students appealed and the appeals court ruled in their favor. The school district then appealed the case. The school district advocated that the newspaper was not a public forum, and therefore school officials had the right to impose reasonable restrictions. They stated that the students' First Amendment rights had not been violated.

Decision

The Court ruled for the school district, stating "First Amendment rights of students in the public schools are not automatically coextensive with the rights of adults in other settings, and must be applied in light of the special characteristics of the school environment. A school need not tolerate student speech that is inconsistent with its basic educational mission, even though the government could not censor similar speech outside the school."

The Court determined that the school newspaper was not a forum for public expression and that school facilities could be deemed public forums only if "school authorities have by policy or by practice opened the facilities for indiscriminate use by the general public, or by some segment of the public, such as student organizations." The Court went on to state that, if no such public forum had been created, school officials had the right to impose speech restrictions on students, teachers, and other members of the school community.

Impact

This case answered many questions across the country regarding censorship of school publications. Students would continue their campaign to hold greater control over their school activities; however, administrators held Supreme Court guidelines that gave them the power to censor within the school environment.

Censorship

TEXAS V. JOHNSON, 491 U.S. 397 (1989)

Background

Gregory Johnson took part in a march and rally to protest Reagan administration policies. During the march, approximately 100 protesters chanted political slogans and staged "die-ins" to demonstrate their concern over nuclear war. At the end of the demonstration, in front of Dallas City Hall, Johnson was handed a flag. He poured kerosene over the flag and set it ablaze while he and other demonstrators declared, "America, the red, white, and blue, we spit on you."

There was neither injury nor threat of injury during this demonstration. Johnson was the only demonstrator arrested. He was charged with the crime of desecration of a venerable object and was convicted in the state court.

Legal Issues

The Court was faced with determining whether Johnson's conviction was "consistent with the First Amendment." The state defended the desecration statute by arguing that the flag should be preserved as a symbol of unity. The state further asserted that the law was designed to prevent a breach of the peace.

Johnson argued that his actions constituted expressive conduct entitled to protection under the First Amendment.

Decision

The Court disagreed with the state's arguments and held for Johnson, stating: "Johnson was not . . . prosecuted for the expression of just any idea; he was prosecuted for his expression of dissatisfaction with the policies of this country, expression situated at the core of our First Amendment values . . . If he had burned the flag as a means of disposing of it because it was dirty or torn, he would not have been convicted of flag desecration under this Texas law. . . . We never before have held that the Government may ensure that a symbol be used to express only one view of that symbol or its referents."

Impact

Flag desecration raises the ire of many. Just after the *Johnson* decision, the United States Congress enacted the Flag Protection Act in 1989, which was promptly struck down by the Supreme Court in *U.S. v. Eichman* (1990). By 1995, the U.S. House had passed the Flag Desecration Amendment—which failed in the Senate. New flag desecration laws were being promulgated by 1997.

FINLEY ET AL. V. NATIONAL ENDOWMENT FOR THE ARTS, U.S. CT. OF APPEALS, 9TH CIR., NO. 92-56028, D.C. NO. CV-90-5236-AWT (1996)

Background

During the 1980s and 1990s, controversy raged over federal arts funding. Debates were fueled by funding for exhibits featuring such works as Robert Mapplethorpe's homoerotic photographs and Andres Serrano's "Piss Christ," which depicted Christ in a bottle of urine.

In 1990, a statute mandating that the National Endoment for the Arts (NEA) consider "general standards of decency and respect" when dispensing grants was passed. Prior to the enactment of the statute, the standard had been "artistic excellence and artistic merit." Proponents of the new law were glad to see regulation on the horizon. Opponents railed against the statute, calling in vague and unenforceable, stating that political influence should keep its nose out of the arts.

In 1996, four performance artists and the National Association of Artists' Organizations (NAAO) filed a lawsuit against the NEA. They challenged the constitutionality of the statute.

Legal Issues

Those who challenged the statute stated that it was vague and should be voided under the void-for-vagueness doctrine. They further stated that there could be no due process under such a vague statute because it is impossible to know how to observe it. Thus the statute violates due process rights.

Those wishing to enforce the statute first stated that the plaintiffs did not have a property right in NEA grants and that their "liberty to express themselves is not regulated by the grants." They further advanced the theory that the vagueness doctrine applied only if "the government regulates speech or places conditions on a generally available benefit."

The Court rejected both arguments, holding "the scarcity of a government benefit does not render it immune from constitutional limitations."

Additionally, the NEA stated that the vagueness of the "decency and respect" clause was not an issue. It advocated that the clause only required that the chairperson consider "general standards of decency and respect for diverse beliefs and values" when assessing procedures for determining grants. The Court also rejected this argument.

Decision

The Court held that the plaintiff's due process rights and First Amendment rights had been violated because the statute was vague and its requirements were unclear. "The twin dangers of a vague law—lack of notice and arbitrary or discriminatory application—may chill the exercise of important constitutional rights."

Impact

Federal arts funding decisions were not to be based on a vague law. Many arts supporters cheered the decision, considering it a blow against restraint of intellectual freedom. Many of those who had supported the statute set about promulgating new legislation to address the growing arts funding controversy.

RENO, ATTORNEY GENERAL OF THE UNITED STATES ET AL. V. ACLU ET AL., NO. 96-511 U.S. SUPREME COURT (1997)

Background

In 1995 and 1996, a variety of bills focusing on Internet issues found their way to the legislative floor. Two of the most controversial were the Telecommunications Act of 1996 and the Communications Decency Act of 1996 (which amended the Telecommunications Act).

The Telecommunications Act of 1996 addressed four areas relating to the transmission of material via interactive computer services. The first provision criminalized the use of interactive computer services and telecommunications services to send harassing communications or to display "indecent" material to a minor. An additional section made it a crime to use a facility to coerce or entice minors to engage in criminal sexual activity.

The Communications Decency Act of 1996 (CDA) mandated criminal penalties for those who displayed "indecent" material to minors. Critics charged that the Act was vague, that there was no way to determine the meaning of "indecent" and "patently offensive." Would sex education materials sent over the Internet be considered indecent?, for example. When the CDA passed on February 1, 1996, the internet dubbed the day Black Thursday. Thousands of websites turned their backgrounds black in protest.

On the same day, the American Civil Liberties Union (ACLU) filed a lawsuit seeking a temporary restraining order against enforcement of the CDA. The temporary restraining order was granted. Attorney General Janet Reno agreed not to "initiate any investigations or prosecutions" under the challenged provisions of the CDA until the case was heard by the District Court. The American Library Association joined in the action in the U.S. District Court for the Eastern District of Pennsylvania.

The Law of Censorship

Legal Issues

The opinion stated, "All parties agree that in order to apprehend the legal questions at issue in these cases, it is necessary to have a clear understanding of the exponentially growing, worldwide medium that is the Internet, which presents unique issues relating to the application of First Amendment jurisprudence and due process requirements to this new and evolving method of communication."

The opinion went on to describe, in great detail, the nature of cyberspace. A cyberspace expert actually gave an Internet tour before the opinion was rendered.

At issue was whether the terms "indecent" and "patently offensive," which were not defined in the statute, were unconstitutionally vague, thus impinging on First Amendment rights.

The government contended, "shielding minors from access to indecent materials is the compelling interest supporting the CDA." The court rejected this argument, citing earlier cases dealing with film nudity at drive-in movie theaters.

The plaintiffs stressed "the possibility of arbitrary enforcement of the Act" due to its vagueness.

Decision

In a very lengthy decision, the lower court ruled for the plaintiffs, stating, "There is no doubt that the CDA requires the most stringent review for vagueness, since it is a criminal statute that 'threatens to inhibit the exercise of constitutionally protected rights.'"

In its analysis, the court referred to an AIDS project website that offered safe sex instructions in "street language" so that they were easily comprehensible. It referred to a variety of previous cases, including a 1957 case that held that adults had been denied their free speech rights because they were allowed "to read only what was acceptable for children."

Pertinent passages from the decision include the following:

After the CDA, however, the content of a user's speech will determine the extent of participation in the new medium. . . . If a speaker's content is even arguably indecent in some communities, he must assess, inter alia, the risk of prosecution and the cost of compliance with the CDA. Because the creation and posting of a Web site allows users anywhere in the country to see that site, many speakers will no doubt censor their speech so that it is palatable in every community. . . . Unlike other media, there is no technologically feasible way for an Internet speaker to limit the geographical scope of his speech. . . . The CDA will, without doubt, undermine the substantive, speech-enhancing benefits that have flowed from the Internet . . . The diversity of the content will necessarily diminish as a result.

The court went on to discuss the fact that the CDA would "skew the relative parity among speakers on the Internet." Those commercial entities who could afford and who required verification and/or a fee would be relatively unaffected by the act, as their websites would generally remain inaccessible to children. Those entities who could not afford to charge or require verification, such as the ACLU, would be "profoundly affected."

"Perversely," the Court stated, "commercial pornographers would remain relatively unaffected by the Act, since we learned that most of them already use credit cards for adult verification anyway." Though the CDA would mandate removal of free "teaser" photos, the court reasoned that the "core" would remain in place as it had before.

Finally, the decision stated, "Just as the strength of the Internet is chaos, so the strength of our liberty depends upon the chaos and cacophony of the unfettered speech the First Amendment protects.

"For these reasons, I without hesitation hold that the CDA is unconstitutional on its face."

The United States Supreme Court agreed with the lower court ruling and held the CDA unconstitutional. The Supreme Court opinion stated, "It is true that we have repeatedly recognized the governmental interest in protecting children from harmful materials. But that interest does not justify an unnecessarily broad suppression of speech addressed to adults."

Impact

This decision met with a resounding cheer from intellectual freedom activists nationwide. It was hailed as one of the most significant First Amendment decisions in history. Proponents of the CDA, however, continued to work vigilantly to promulgate a similar statute.

CHAPTER 3

CHRONOLOGY

This chapter provides a chronology of important events relevant to censorship. The history of censorship is vast, so this chronology focuses on representative occurrences. History, culture, politics, and legal viewpoints are all taken into consideration.

Because censorship has roots in the distant past, the chronology begins there and it wends its way through the centuries and around the globe.

443 BCE

■ The Office of the Censor is established in Rome. The censor's job is to take the census and regulate citizens' morals.

399 BCE

■ Socrates is accused of corrupting youth and insulting the gods. He is condemned to death, being forced to drink hemlock. Socrates maintains that he had no intention of corrupting, that his goal was only to seek the truth.

213 BCE

■ In order to deal with political and intellectual opposition, Shi Huang Ti, the Chinese emperor who built the Great Wall of China, orders that certain books be destroyed.

204 BCE

■ Naevius, a Roman comic poet, is found guilty of slander for having mocked public officials. This is the first theater censorship case to be recorded.

1209 CE

■ The Synod of Paris condemns the works of David Dinant (de Nantes). Anyone reading the unexpurgated text of *De Metaphysica* is ordered excommunicated.

1215

- The Magna Carta is signed, granted new rights to citizens; however, laws still remain in force limiting freedom of expression.

1231

- Aristotle's writings are banned by Pope Gregory IX

1459

- In Germany, Johann Gutenberg "invents" the printing press for the Western world, leading to wide dissemination of ideas through books and pamphlets.

1529

- King Henry VIII issues a proclamation against heretical books. He creates a licensing system requiring prior review of all material to be printed.

1538

- The Church of England declares that prior approval, in the form of a license, is required before a book can be published. Those who fail to obtain a license prior to publication can be sentenced to death.

1551

- Theatre censorship begins in the United Kingdom; it continues until the mid-twentieth century.

1559

- The Congregation of the Index, a censorship board, is established by Pope Paul IV. Its purpose is to censor all books written in Roman Catholic countries.

1564

- The *Index of Forbidden Books* is published; the Roman Catholic church places more than 4,000 works on the list. The index is renewed and utilized until the mid-twentieth century.

1579

- Queen Elizabeth I plans to marry a man of French extraction. John Stubbs publicly decries this action. His right hand is cut off and his lawyer is imprisoned.

1621

- The first *Coranto*, a weekly newspaper offering translations into English from European publications, is published in Britain.

Chronology

1632

- The *Coranto* is outlawed by the British government.
- Galileo, against admonitions from the Church, publishes his findings that the earth is not at the center of the universe, but is one of many planets revolving around the sun. After his arrest and threats of torture, he publicly states that his findings were erroneous and foolish. Galileo's works on the topic are banned.

1643

- The British Licensing Act is passed. The act requires that government approval must be sought before printed material may be published.

1644

- Poet John Milton writes "Areopagitica," an essay in which he beseeches the government to permit the "liberty to know, to utter, and to argue freely according to conscience." Milton expresses a staunch belief in the positive power of the truth. The arguments he advances against censorship remain pertinent throughout time. Though Milton admits that criminal sanctions may be in order subsequent to publication, he argues vehemently against prior restraint of the written word.

1651

- Thomas Hobbes's *Leviathan* is banned. The book questions the divine right of kings and advocates that the state should control the clergy.

1689

- British Parliament gains the right to debate on the Parliament floor.
- The English Bill of Rights is adopted. It helps lay the foundation for its American counterpart.

1690

- *Publick Occurrences Both Foreign and Domestick*, the first newspaper in British North America, is censored by Maryland's governor.

1695

- The Licensing Act lapses and is not renewed by the British Parliament. Though seditious libel remains as law, the prior restraint provided for under the Licensing Act is abolished.

1700s

- Laws of Seditious Libel are passed; citizens are imprisoned, fined and whipped for ordinary political discussion.

1702

- The *Daily Courant*, England's first daily newspaper, begins publication.

1734

- John Peter Zenger is found innocent of seditious libel after having been charged with defaming the governor through articles in the *New-York Weekly Journal*. Even though Zenger is found not guilty, the law is not changed and "truth" is not established as a defense to libel until many years later.

1762

- *Du Contrat social (The Social Contract)* by Jean-Jacques Rousseau is published in the Netherlands after having been banned in France. The book opens with the sentence: "Man is born free and everywhere, he is in chains."

1771

- British newspapers gain the right to publish articles about debates in Parliament.

1789

- France proclaims freedom of thought, communication, and printing (with specified limitations) when it issues the *Declaration of the Rights of Man*.

1791

- In December, the United States Bill of Rights is ratified. The First Amendment guarantees freedom of speech and press.

1792

- Thomas Paine's *The Rights of Man* is published in England. The book is wildly popular, selling approximately 200,000 copies. The government accuses Paine of blasphemy and treason due to his criticisms of the monarchial system and other governmental practices. Though Paine escapes safely to France, others who have printed and distributed his book are routinely jailed.
- In Great Britain, Fox's Libel Act is passed; it provides that a jury will determine if material is libelous.

1798

- The Alien and Sedition Acts of 1798 are passed in the United States. They make it a crime to "write, print, or speak any false or scandalous criticism of the government with the intention to harm reputations or to incite against the government the hatred of the good people of the U.S."

Chronology

1800

- Thomas Jefferson defeats President John Adams. He pardons all those who were convicted under the Alien and Sedition Acts.

1802

- In Great Britain, Thomas Bowdler establishes the Society for the Suppression of Vice. He plucks language he deems indecent from literature—and the term "bowdlerizing" is coined.
- In France, publications, plays, personal correspondence, and newspapers are censored by Napoleon.

1805

- Following a legal argument made by attorney Alexander Hamilton in a court case, the New York legislature establishes truth as a defense to libel. Many other states follow suit.

1818

- *The Family Shakespeare* is published by Thomas Bowdler in England. Bowdler has edited the bard's works to make them more "acceptable and appropriate."

1836

- Emile de Girardin establishes La Presse in France, beginning a new era of the free press.

1857

- British Parliament adopts the Obscene Publications Act; the act defines obscene publications and provides for such material to be seized.

1884

- Mark Twain's *Huckleberry Finn* is banned in a Massachusetts library; sales skyrocket. The book is subsequently banned many times.

1902

- George Bernard Shaw's play *Mrs. Warren's Profession* is finally produced in Great Britain after years of suppression because of the profession alluded to in the title—prostitution.

1907

- Chicago passes the first film censorship law.

1917

- In the United States, Congress passes the Espionage Act, providing criminal penalties for making false reports or statements designed to interfere with the war effort. The act also makes it illegal to obstruct recruitment or enlistment.

■ In Australia, the Commonwealth Film Censorship Board is established. A rating system to protect children is promulgated.

1918

■ The United States Congress passes the Sedition Act of 1918, which provides criminal penalties for those who say, print, write, or publish anything disloyal, profane, or abusive about the United States service, flag, or uniforms. It further provides criminal penalties for offering financial advice that could have a negative impact on the sale of war bonds.

1919

■ The United States Supreme Court enunciates the "clear and present danger" test and upholds the Espionage Act of 1917. The Court draws a distinction between speech that is permissible during wartime and speech that is permissible during peacetime.

1922

■ Import of James Joyce's novel *Ulysses* is prohibited in the United States. The ban is not lifted until 1933.

■ The motion picture industry forms the Motion Picture Producers and Distributors of America (MPAA) in order to circumvent imminent federal regulation. The MPAA promulgates a Production Code containing regulations for the film industry.

1925

■ The American Civil Liberties Union (ACLU) is founded. Its members fight vigorously for civil rights and are strong advocates of intellectual freedom.

■ In the famous Scopes trial, John Scopes is convicted for violating a state law that prohibits the teaching of Darwinism.

■ The Minnesota Gag Law is passed as a result of the proliferation of tabloids that print libelous material. The law allows prior restraint of printed defamatory statements and remains in effect until it is struck down by the United States Supreme Court in 1931.

1927

■ Congress passes the Radio Act of 1927, which provides for a commission to regulate radio communications. The act is passed in response to industry pleas, as a plethora of stations has begun to flood the airwaves, making broadcasting difficult to control.

Chronology

1931

■ The United States Supreme Court decides *Near v. Minnesota*, stating that prior restraint of newspapers and periodicals is unconstitutional except in extreme circumstances.

1933

■ *May 10:* In Nazi Germany, approximately 20,000 books are burned in Berlin; Josef Goebbels, propaganda minister, is instrumental in this and other book burnings.

1934

■ The Federal Communications Commission (FCC) is established in the United States. Although it holds no prior restraint power, the FCC does have the right to review broadcasters' operating licenses. The FCC is granted the power to deny renewal when broadcasters are deemed to have disregarded the public interest. The FCC seldom utilizes its powers to revoke, but one of its rare decisions to do so is upheld by the United States Supreme Court.

1938

■ The United States House establishes the House Un-American Activities Committee (HUAC). The committee investigates people from all walks of life for "anti-American" activities; performers in particular are targeted. Many people are deemed Communist sympathizers. The committee's activities act as a precursor to the McCarthy era.

■ The United States Supreme Court decides *Lovell v. Griffin* and finds unconstitutional a statute that prohibits distribution of literature without a city manager's prior approval.

1940

■ The Smith Act, the first peacetime sedition act since 1918, is passed in the United States. A violation occurs under the act when a person orally or through printing, publishing, or distributing written material advocates or teaches the violent overthrow of any government in the United States.

1942

■ Obscenity, libel, and "fighting words" are declared by the United States Supreme Court (*Chaplinsky v. New Hampshire*) to be forms of unprotected speech under the First Amendment.

1943

■ Theaters and publishers in Germany are closed down by the Nazi propaganda minister.

Censorship

1948

- The United Nations promulgates its Universal Declaration of Human Rights, advancing the tenet that all people have the right to freedom of expression.

1950–54

- McCarthyism runs rampant across the United States as Wisconsin senator Joseph McCarthy hurls accusations of "Communist!" at teachers, members of government, actors, musicians, and those from numerous other walks of life.

1950

- In South Africa, those who express opposition to apartheid are banned from public meetings, schools, and universities; it becomes illegal to quote them. The ban remains in effect until 1990.

1954

- The Comics Code Authority is established to regulate comic books.

1957

- The United States Supreme Court enunciates the "prurient interest" test for obscenity in *Roth v. United States.*
- The United States Supreme Court holds that it is "not illegal to speak or write in favor of violent revolutions."

1958

- At the direction of the Soviet government, Boris Pasternak declines the Nobel Prize for Literature for his novel *Doctor Zhivago.*

1959

- *Lady Chatterly's Lover* by D. H. Lawrence is deemed obscene and banned from the mail by the United States Postmaster General. In 1960, a court lifts the ban. The film version of the book is found to be obscene by a New York state court. On appeal, the Supreme Court finds that the film is protected under the First Amendment.

1961

- *May 1:* The University of California at Berkeley refuses to allow Black Muslim leader Malcolm X to appear for a speaking engagement.
- Amnesty International is established. The group's goal is to offer aid to those suffering from censorship and other rights abuses.

Chronology

1963

- *May 6:* In Birmingham, Alabama, thousands are arrested during a civil rights march.

1966

- Congress passes the Freedom of Information Act (FOIA) allowing access to thousands of previously classified government documents.

1967

- The United States Commission on Obscenity and Pornography is established on October 23. The commission does not find a link between pornography and crime. (Some speculate that President Nixon had hoped it would).

1968

- A sponsor calls for television censorship after Petula Clark, a white singer touches black musician Harry Belafonte's arm during the taping of a duet.

1969

- Armbands in public schools are deemed constitutional symbolic speech in *Tinker v. Des Moines School District.* The case arises after students who wear black armbands to protest the Vietnam War are suspended; the Supreme Court finds that their conduct did not interfere with school activities and that they had a First Amendment right to wear the armbands.
- Denmark abolishes all adult film censorship.

1971

- *June 13:* The *New York Times* prints the first installment of the *Pentagon Papers*, a classified government document revealing deceitful activities leading U.S. involvement in the Vietnam War.
- *June 30:* The United States Supreme Court strikes down injunctions against the *New York Times* for publishing the Pentagon Papers (*New York Times Co. v. U.S.*).

1973

- The *Miller* case before the United States Supreme Court results in the three-pronged test to determine obscenity. For the first time, the geographic (community) standard is applied.
- George Carlin appears before a live audience and records his twelve-minute monologue entitled "Filthy Words." The monologue is subsequently aired on a radio station, and the station is cited by the FCC. The Supreme Court does not find the monologue obscene.

Censorship

1976
- The United States Supreme Court finds the film *Deep Throat* obscene.

1977
- A neo-Nazi group is granted the legal right to march in Skokie, Illinois, a city with a large Jewish population.

1980
- Reverend Jerry Falwell establishes the Moral Majority, a fundamentalist group with a number of agendas, including frequent calls for censorship.

1981
- Carol Burnett wins a $1.6 million dollar judgment (though the amount was later reduced) against the *National Enquirer* for libel. (The *Enquirer* published an erroneous story with a variety of allegations, including a suggestion that Burnett had been intoxicated at a restaurant.)

1983
- The United States bars the press from covering the Grenada invasion.
- Foreign reporters are banned from Ethiopia and Ethiopian local reporters are banned from writing stories about famines, which are causing widespread starvation.

1985
- The Chinese government creates a state agency to control all publications.

1986
- The United States Attorney General's Commission on Pornography is established by William French Smith. It finds that erotic matter is not a significant cause of crime or sexual deviance; it further finds a connection between the pornography industry and organized crime.

1987
- Oscar Arias Sánchez, who wins the 1987 Nobel Peace Prize, orchestrates the Arias Peace Plan in Costa Rica which calls for a variety of action, including cease-fires and an end to media censorship.
- The FCC determines that it has the right to revoke a station's license for the broadcast of indecent material.

1988
- The U.S. Supreme Court finds the right of administrators to censor a school newspaper constitutional in *Hazelwood School District v. Kuhlmeier*.
- The Soviet Union ceases jamming Radio Free Europe broadcasts.

Chronology

1989

- Author Salman Rushdie goes into hiding after Islamic religious leaders order his death and denounce his novel *The Satanic Verses* as blasphemous.
- The United States Supreme Court decides *Texas v. Johnson* and determines that flag-burning is a protected category of nonverbal expression under the First Amendment.
- After the *Texas v. Johnson* decision, the United States Congress enacts the Flag Protection Act, which provides criminal sanctions for flag desecration. The act is struck down in 1990 in *United States v. Eichman.*
- Robert Mapplethorpe's homoerotic art fans a blaze of controversy over federal funding and the National Endowment for the Arts.

1990

- In Florida, a federal district court judge rules that *As Nasty As They Wanna Be*, an album by the rap group 2 Live Crew, is obscene; this provides the framework for criminal penalties against store owners who sell the album. Several days later, the members of the group are arrested for obscenity during a performance. They are later found not guilty.
- The director of the Cincinnati Contemporary Arts Center is charged with obscenity for exhibiting Robert Mapplethorpe's work.

1995

- German officials demand that CompuServe cease offering access to specific Internet bulletin boards that include content deemed obscene by the German government. CompuServe complies. As it does not have the capability to censor the Internet for portions of its users, CompuServe discontinues the newsgroups for all of its subscribers worldwide. Its action is met with explosive disapproval around the globe.
- President Clinton voices his approval of the antiviolence v-chip while addressing the Conference on the Family and the Media in Nashville. The v-chip offers technology that allows parents to lock out programs whose content has been deemed to rise above a specified level of violence.
- The Flag Desecration Amendment passes in the House. The Senate does not vote on the amendment and similar legislation fails in the Senate.

1996

- *February 8:* Congress passes the Telecommunication Reform Bill and attaches the Communications Decency Art (CDA). President Clinton signs the act into law. The CDA provides criminal sanctions (punishable by up to two years in jail and/or a $250,000 fine) for those who engage in "indecent" or "patently offensive" speech on a computer network in situations where such "speech" could be seen by minors. The CDA is strongly opposed and February 8, 1996, becomes known as Black Thursday on the Internet, and thousands of websites are turned black in protest.

- The ACLU files a legal challenge to the CDA. Within weeks, nearly thirty more plaintiffs, including the American Library Association (ALA), join the ACLU.

- *November 1:* A New York law providing criminal sanctions for disseminating "indecent" content "harmful to minors" via computer network becomes effective.

- *November 5:* The Ninth Circuit Court of Appeals holds unconstitutional a law mandating that the National Endowment for the Arts consider "general standards of decency" when making grant decisions.

1997

- *February 12:* Internet missives explicitly detailing torture, rape, and murder written by Jake Baker, a former Michigan University student, are determined by the Sixth Circuit Court to be constitutionally protected speech. Baker serves as the test case; he is the first person to have been criminally charged for such communications over the Internet.

- *early June:* A law is introduced to the North Carolina legislature that would mandate felony penalties for anyone convicted of providing material to a child that "condones or advocates . . . alternate lifestyles" unless the child's parent gives prior permission.

- *June 26:* The U.S. Supreme Court upholds a lower court ruling and finds the Communications Decency Act (CDA) vague, and hence, unconstitutional.

- *July 11:* A Johnson City, Tennessee, art exhibit opens. Among the exhibits is Emerson Zabower's oil painting *The Philly Flasher*. The painting depicts a man clothed only in sagging socks and a raincoat, which he is holding open. In mid-July, the painting is removed from the main exhibit and placed in a back room—where it may be viewed by request only.

- *September 23:* The Military Honor and Decency Act (under the umbrella of the Defense Authorization Act) is signed into law. The law prohibits military PXs from selling recordings, magazines, and videos that depict or describe "lascivious" nudity. *Penthouse* magazine files a lawsuit challenging the new law.

- *September 30:* President Clinton signs an omnibus appropriation package that expands the federal definition of child pornography. The law provides that child pornography is to include adults who "appear to be" minors engaging in sexual activities, as well as computer-generated images.

- *November 6:* A subcommittee of the Senate Governmental Affairs Committee convenes hearings to examine music violence and its impact on the behavior of America's youth.

CHAPTER 4

BIOGRAPHICAL LISTING

This chapter offers brief biographical information on people who have played a role in the history of censorship. This listing is representative, and offers biographies of a diverse group, as censorship involves people from a variety of philosophies and backgrounds. Because censorship is a topic of such historical significance, figures from the distant past to the present day are included.

John Adams, second president of the United States (1797–1801). A Harvard University graduate, Adams served as an American diplomat in Europe and as vice president before becoming president of the United States. Adams was a passionate proponent of independence and assisted in drafting the Declaration of Independence. Even so, Adams considered the Alien and Sedition Acts necessary for national security. He served only one term as president.

Samuel Adams, American politician and writer. A graduate of Harvard University with a master's degree, Samuel Adams worked tirelessly for the American Revolution. He gave many impassioned speeches and his writings are part and parcel of the American annals of freedom. Adams penned the Boston protest against the proposed Stamp Act. A signer of the Declaration of Independence, Adams served as governor of Massachusetts.

Jane Alexander, American actress and chair of the National Endowment for the Arts. Jane Alexander has worked to maintain federal funding for the arts. She has appeared before the government to testify in regard to federal arts funding. During major debates in the 1990s, she appealed to Congress, asking that funding not be withdrawn, and that artists be permitted to retain their freedom in choice of subject matter.

Hugo Black, Supreme Court associate justice (1937–71). Justice Black led a controversial career, including a stint as a member of the Ku Klux Klan; he later said that he had joined because many Alabama jurors belonged to the group. He resigned as a KKK member before running for the U.S. Senate. Black held an absolutist view regarding free speech. He opposed the "clear and present danger" test, as well as controls over libel and obscenity. He did not, however, believe that First Amendment rights extended to symbolic speech.

Judy Blume, contemporary American author. Blume, renowned author of books for young people, many of which have been banned or removed from libraries, is a staunch supporter of intellectual freedom. Her novels present adolescent problems in a frank, forthright fashion. Blume's many awards include the Children's Choice Award and the Carl Sandburg Freedom to Read Award. Blume is a member of the Author's Guild, the Society of Children's Book Writers and Illustrators, and the National Coalition Against Censorship. Among her well-known works are *Are You There God? It's Me, Margaret* and *Here's to You, Rachel Robinson*.

Thomas Bowdler, 18th/19th-century English editor and founder of the Society for the Suppression of Vice. Bowdler went to great lengths to produce expurgated volumes of works such as *Decline and Fall of the Roman Empire* and many Shakespearean plays, as well as the Old Testament. His zeal to remove indecency coined the term *bowdlerizing*. Bowdlerizing today means that a work has been so altered that its original meaning has been lost. Even in Bowdler's own time, many felt that his censorship was extreme.

Patrick Buchanan, journalist and broadcast commentator, adviser to President Nixon and President Reagan, Republican primary candidate for president of the United States. Buchanan espoused his conservative views through newspaper columns and radio and television programs. He advocated morality founded on a strict interpretation of the Bible and frequently advanced the cause of censorship based on his beliefs.

George Carlin, American actor, comedian, and satirist. Carlin exhibits a biting wit. His irreverent material came under fire in 1973, when he appeared before a live audience and recorded a twelve-minute monologue entitled "Filthy Words." Carlin, quite frankly and in comic style, recited the seven words that "cannot be uttered on public airwaves." When Carlin's monologue was played on a radio station, the station was cited by the Federal Communications Commission (FCC), and the Supreme Court upheld the right of the FCC to cite the station. The Supreme Court did not, however, find the monologue obscene.

Samuel Langhorne Clemens, American author, lecturer, and humorist. Writing under the name Mark Twain, Clemens was known for his insightful, vivid characterizations and ironic humor. Clemens worked as a printer and an editor. He first began writing under the pseudonym Josh. Ultimately, he used the pseudonym Mark Twain, which refers to a safe depth of water for a steamboat. Clemens's novel *Huckleberry Finn* is a frequently banned book. It was first banned from a Massachusetts library in 1884.

Daniel Ellsberg, deputy secretary of defense during the Johnson administration. Though no longer deputy secretary of defense in 1971, Ellsberg was familiar with the contents of the *Pentagon Papers*, the voluminous top-secret document revealing deceit in the inception of the Vietnam War. Ellsberg leaked the papers to the *New York Times*, which published the first installment on June 13, 1971.

Desiderius Erasmus, scholar, author, Augustinian monk. Considered the founder of humanism, Erasmus, born in Rotterdam, became one of the most popular authors in Europe in the late fifteenth and early sixteenth centuries. He was a contemporary of Luther and Calvin, and wrote in support of the Protestant Reformation as he detailed problems in the church. Initially, Erasmus's work was only rarely censored; however, as the Counterreformation became more powerful, all of his work was banned.

James Exon, Jr., United States senator. Exon introduced the Communications Decency Act of 1996 (CDA), which provided criminal penalties for those who displayed indecent material to minors over the Internet. Exon and the act were strongly criticized by liberals and conservatives alike. A temporary injunction was granted against enforcement of the act in a California court on the day the act passed.

Jerry Falwell, Baptist minister and television evangelist. Falwell began broadcasting religious shows espousing his Christian beliefs in 1956. In 1979, he founded the Moral Majority, a political group dedicated to upholding a fundamentalist agenda. The Moral Majority evolved into the Liberty Federation in 1986. Falwell and his supporters frequently called for censorship of material they deemed dangerous to moral welfare. They supported teaching the theory of creationism in schools and opposed abortion, the U.S.–Soviet SALT treaties, and the Equal Rights Amendment.

Galileo Galilei, 16th/17th-century Italian scientist and astronomer. Against the admonition of the Church, Galileo published his *Dialogue Concerning the Two Chief World Systems*. Galileo stated that the earth was not at the center of the universe, but was a planet that revolved around the sun, along with other planets. The Inquisition sentenced him to life in prison; however, after Galileo met demands and fell to his knees before a crowd to disavow his findings, he was allowed to serve his sentence in his home. All of his works were banned.

Mikhail Gorbachev, president of the Union of Soviet Socialist Republics (1988–91). Gorbachev instigated the end of communism as a major world political system. When he came to office, Gorbachev designed programs to stimulate the economy (*perestroika*) and to lift the veil from previously censored material (*glasnost*). As a result, a wealth of historical and cultural documents that had been hidden from his own people—and certainly from the rest of the world—became available.

Johannes Gutenberg, 15th-century printer, inventor of movable type for the western world. Though movable type was actually invented by the Chinese, Gutenberg's movable type became the standard for the Western world. His movable type made it possible for books to be printed, rather than copied by hand. Some of the first printed works were Bibles from a Gutenberg press.

Oliver Wendell Holmes, Supreme Court associate justice (1902–32). A graduate of Harvard College and Harvard Law School, Holmes served in the federal army during the Civil War before attending law school. He enunciated the now-famous "clear and present" danger test and is well-known for his dissents in early freedom of speech cases where he disagreed with restrictive rulings.

Molly Ivins, 20th-century political columnist, author. Ivins holds a B.A. from Smith College and a master's degree in journalism from Columbia University. She has studied at the Institute of Political Science in Paris. Ivins, who is outspoken on intellectual freedom issues, is active in the Amnesty International's Journalism Network and the Reporters Committee for Freedom of the Press. She has written on press issues for the American Civil Liberties Union (ACLU) and journalism reviews. Ivins, who is trilingual, has won a variety of awards and has three times been a finalist for a Pulitzer Prize. Her famous quotes include: "In this country, we get so scared of something terrible—of Communists or illegal aliens or pornography or crime that we decide the only way to protect ourselves is to cut back on our freedom. . . . Well, now, isn't that the funniest idea—that if we were less free we could be safer? . . . The cure for every excess of freedom of speech is more freedom of speech."

Thomas Jefferson, United States president (1801–9). Jefferson's list of accomplishments is enormous. Appointed to head the committee that prepared the Declaration of Independence, Jefferson was its primary author. He addressed intellectual freedom issues in his writings and his actions, including his decision not to renew the Sedition Act of 1798 and his pardoning of all those who had been convicted under it. Before serving as president, Jefferson served as governor of Virginia, minister to France, secretary of state and vice president. Jefferson directed that the following words be inscribed on his tombstone: "author of the Declaration of American Independence, of the Statute of Virginia for religious freedom, and Father of the University of Virginia."

James Joyce, Irish poet and novelist. Joyce was one of the strongest influences on the twentieth-century novel. He dealt very straightforwardly with sexual content; this led to the banning of perhaps his greatest work, *Ulysses*. This novel, published in 1922, recounted a day in the life of two Dubliners. It was banned from import to the United States until 1933.

Judith Fingeret Krug, present-day director of the Office for Intellectual Freedom (ALA) and executive director of the Freedom to Read Foundation (ALA). Krug heads two of the most influential First Amendment rights organizations in the United States. She has served on the board of directors for a variety of agencies, including the ACLU-Illinois Division, the Fund for Free Expression, and the Council of Literary Magazines and Presses. She has received awards for her work from many intellectual freedom organizations.

D. H. Lawrence (David Herbert Lawrence), early 20th-century British author and visual artist. Many view Lawrence, a prolific writer, as an author who deeply affected the direction of the British novel. His work often featured sexual relationships as the most important motivation in human behavior. As a result, his work was frequently banned. Perhaps his best-known work is *Lady Chatterly's Lover*. Not only were Lawrence's writings banned; his paintings, while critically acclaimed, met with similar disapproval.

Catharine A. MacKinnon, 20th-century attorney, professor, author. MacKinnon's degrees include a B.A. from Smith College, a J.D. from Yale Law School, and Ph.D. in political science from Yale. She has taught at Yale, the University of Chicago, UCLA, Minnesota, Harvard, York, and Stanford. MacKinnon specializes in constitutional law and political theory. She is active in feminist and pornography issues, and her books and articles include *Toward a Feminist Theory of the State*.

Robert Mapplethorpe, American photographer and artist. Mapplethorpe's early artistic career included time at the Pratt Institute in Brooklyn and works in sculpting as well as photography. His black-and-white photography was praised for its intensity and ability to portray its subject. Mapplethorpe worked as a fashion photographer and became well-known in the area of celebrity portraits. By the end of the 1980s, controversy began to rage over Mapplethorpe's explicit, and sometimes sadomasochistic, homoerotic art. The controversy fueled a debate over funding and the National Endowment of the Arts. Mapplethorpe died of AIDS in 1989.

Thurgood Marshall, Supreme Court associate justice (1967–91). The first African-American on the United States Supreme Court, Marshall was the great-grandson of a slave. He was active in the National Association for the Association of Colored People (NAACP) and won twenty-nine Supreme Court cases as he pursued litigation that challenged racial oppression. On the Court, he was a part of many decisions that emphasized civil rights, including equal protection and intellectual freedom cases.

Censorship

Joseph McCarthy, United States Senator. McCarthy was the major figure in a period in history now known as the McCarthy Era. In the 1950s McCarthy made wild and flamboyant charges of Communist sympathy against American citizens. No one was immune from McCarthy's long finger of accusation. From 1950 to 1954, McCarthy's efforts surged forward, virtually unchecked, but in 1954, he was investigated and ultimately censured by the Senate for his activities.

Thelma McCormack, 20th-century professor and author. McCormack is the founding director of York University's Centre for Feminist Research in Canada. She is Professor Emerita at York University and former president of the Canadian Women's Studies Association and the Canadian Sociology and Anthropology Association. McCormack is a York University research associate at the Institute for Social Research and has taught at McGill, the University of Amsterdam, the Hebrew University of Jerusalem, and the University of British Columbia. Active in intellectual freedom issues, McCormack focuses on political sociology, communication, and women's studies. She is "very critical of the Dworkin-MacKinnon thesis and other pro-censorship feminists."

Robert McNamara, secretary of defense during the Vietnam War. McNamara served under Presidents Kennedy and Johnson. He was the author of the ill-fated *Pentagon Papers*, a classified document that detailed deceitful activities leading to the Vietnam War. In 1995, McNamara stated that he and his colleagues had been "wrong, terribly wrong" in regard to Vietnam policy.

John Milton, 17th-century English poet. Milton was a major force in literature; he authored works including *Paradise Lost*. A strong advocate of freedom of expression, Milton wrote "Areopagitica," an essay that advanced the cause of freedom of speech and decried government censorship. He was greatly praised by the public for his views.

J. M. Near, newspaper publisher. In the early 1930s, an action was brought against Near, the publisher of the *Saturday Press*, to stop him from publishing defamatory statements. Near's case challenged the Minnesota Gag Law, which required prior approval for printing. The United States Supreme Court found the Minnesota law unconstitutional.

Ovid (Publius Ovidius Naso), Roman author (43 B.C.–A.D. 18). *The Art of Love*, *Loves*, and *Cure for Love*—Ovid's best-known works, were considered scandalous by many. Throughout the centuries, Ovid's works have been burned and banned around the world. Emperor Augustus declared Ovid's books obscene. The United States banned his work until 1929.

Thomas Paine, patriot and philosopher. Paine arrived in America from England in 1774, upon the advice of his friend Benjamin Franklin. Paine wrote the pamphlet "Common Sense" and a series of pamphlets entitled

"The Crisis" in passionate support of American independence; the language was easy to understand and inspired thousands. Paine also wrote *The Rights of Man* and *The Age of Reason*, an attack on Christianity. Paine's writings were banned or censored in America, France, and England.

François Rabelais, French author, satirist, physician, and Franciscan and Benedictine monk. Rabelais's work spanned a spectrum from pieces on academics, medicine, and archaeology to ribald, biting satire of human nature in *Pantagruel* (1534). Rabelais frequently criticized the Roman Catholic church and his work was often considered obscene. His books were banned in France, the United States, and South Africa, among others.

Salman Rushdie, British author. Rushdie, born in India, wrote several works prior to *The Satanic Verses*. None of his early fiction gained international notoriety, but in 1989, when he was forced to go into hiding after the publication of *The Satanic Verses*, his name was heard all over the world. The Islamic leader of Iran, the Ayatollah Khomeini, banned Rushdie's novel, claiming it to be blasphemous, and ordered Rushdie's death. Khomeini's action strongly influenced the literary world. Many booksellers around the world refused to carry *The Satanic Verses* after threats of bombings; writers and supporters of intellectual freedom expressed outrage at the ayatollah's action.

Marquis de Sade (Donatien Alphonse François), French author. The Marquis de Sade lived during the late eighteenth and early nineteenth centuries. His works include *Justine; or, the Misfortunes of Virtue*, in which a young woman is victimized sexually and morally. The term *sadism* is derived from this novel. Marquis de Sade himself spent time in prison for sexually oriented crimes. De Sade's work has alternately been deplored as depraved and held in esteem as important historical and philosophical material. The work has been extensively banned throughout the centuries.

Oscar Arias Sánchez, president of Costa Rica (1986–90). Arias Sánchez, who had been a professor and served as minister of planning, rose to power when Central America was in turmoil. His Arias Peace Plan called for a variety of action, including cease-fires and an end to censorship. Arias Sánchez won the Nobel Peace Prize in 1987.

Charles Schenk, general secretary of the Socialist Party. When Schenk was arrested in 1917 for violating the Espionage Act, he became part of a case that would make United States Supreme Court history. After printing and mailing more than 15,000 leaflets encouraging men registered for the draft not to submit, he was charged with a crime and brought to trial. He was convicted in a lower court, and the Supreme Court upheld his conviction, holding that his actions created a "clear and present danger" in wartime.

George Bernard Shaw, late 19th/early 20th-century, Irish-born playwright. Often referred to by his initials, this accomplished playwright held atheistic and Darwinist beliefs in his younger days. He progressed to other views, on topics including socialism and communism, though he did not totally endorse any one philosophy. His play *Mrs. Warren's Profession* was banned for many years in Great Britain as it involved reminiscences of the title character's life as a prostitute.

William French Smith, attorney general (1981–85). Smith served as personal attorney to President Reagan prior to his election; he was also a key organizer of Reagan's campaign. Smith acted as chair of the University of California Board of Regents. In 1986, he established the United States Attorney General's Commission on Pornography. The commission found no substantiated connection between erotica and sexual deviance or violence. The commission did find a connection between organized crime and pornography.

Socrates, ancient Greek philosopher and teacher. In 399 BCE, when Socrates was approximately seventy years old, he was charged with corrupting the morals of children and offending the gods; his defense was that he was only trying to teach the truth. Socrates was sentenced to death; he refused plausible escape plans set out by supporters and died after accepting his sentence by drinking hemlock.

Alexander Solzhenitsyn, Soviet author and historian. Solzhenitsyn often chronicled and criticized Soviet government. He was arrested in 1945 after attacking Stalin in a letter; he served eight years in prison, and was released the day Stalin died, though he then spent three years in exile. Solzhenitsyn's *One Day in the Life of Ivan Denisovitch* (1962), which detailed life in a Soviet labor camp, brought him acclaim, but his short stories published a year later spurred the banning of the author's work in the Soviet Union. Solzhenitsyn was awarded the Nobel Prize for Literature in 1970. After initial publication of *The Gulag Archipelago*, he was taken into custody for treason and exiled. Solzhenitsyn ultimately moved to the United States.

Nadine Strossen, attorney, author, president of the ACLU. Strossen became ACLU president in 1991. Her career includes a professorship of constitutional law at New York Law School. She was among the 100 Most Influential Lawyers in America named by the *National Law Journal* in the mid-1990s. Strossen, an honors graduate of Harvard Law School, has published many journal articles and books; she appears around the world as a lecturer. A strong advocate of civil rights, Strossen is the author of *Defending Pornography: Free Speech, Sex, and the Fight for Women's Rights*.

Carole S. Vance, anthropologist, author. Vance is an anthropologist at the Columbia University School of Public Health. She is the editor of *Pleasure and Danger: Exploring Female Sexuality* (1990). Active in women's rights and censorship issues, Vance is the co-founder of FACT, the Feminist Anti-Censorship Task Force.

Biographical Listing

John Peter Zenger, publisher. In the 1700s, in New York, Zenger printed a newspaper that voiced strong opposition to a variety of government policies. He was jailed under the charge of seditious libel. When his case was tried, Zenger's lawyer used the truth of the statements as a defense, even though such a defense did not legally exist at the time. Zenger was acquitted, perhaps more because of anti-government sentiment than because of any great belief by the jury in the truth defense. Zenger remained a publisher until his death.

PART II

GUIDE TO FURTHER RESEARCH

CHAPTER 5

HOW TO RESEARCH CENSORSHIP

The topic of censorship has given rise to a wealth of material. Because censorship issues include a wide variety of subtopics, researchers may want to consider narrowing their search after becoming familiar with the topic in general. With an eye to that end, this chapter includes not only a discussion of resources, but also a discussion of subtopics to consider while researching.

Many traditional research tools work quite efficiently for researching censorship. This chapter includes reference to these traditional tools, as well as information on lesser-known avenues of research.

SUBTOPICS TO INCLUDE FOR CENSORSHIP RESEARCH

Although the topic of censorship is a good starting point, other topics and subtopics will also lead to valuable information. These include Alien and Sedition Acts, Arts, Bill of Rights, Broadcasting, Film, First Amendment, Freedom of the Press, Freedom of Speech, Hate Speech, Internet, Journalism, Music, Obscenity, Pornography, President John Adams, Recording Industry, Sculpture, Speech Codes, Technology, Television, Theater, United States Constitution.

Using these subtopics not only provides access to additional references, but also may assist in narrowing focus. Because censorship is such a broad topic, a search launched with this word alone may bring forth thousands of references. Subtopics will help define the sought-after information.

CARD CATALOGS

The card catalog continues to be a valuable tool. It references the resources in a library. Most libraries offer one card catalog indexed by subject and another indexed by author's last name. In the card catalog can be found the author, title, and call number of a work, as well as subjects covered in the work. Many libraries reference all of the works they own in the same catalog; others maintain separate catalogs for specific collections, as well as government documents, research materials that cannot be checked out, and audiovisual materials.

Although most libraries provide manual card catalogs, many also offer an automated system. Through this system, patrons often can reference and obtain titles through interlibrary loan. Many automated search systems allow researchers to enter subject, title, or author to locate references. Once references are located, patrons may see a list of locations where titles are available.

AUTOMATED SYSTEMS

A wide variety of automated systems, accessible through computer and modem, make today's research more fruitful and infinitely more expedient. Many libraries now offer access via modem, both in the library and from remote locations.

To obtain information via modem away from the library, the researcher brings up the modem access window, types in the telephone number, and receives prompts to enter the system. Many systems offer general access to anyone who dials in; they may then require a library card or other identification number if the patron wishes to access specific databases, such as article indexes.

Systems such as *Carl*, *EBSCO*, and *SIRS*, are available in many libraries. Additionally, some libraries provide access to them via modem. Researchers should check with a local library to learn which systems are available and how to gain access from a remote location.

The *Carl* system is one of the largest automated systems in the country. It provides access to information in libraries from coast to coast, including some public and school libraries. Researchers who don't own modems may use the library computers to access *Carl* and other valuable systems. *Carl* offers search by word (including title) or name (including author). Resources available through most *Carl* systems include books, articles (some with text), and audiovisual references. *Carl* also provides links to other systems.

Many other automated systems are very helpful in researching censorship. One of these is *Uncover*, a database that allows researchers to order full text of available articles for a fee. Delivery is usually via fax and generally within forty-eight hours. Although *Uncover* charges a fee for its service, it provides a wide selection of material.

Another valuable resource for article research is *SIRS*. *SIRS* offers article abstracts and full text with complete citation information. It is a searchable database offered through libraries and businesses.

Electric Library is another tool for article research. Though *Electric Library* offers full text, not all versions offer full citation information. This can make the research process lengthier, because *Electric Library* may offer the date of publication and title of a periodical, but not the volume number. The researcher must then manually pull the article or read the microfilm in order to complete a required citation.

The *EBSCO* database provides full article citation information with an abstract. It also provides full text for some articles.

INDEXES

Though many indexes are available online, others must be researched manually. Additionally, not all libraries are equipped to provide access to the online versions of indexes.

The *Reader's Guide to Periodical Literature* indexes more than two hundred United States periodicals. The *Magazine Index* indexes many of the same popular magazines referenced by the *Reader's Guide to Periodical Literature*, but also includes citations to professional journals.

The *Newspaper Index* is a truly valuable tool for researching censorship. Because censorship issues are so frequently at the forefront of the news, newspaper articles can be a key to obtaining the latest information. With the emerging legislation regarding Internet content, newspapers can provide up-to-date information on the ever-changing legal scene with respect to online intellectual freedom issues.

INTERNET

Because censorship issues are so influenced by current events and because specific-needs organizations frequently emerge and disband in response to the climate prevailing at the time, the Internet is an ideal research tool for censorship. Internet addresses, also known as URLs, are listed where available in chapter 7, Organizations. A summary of some of the most valuable Internet sites for censorship research appears below.

The EFF (Electronic Frontier Foundation) *(http://www.eff.org/)* is an excellent resource for current information. This organization focuses on the needs and interests of online users. Its website provides links to a variety of other sites concerned with censorship issues.

The National Campaign for Freedom of Expression *(http://www.tmn.com/Artswire/www/ncfe/ncfe.html)* is another valuable Internet resource. It offers current information and links to other sites.

Congressional Quarterly, *(http://www.cq.com/)* a publication that offers analyses of government activities, including legislation and Supreme Court decisions, has a strong online presence. In addition to listing online and offline publications, *CQ* offers "chat sessions" where students and others may ask questions on governmental issues.

Other valuable websites are the National Coalition Against Censorship *(http://www.ncac.org/)* and the American Civil Liberties Union *(http://www.aclu.org/)*. These organizations and many others are listed in chapter 7. URLs are included where possible. It is important to note that websites are sometimes updated or moved altogether. If it is not possible to access an organization by the listed URL, the researcher can search engine such as Yahoo! *(http://www.yahoo.com)* can be used to locate the new Internet address by typing in the name of the organization.

GOVERNMENT DOCUMENTS

Because government action often comes into play in censorship issues, government documents can be quite useful for researchers. Transcripts of hearings before the Senate and House, as well as inventories of important wartime documents, commission reports, and agency publications are available through the government.

The *Index to U.S. Government Periodicals* provides listings of federal government periodicals. The *Congressional Information Index* (CIS) indexes congressional publications. The *Monthly Catalog of United States Government Publications* references documents published by federal agencies.

Because the Federal Communications Commission (FCC) plays such a large role in broadcast censorship, its publication *Information Seekers Guide: How to Find Information at the FCC* is also very helpful. The guide lists services for FCC hearing transcripts, FCC databases, and other important information.

IMPACT/GDCS (Government Documents Catalog Service) provides full citations and full text of government documents through CD-Rom.

Because of the large number of congressional hearings and agency reports resulting from censorship issues, this tool is particularly useful.

The Government Publication Office, (212) 512-1530, is also accessible via the Internet, at *http://www.access.gpo.gov/*. The GPO offers a full complement of government publications, including transcripts of hearings before Congress. A variety of such hearings is listed in the following annotated bibliography under the heading Government Documents.

BASIC SOURCES

Because censorship includes such a wide variety of issues, it is difficult for one book to provide a complete overview of the topic. *Speech Acts and the First Amendment* by Franklyn Haiman, however, is an excellent resource. Susan and Paul Lang's *Censorship* provides a succinct overview. Nat Henthoff's *Free Speech for Me—But Not For Thee* focuses on some intellectual freedom realities and characterizes some of the debate on the issue. Herbert N. Foerstel's *Free Expression and Censorship in America* offers a wide variety of material on a plethora of topics, with a strong treatment of the Internet.

Censorship: Opposing Viewpoints, edited by Lisa Orr, offers essays by prominent Americans exploring different perspectives on censorship. It covers a variety of topics, including news media, school and library censorship, and pornography.

For legal analysis, Edmund Lindpop's *The Bill of Rights and Landmark Cases* provides a framework. *Censorship Landmarks* by Edward DeGrazia is also pertinent. An interesting work in censorship and recent law is *SLAPPS: Getting Sued for Speaking Out* by George Pring and Penelope Canan. This book was written by a law professor and a sociology professor and discusses "strategic lawsuits against public participation," a phenomenon in which retaliatory lawsuits are filed against those exercising First Amendment rights.

In regard to censorship outside the United States, references abound. They include Robert Darton's *The Forbidden Best-Sellers of Pre-Revolutionary France*, Gunilla Faringer's *Press Freedom in Africa*, Richard Mitchell's *Censorship in Imperial Japan*, and Girja Kumar's *Censorship in India*.

As hate speech and campus speech codes have become more prominent issues in the public eye, a number of authors have addressed this form of expression, along with its legal and moral implications. Among them are Richard Delgado and Jean Stefanic in *Must We Defend Nazis?: Hate Speech, Pornography, and the New First Amendment*, Louis Gates, Jr. in *Speaking of Race, Speaking of Sex: Hate Speech, Civil Rights, and Civil Liberties*, and Samuel Walker in *Hate Speech: The History of an American Controversy*.

Censorship

With the advent of the Internet, cyberspace becomes uniquely important in the censorship arena. From bomb-making instructions, to fictional stories of explicit sexual torture, to detailed instructions on "how to murder", Internet offerings have tested the limits in the censorship debate. Though the bulk of resources in this area are magazines, books such as Richard Sclove's *Democracy and Technology* and Jonathan Wallace and Mark Manga's *Sex, Laws and Cyberspace: Freedom and Censorship on the Frontiers of the Online Revolution* offer information on emerging technology.

The topic of pornography has sharply divided people for centuries and continues to be controversial. Good references in this area include Edward DeGrazia's *Girls Lean Back Everywhere: The Law of Obscenity and the Assault on Genius* and Nadine Strossen's *Defending Pornography: Free Speech, Sex, and the Fight for Women's Rights.*

Library and textbook censorship constantly provide forums for debate: political campaigns often focus on this area. Resources for research abound. The Intellectual Freedom Office and the Freedom to Read Foundation of the American Library Association offer a variety of publications in this area. Good books are readily available, and include Herbert Foerstel's *Banned in the U.S.A.: A Reference Guide to Book Censorship in Schools and Public Libraries*, Joan DelFattore's *What Johny Shouldn't Read: Textbook Censorship in America*, and Lee Burress's *Battle of the Books: Literary Censorship in the Public Schools, 1950–1985.*

Debate has risen to fever pitch over the relationship among arts, censorship, and funding. In the 1980s and 1990s, Robert Mapplethorpe's homoerotic art and NEA funding brought this issue under closer scrutiny than at any time in the past. Excellent periodicals on this topic are available from the National Campaign for Freedom of Expression (NCFE) in Seattle, Washington. A strong reference is *The Cultural Battlefield: Art Censorship and Public Funding.*

The magazine *Index on Censorship*, founded in 1972, is an excellent resource. *Index on Censorship* is published six time a year in London, and boasts an international readership and contributorship. The publication's purpose is "to report on the many ways in which freedom of expression is curtailed around the world; to publish literature and other forms of writing that are censored in their country of origin; and to provide a platform for the discussion and debate of contentious issues, whether related to censorship or not."

For the most current information on a wide variety of topics, many of the organizations listed in chapter 7 offer excellent resources.

LEGAL RESEARCH

Censorship issues have frequently been addressed in legal arenas. Legal research can seem daunting to those without a legal background. State and federal statutes and court decisions, as well as law journal articles, digests (which elaborate on decisions and refer researchers to other relevant material) can seem inaccessible. However, a variety of resources are available to guide researchers in this area. *Legal Research: How to Find and Understand the Law* by Steven Elias and *Law on the Net* by James Evans, both from Nolo Press, provide strong foundations for legal research. Additionally, Nolo Press offers the video *Legal Research Made Easy*. *Legal Research Made Easy* is also the title of a book by Suzan Herskowitz, from Sphinx Press. This book offers information on state and federal legal research, as well as sample research problems that help initiate the inexperienced.

Within their holdings, public libraries frequently offer books containing state and federal statutes. Some offer books, called reporters, that reproduce the text of decisions from the courts. The citation, or "cite," is used to locate a case in a reporter. For example, the citation *New York Times Co. v. United States*, 403 U.S. 713 (1971) refers to a case handed down in 1971 that can be located in volume 403 of the *Supreme Court Reports* (the official reporter of the United States Supreme Court) at page 713. The name of the case, *New York Times Co. v. United States*, is also called the "style." The *Supreme Court Reporter*, a private publication by West Publishing, includes the text of the case preceded by a summary and notations referring to relevant areas of law. For example, headings might include "Libel and Slander" or "Constitutional Law." Other reporters offer regional and state court opinions.

Code, or statute sections, are cited in much the same way as cases. For example, the Flag Desecration Act of 1989 is cited at 18 U.S.C. Sec. 700. This is a reference to volume 18, section 700 of the *United States Code*.

Statutes and court decisions are referred to as primary sources because they have been handed down by legislatures or courts. These statutes and decisions are the law. Law journal and law review articles, as well as digests and treatises, are referred to as secondary sources because they interpret the law but do not serve as law themselves. These secondary sources exhibit a variety of writing styles. Some pieces may be esoteric, while others may be easy to understand. In any event, secondary sources are worthwhile resources because they frequently provide insight and assist in melding and then sorting through copious quantities of material on a given topic. One of their most valuable functions is that they frequently refer researchers to additional authoritative material.

Censorship

It is important to remember that a court decision may no longer be the law, as it may have been overruled by a subsequent case. A process known as shepardizing determines whether a case has been overruled; this involves looking up the case in *Shepard's Citations* from Shepard's Company or using a computerized search to complete the same process.

Two companies, LEXIS and WESTLAW, are widely used for computerized legal research. They include functions that check current validity of court decisions, and allow information to be retrieved through a variety of methods, including a key word search. Researchers are able to input a word such as "libel" or "obscenity" and retrieve a variety of legal resources. LEXIS and WESTLAW, which are often used in law schools and law firms, may be difficult for nonlegal personnel to access. If the opportunity is available, however, *Using Computers in Legal Research: A Guide to LEXIS and WESTLAW* by Christopher G. Wren and Jill Robinson Wren from Adams and Ambrose provides valuable information.

With the advent of the Internet, legal material has become even more accessible. THOMAS: Legislative Information on the Net *(http://thomas.loc.gov/)* provides access to bill summary, full text, status, and legislative history of recent Senate and House bills. Searches may be performed through the following categories: topic, popular/short title, bill number/type, enacted into law.

The United States House of Representatives, through its Internet Law Library home page *(http://law.house.gov/1.htm)*, provides links to a wealth of resources, including the U.S. Code at *http://law.house.gov/usc.htm*, which can be searched by key word, and state statutes and other legal material at *http://law.house.gov/17.htm*.

Cornell Law School offers a strong Internet resource for Supreme Court decision research. Supreme Court decisions from 1990 to the present may be found at *http://supct.law.cornell.edu/supct* and are arranged by date, topic, and party name. Cornell links to older Supreme Court decisions, as well as a great variety of other legal material, including United States Code sections. These can be found at *http://lcweb.loc.gov/global/judiciary.html*.

FindLaw *(http://www.findlaw.com/)* provides links to a wide variety of legal resources, including law review articles, state statutes, and Supreme Court opinions. FindLaw also refers researchers to other court cases relevant to the topic being researched.

Many of the organizations listed in chapter 7 offer summaries and text of legislation and court decisions through their Internet sites. URLs are provided in the listings.

CHAPTER 6

ANNOTATED BIBLIOGRAPHY

This chapter references a wide variety of material on censorship. This is a representative sampling, and categories include

- Bibliographies

- Books

- Encyclopedias

- Periodicals

- Articles

- Government documents

- Films

- Transcripts of broadcasts

Brief annotations are provided. The annotations are not meant to comment on the quality of the resources, but only to summarize the information found in each one.

Within the major categories of "Books" and "Articles," subheadings also appear; the purpose of the subheadings is to facilitate the search for reference material. It should be noted, however, subheadings will overlap, that is, material on a variety of aspects of censorship will often be found in one reference. The subheadings point to the major focus of the book or article. Subheadings differ in the "Book" and "Article" listings, due to the differences in the content of material in each category.

Transcripts of news programs are included along with film listings because, collectively, news programs have their finger on the pulse of the world. Reading a transcript or watching a film or a television broadcast from the past enables researchers to "walk through history" and gain a realistic flavor of the time period, the issues, and the people involved.

BIBLIOGRAPHIES

Bennett, James R. *Control of Information in the United States: An Annotated Bibliography*. Westport, Conn.: Meckler, 1987.
Nearly 3,000 entries; also includes global references.

Byerly, Greg, and Rick Rubin. *Pornography: The Conflict Over Sexually Explicit Materials in the United States*. New York: Garland, 1980.
Reports on a wide variety of resources for pornography research.

Censored Japanese Serials of the Pre-1946 Period: A Checklist of the Microfilm Collection—Ken'Etsu Wazasshi (1945-nen Izen: Maikurofirumu Chekkurisuto. Library of Congress, 1944.
U.S. Government document cataloging the microfilm collection of censored Japanese serials.

Christensen, John O. *Intellectual Freedom and Libraries: A Selective Bibliography*. Monticello, Ill.: Vance Bibliographies, 1991.
Censorship and the Freedom of Information Act.

Cooper, Thomas W. *Television and Ethics: A Bibliography*. Boston: G. K. Hall, 1988.
Includes a wide array of references on television programming, broadcasting, and other areas.

The Freedom of Information Act: A Comprehensive Bibliography of Law and Related Matters, rev. ed. Austin, Tex.: Tarlton Law Library, University of Texas School of Law, 1981.
A variety of entries relating to the Freedom of Information Act.

Hoffman, Frank. *Intellectual Freedom and Censorship: An Annotated Bibliography*. Metuchen, N.J.: Scarecrow, 1989.
First Amendment entries.

Houder, Frank G. "Constitutional Limitations on Libel Actions: A Bibliography of *New York Times v. Sullivan* and Its Progeny." *Law Journal*, Winter 1984, vol. 6, pp. 447–49.
Reviews documents relative to the *New York Times* case.

Lindeen, Ellen, Merryn Rutledge, Lee Woolman, Lou Orfanella, Nancy Lewis-House, Becky Dennis, Gary Kerley, Robert C. Hanna, Thomas G. Lisack. "Books Worth Teaching Even Though They Have Proven Controversial." *English Journal*, April 1993, vol. 82, pp. 86–90.
Lists controversial books and discusses how to choose from the list, thereby obviating censorship.

McCoy, Ralph E. *Freedom of the Press: An Annotated Bibliography*. Carbondale, Ill.: Southern Illinois University Press, 1968.
———. *Freedom of the Press: An Annotated Bibliography, Second Supplement*. Carbondale, Ill.: Southern Illinois University Press, 1993.

———. *Freedom of the Press: A Bibliocyclopedia. Ten-Year Supplement (1967–1977)*. Carbondale, Ill.: Southern Illinois University Press, 1979.
Annotated bibliographies of books, pamplets, journal articles, dissertations, films, and other material relating to freedom of the press in the English-speaking world.

Rao, Rama K. *An Annotated Bibliography on Pornography: Current Literature, 1980–1986*. Monticello, Ill.: Vance Bibliographies, 1990.

Rogers, Denise. *Selected Bibliography of Books and Articles on Censorship (1950–1983)*. Compiled by Washington University Law Library. St. Louis, Miss.: Washington University Law Library, 1983.
Contains wide array of references.

Schroeder, Theodore A. *Free Speech Bibliography*. New York: New Benjamin Franklin House, 1969.
Provides selection of references.

Schladweiler, Chris. "The Library Bill of Rights and Intellectual Freedom." *Library Trends*, Summer 1996, vol. 45, pp. 97–126.
Entry subjects include "libraries," "selection process," and others.

Sellen, Betty-Carol, and Patricia Young. *Feminists, Pornography, and the Law: An Annotated Bibliography of Conflict, 1970–1986*. Hamden, Conn.: Library Professional Publications, 1987.
Entries represent a balance between viewpoints.

Simmons, Joan S., ed. *Censorship: A Threat to Reading, Learning and Thinking*. Newark, Del.: International Reading Association, 1994.
Refers to selected readings relating to intellectual freedom.

Women's Annotated Legal Bibliography: 1984–1992. Buffalo, N.Y.: W.S. Hein, 1984.
Cites bibliographic references pertaining to women and the law; includes First Amendment references.

BOOKS

GENERAL

Bartlett, Jonathan, ed. *The Reference Shelf: The First Amendment in a Free Society*. New York: H. W. Wilson, 1979.
Contains reprints of articles, book excerpts, and oral presentations on U.S. censorship and censorship in other countries. Examines debates over a wide range of topics from *Hustler* magazine to national security.

Boardman, Edna M. *Censorship: The Problem that Won't Go Away*. Worthington, Ohio: Linworth, 1993.

Advice for building support for freedom of access to information; topics include Parents and the Library, Administrators and the Library, Professionalism, Statements and Policies, et al.

Censorship: 500 Years of Conflict. New York: New York Public Library, 1984. Profiles exhibition held at the New York Public Library in 1984; exhibits covered freedom of the press and condemned books.

Coetzee, J. M. *Giving Offense: Essays on Censorship*. Chicago: University of Chicago Press, 1996. Includes a variety of essays.

DeGrazia, Edward. *Censorship Landmarks*. New York: R. R. Bowker, 1969. Examines historical, political, and legal issues and events.

DeMac, Donna. *Liberty Denied: The Current Rise of Censorship in America*. 2d ed. New Brunswick, N.J.: Rutgers University Press, 1990. Profiles freedom of press and speech in the twentieth century.

Dewhirst, Martin and Robert Farrel. *The Soviet Censorship*. Metuchen, N.J.: Scarecrow Press, 1973. Deals with freedom of the press and freedom of speech in the twentieth century.

Garry, Patrick. *An American Paradox: Censorship in a Nation of Free Speech*. Westport, Conn.: Greenwood Press, 1993. Examines historical and contemporary views of censorship.

Haiman, Franklyn S. *"Speech Acts" and the First Amendment*. Carbondale, Ill.: Southern Illinois Press, 1993. Focuses on free speech; includes symbolic expression.

Harer, John B., and Steven R. Harris. *Censorship of Expression in the 1980s: A Statistical Survey*. Westport, Conn.: Greenwood Press, 1994. Details instances of censorship and their implications.

Henthoff, Nat. *Free Speech for Me—But Not for Thee*. HarperCollins, New York: 1992. Analyzes First Amendment conflicts; looks at specific instances of censorship, and offers author's hope that the First Amendment can emerge "unfettered."

Intellectual Freedom Manual. 5th ed. Chicago: American Library Association, 1995. Provides practical information regarding First Amendment rights.

Jansen, Sue C. *Censorship: The Knot that Binds Power and Knowledge*. New York: Oxford University Press, 1991. An examination of politics and censorship issues.

Kane, Peter E. *Murder, Courts, and the Press: Issues in Free Press/Fair Trial*. Carbondale, Ill.: Southern Illinois University Press, 1992. Case studies in the areas of freedom of press and fair trial.

Annotated Bibliography

Klinker, Philip A. *The American Heritage History of the Bill of Rights: The First Amendment*. Englewood Cliffs, N.J.: Silver Burdett, 1991.

Discusses specific provisions of the First Amendment and looks at the history behind the provisions, as well as specific instances in history that have derived from challenges of First Amendment rights. Includes a foreword by Supreme Court Justice Warren Burger, a time line, and chapters on symbolic speech, prior restraint, libel, and obscenity

Knowlton, Steven R., and Patrick R. Parsons, eds. *The Journalist's Moral Compass: Basic Principles, Ethics in Journalism*. Westport, Conn.: Praeger, 1995.

Includes a variety of essays by philosophers, politician, authors, and others.

Levy, Leonard W. *Legacy of Suppression: Freedom of Speech and Press in Early American History*. Cambridge, Mass.: Belknap Press, 1990.

Explores the history of censorship in the United States.

Lindpop, Edmund. *The Bill of Rights and Landmark Cases*. New York: Watts, 1989.

Looks at prominent Supreme Court cases and their effect on the Bill of Rights. Discusses the Bill of Rights as "living law" and stresses its flexibility in meeting ongoing challenges.

MacArthur, John. *Second Front: Censorship and Propaganda in the Gulf War*. New York: Hill and Wang, 1992.

Explores the government's role in Persian Gulf War censorship.

Marsh, Dave. *50 Ways to Fight Censorship*. New York: Thunder's Mouth Press, 1991.

Includes practical suggestions and methods of fighting censorship; suggests specific groups and organizations to contact.

Meltzer, Milton. *The Bill of Rights: How We Got It and What It Means*. New York: Thomas Y. Crowell, 1990.

Examines the history of the Bill of Rights and discusses the connection between Great Britain's freedom documents—such as the Magna Carta —and the Bill of Rights. Also looks at how our freedoms under the Bill of Rights have been challenged.

Orr, Lisa, ed. *Censorship: Opposing Viewpoints*. San Diego: Greenhaven Press, 1990.

Offers essays by prominent Americans. Explores both sides of the censorship issue, including analyses of regulation of news media, justification of school and library censorship, and pornography censorship.

Pring, George W., and Penelope Canan. *SLAPPS: Getting Sued for Speaking Out*. Philadelphia, Penn.: Temple University Press, 1996.

Written by a law professor and a sociology professor, this book describes what its authors refer to as SLAPPs, also known as "strategic lawsuits against public participation;" the material provides accounts of retaliatory lawsuits filed by teachers, police, politicians, and opponents of civil rights. The book also offers solutions for preventing, managing, and curing SLAPPS.

Robins, Natalie. *Alien Ink: The FBI's War on Freedom of Expression.* New Brunswick: N.J.: Rutgers University Press, 1993.

Details the role of the FBI in First Amendment issues.

Schwartz, Bernard. *Constitutional Issues: Freedom of the Press.* New York: Facts On File, 1992.

Focuses on issues such as prior restraint, history of free speech, sedition, obscenity, and libel. Includes full text of Supreme Court cases.

Sheehan, Neil, et al. *The Pentagon Papers.* New York: Bantam Books, 1971.

Details First Amendment issues and the *Pentagon Papers.*

Shiffrin, Steven H. *The First Amendment, Democracy, and Romance.* Princeton, N.J.: Princeton University Press, 1990. A philosophical examination of the First Amendment that includes historical analysis from a philosophical perspective, including specific theories.

Smith, Reed W. *Samuel Medary and the "Crisis." Testing the Limits of Press Freedom.* Columbus, Ohio: Ohio State University Press, 1995.

In-depth examination of freedom of the press.

Wilson, John K. *The Myth of Political Correctness: The Conservative Attack on Higher Education.* Durham, N.C.: Duke University Press, 1995.

Reports on political aspects of higher education in the United States; includes discussions of multicultural education and discrimination in higher education.

Wildmon, Donald, and Randall Nulton. *Don Wildmon: The Man the Networks Love to Hate.* Wilmore, Ky.: Bristol, 1989.

The author focuses on his life as a Methodist minister campaigning against violence, obscenity, and other issues.

Wilson, Quintus C. *Censorship in Civil War.* Great Neck, N.Y.: Todd and Honeywell, 1988.

Focuses on censorship from 1861 to 1865.

FOREIGN CENSORSHIP

Ashbee, Henry S., and Peter Fryer. *Forbidden Books of the Victorians.* London: Odyssey Press, 1970.

Discusses books banned in Victorian England.

Bertrand, Ina. *Film Censorship in Australia.* St. Lucia: University of Queensland Press, 1978.

Raises issues regarding censorship of films in Australia.

Darnton, Robert. *The Forbidden Best-Sellers of Pre-Revolutionary France*. New York: W. Norton, 1995.

Examines clandestine literature in prerevolutionary France.

Faringer, Gunilla L. *Press Freedom in Africa*. Westport, Conn.: Greenwood Press, 1991.

Focuses on censorship of mass media in Africa.

Goldstein, Robert J. *Censorship of Political Caricature in Nineteenth Century France*. Kent, Ohio: Kent State University Press, 1990.

Deals with freedom of the press in Europe and focuses on France.

Grendler, Paul F. *The Roman Inquisition and the Venetian Press, 1540–1605*. Princeton, N.J.: Princeton University Press, 1977.

Examines censorship during the Roman Inquisition; discusses historical and political implications.

Hale, Orton J. *The Captive Press in the Third Reich*. Princeton, N.J.: Princeton University Press, 1964.

Examines German censorship under Hitler.

Hester, Al, and Kristina White. *Creating a Free Press in Europe*. Athens, Ga.: Cox International Center at the University of Georgia, 1994.

Profiles the ever-changing press of eastern and Central Europe. Includes chapters by U.S. and foreign journalists and academicians.

Kumar, Girja. *Censorship in India*. New Delhi: Vikas Publishing House, 1990.

Examines politics and government in India relating to censorship from 1947 to the late 1980s.

Mitchell, Richard H. *Censorship in Imperial Japan*. Ann Arbor, Mich.: Books on Demand, 1983.

Explores freedom of expression issues in Imperial Japan.

Moore, Robert C. *The Political Reality of Freedom of the Press in Zambia*. Lanham, Md.: University Press of America, 1992.

Reports on censorship in Zambia.

Putman, George H. *Censorship of the Church of Rome and its Influence upon the Production and Distribution of Literature*. New York: B. Blom, 1967.

A comprehensive study of freedom of the press and banned books.

Roth, Cecil. *The Spanish Inquisition*. New York: Norton, 1964.

An in-depth examination of the Spanish Inquisition focusing on individual liberties and freedoms.

Collins, Irene. *The Government and the Newspaper Press in France, 1814–1881*. Oxford: Oxford University Press, 1959.

Explores the French press in the late nineteenth century.

FREEDOM OF THE PRESS

Baker, Edwin. *Advertising and a Democratic Press*. Princeton, N.J.: Princeton University Press, 1994.
Examines pressure groups, advertising law, and censorship.

Califia, Pat, and Janine Fuller, eds. *Forbidden Passage: Writings Banned in Canada*. Pittsburgh: Cleis Press, 1995.
Details censorship in Canada.

Chen, Constance M. *"The Sex Side of Life:" Mary Ware Dennett's Pioneering Battle for Birth Control and Sex Education*. New York: New Press, 1996.
An examination of the life and times of an early 1800s activist who was prosecuted for publishing a sex education pamphlet.

Cortner, Richard C. *The Kingfish and the Constitution: Huey Long, the First Amendment and the Emergence of Modern Press Freedom in America*. Westport, Conn.: Greenwood Press, 1996.
From the series Global Perspectives in History and Politics, this book profiles Louisiana politics and government in the framework of U.S. freedom of press rights.

Craig, Alec. *The Banned Books of England and Other Countries*. London: George Allen & Unwin, 1962.
Looks at book censorship through the mid-twentieth century.

Garry, Patrick. *The American Vision for a Free Press: A Historical and Constitutional Vision of the Press as a Marketplace of Ideas*. New York: Garland, 1990.
Examines censorship in the United States.

Harrison, Maureen, and Steven Gilbert, eds. *Freedom of the Press: Decisions of the United States Supreme Court*. San Diego: Calif.: Excellent Books, 1996.
Reviews Supreme Court freedom of the press decisions.

Levy, Leonard W. *Freedom of the Press from Zenger to Jefferson: Early American Libertarian Theories*. Durham, N.C.: Carolina Academic Press, 1966.
Examines freedom of the press and other civil liberties issues.

Noble, William. *Bookbanning in America: Who Bans Books—and Why*. Middlebury, Vt.: Paul S. Ericksson, 1990.
Deals with censorship and banned books in the United States.

FREEDOM OF SPEECH

Delgado, Richard, and Jean Stefanic. *Must We Defend Nazis?: Hate Speech, Pornography, and the New First Amendment*. New York: New York University Press, 1997.
Raises issues regarding pornography and hate crimes; discusses how they are addressed in the framework of freedom of speech.

Fiss, Owen M. *The Irony of Free Speech*. Cambridge, Mass.: Harvard University Press, 1996.

Examines the law and pornography, campaign funds, and other legal and political issues.

John J. Makay, ed. *Free Speech Yearbook*. Carbondale, Ill.: Southern Illinois University Press, 1995.

Published annually, this is a collection of First Amendment studies for the Speech Communication Association.

Freedman, Monroe H., and Eric M. Freedman. *Group Defamation and Freedom of Speech: The Relationship between Language and Violence*. Westport, Conn.: Greenwood Press, 1995.

Examines the influence of defamatory speech on violence.

Garvey, John H., and Frederick Schauer. *The First Amendment: A Reader*. St. Paul, Minn.: West, 1993.

Text with selected readings on freedom of speech, press, and religion.

Gates Jr., Louis, Anthony P. Griffin, Donald E. Lively, Robert C. Post, William B. Rubenstein, and Nadine Strossen. *Speaking of Race, Speaking of Sex: Hate Speech, Civil Rights, and Civil Liberties*. New York: New York University Press, 1994.

Explores hate speech and details states', local, and campus hate speech codes.

Goines, David Lance. *The Free Speech Movement: Coming of Age in the 1960s*. Berkeley, Calif.: Ten Speed Press: 1993.

A personal, inside look at the Free Speech Movement of the 1960s. First-person narrative by a man who experienced the rallies, sit-ins, and arrests of the era.

Kalven Jr., Harry. *A Worthy Tradition: Freedom of Speech in America*. New York: Harper & Row, 1988.

Focuses on historical and contemporary freedom of speech.

LaMarche, Gara, ed., *Speech and Equality: Do We Really Have to Choose?* New York: New York University Press, 1996.

Examines freedom of speech issues in the social and political arenas.

Van Winkle, Harold. *Speaking Freely: Your Right of Free Speech and its Legal Limitations*. Tampa, Fla.: Mancorp Publishing, 1995.

A straightforward look by a Kent State University professor at the history of free speech. Includes references to specific court cases.

Walker, Samuel. *Hate Speech: The History of an American Controversy*. Lincoln, Nebr.: University of Nebraska Press, 1994.

Discusses offensive racial and religious speech. Includes an analysis of Supreme Court decisions and a section on campus speech codes.

RADIO/TELEVISION/INTERNET CENSORSHIP

Campbell, Douglas S. *The Supreme Court and the Mass Media: Selected Cases, Summaries, and Analyses*. Westport, Conn.: Praeger, 1990.
Reviews Supreme Court cases.

Garry, Patrick M. *Scrambling for Protection: The New Media and the First Amendment*. Pittsburgh: University of Pittsburgh Press, 1996.
Examines mass media, freedom of speech, censorship history, and legislation.

Jensen, Carl. *Censored: The News That Didn't Make the News*. New York: Seven Stories, 1996.
Focuses on censorship in the news media.

Lewis, Anthony. *Make No Law: The Sullivan Case and the First Amendment*. New York: Random House, 1991.
Deals with the *Sullivan* case, including libel, slander, and U.S. press laws.

Lipschultz, Jeremy H. *Broadcast Indecency: FCC Regulation and the First Amendment*. Newtown, Mass.: Butterworth-Heinenmann, 1996.
Profiles broadcasting law in a freedom of speech context.

Middleton, Kent, Bill Chamberlin, and Matthew Bunker. *The Law of Public Communication*. New York: Longman, 1988.
Examines freedom and regulation of the press in the context of mass media.

Minow, Newton N., with Craig LaMay. *Abandoned in the Wasteland: Children, Television, and the First Amendment*. New York: Farrar, Straus and Giroux, 1995.
Written by President Kennedy's FCC chairman, this book reprises Minow's famous 1961 "vast wasteland" speech and elaborates on his attack on the mass media for such shortcomings as promoting violence and failing to educate. A discussion of television's effect on children, as well as proposals for reform are important components of this book.

Ross, Henry D. *Free Speech and Talk Radio*. New York: Oleander Publishing, 1996.
Explores censorship issues and broadcasting.

Sclove, Richard E. *Democracy and Technology*. New York: Guilford Press, 1995.
Focuses on the political and social aspects of technology.

Wallace, Jonathan, and Mark Mangan. *Sex, Laws and Cyberspace: Freedom and Censorship on the Frontiers of the Online Revolution*. New York: Holt, 1996.
An examination of legal and ethical issues tied to the Internet and online services. Includes interviews with activists who are for and against cyberspace regulation.

PORNOGRAPHY AND OBSCENITY

Cornog, Martha, ed. *Libraries, Erotica, and Pornography*. Phoenix, Ariz.: The Oryx Press, 1991.
   Examines pornography and erotic material in social and First Amendment contexts.

DeGrazia, Edward. *Girls Lean Back Everywhere: the Law of Obscenity and the Assault on Genius*. New York: Random House, 1992.
   An exploration of artistic freedom focusing on twentieth-century visual and print artists.

Downs, Donald Alexander. *The New Politics of Pornography*. Chicago: University of Chicago Press, 1989.
   Discusses specific obscenity statutes, court cases, and the implications of studies that focus on the effect of viewing pornographic material.

Duggan, Lisa, and Nan D. Hunter, eds. *Sexual Dissent and Political Culture*. New York: Routledge, 1995.
   Includes reprinted articles grouped into themes such as pornography and regulation of homosexuality; appendices include proposed antipornography ordinances and Feminists Anti-Censorship Task Force (FACT) brief.

Heins, Marjorie. *Sex, Sin and Blasphemy: A Guide to America's Censorship Wars*. New York: ACLU Art Censorship Project, 1993.
   Focuses on pornography and the political arena.

Hixon, Richard F. *Pornography and the Justices: The Supreme Court and the Intractable Obscenity Problems*. Carbondale, Ill.: Southern Illinois University Press, 1996.
   An in-depth examination of the legal aspects of pornography in the United States.

Hunter, Ian, David Saunders, and Dugald Williams. *On Pornography: Literature, Sexuality and Obscenity Laws*. New York: St. Martin's Press, 1993.
   While profiling the history of obscenity laws, this book examines the impact of feminism on legal reforms in this area.

Lewis, Felice Flannery. *Literature, Obscenity, and the Law*. Carbondale, Ill.: Southern Illinois University Press, 1976.
   Analyzes a variety of censorship legal cases.

McElroy, Wendy. *XXX: A Woman's Right to Pornography*. New York: St. Martin's Press, 1995.
   Deals with pornography and sexually oriented businesses.

Steiner, Wendy. *The Scandal of Pleasure*. Chicago: University of Chicago Press, 1996.
   Examines twentieth-century aesthetics and controversy.

Strossen, Nadine. *Defending Pornography: Free Speech, Sex, and the Fight for Women's Rights.* New York: Scribner, 1995.
This book by an American Civil Liberties Union president examines the history of obscenity laws from a feminist perspective, claiming that censorship has been and continues to be used as a tool to "repress information vital to women's equality, health, and reproductive autonomy." Argues against the belief that pornography is the root of discrimination and violence against women.

SCHOOL/LIBRARY/TEXTBOOK CENSORSHIP

Burress, Lee. *Battle of the Books: Literary Censorship in the Public Schools, 1950 to 1985.* Metuchen, N.J.: Scarecrow Press, 1989.
Details school censorship; lists specific titles.

DelFattore, Joan. *What Johnny Shouldn't Read: Textbook Censorship in America.* New Haven, Conn.: Yale University Press, 1992.
Provides a firsthand view of ways in which special interest groups influence the content of texts.

Foerstel, Herbert. *Banned in the U.S.A.: A Reference Guide to Book Censorship in Schools and Public Libraries.* Westport, Conn.: Greenwood Press, 1994.
Offers specific titles and suggests courses of action.

Geller, Evelyn. *Forbidden Books in American Public Libraries (1876–1939).* Westport, Conn.: Greenwood Press, 1984.
Reports on the history of book censorship in the United States, focusing on books banned from public libraries.

Lane, Robert W. *Beyond the Schoolhouse Gate: Free Speech and the Inculcation of Values.* Philadelphia, Penn.: Temple University Press, 1995.
Explores First Amendment protection of public school students; examines the aims of public education and values relating to freedom of expression; details and analyzes specific Supreme Court decisions.

Reichman, Henry. *Censorship and Selection: Issues and Answers for Schools.* 2d ed. Chicago: American Library Association, 1993.
Covers student press, library and curricular materials.

Stevens, George E., and John B. Webster. *Law of the Student Press.* Ames, Iowa: Iowa University State Press, 1994.
Deals with collection development of school libraries and freedom of student publications.

Selth, Jefferson P. *Ambition, Discrimination and Censorship in Libraries.* Jefferson, N.C.: McFarland, 1993.

Examines a variety of topics, including library-collection development and discrimination in employment.

VISUAL ARTS

Brownlow, Kevin. *Behind the Mask of Innocence*. New York: Knopf, 1990.
Explores censorship in silent films.

Clapp, J. *Art Censorship*. Metuchen, N.J.: Scarecrow, 1972.
Explores the impact of the social climate on film and stage performance; includes silent films.

Findlater, Richard. *Banned: A Review of Theatrical Censorship in Britain*. London: McGiggin & Kee, 1967.
Examines instances of censorship in the British theater through the mid-twentieth century.

Jacobs, Lea. *The Wages of Sin: Censorship and the Fallen Woman Film, 1928–1942*. Madison, Wis.: University of Wisconsin Press, 1991.
Explores motion picture history; focuses on women in film.

Leff, Leonard, and Jerold Simmons. *The Dame in the Kimono: Hollywood Censorship and the Production Code from the 1920s to the 1960s*. New York: Grove Weidenfeld, 1990.
Profiles Hollywood films and censorship.

Lyons, Charles. *The New Censors: Movies and the Culture Wars*. Philadelphia, Penn.: Temple University Press, 1997.
A contemporary history of controversial films; discusses how cultural policies affect the film industry.

Pally, Marcia. *Sex and Sensibility: Reflections on Forbidden Mirrors and the Will to Censor*. Hopewell, N.J.: Ecco Press, 1994.
An examination of arts censorship and its attempt to alleviate society's woes.

Peter, Jennifer A., and Louis M. Crosier. *The Cultural Battlefield: Art Censorship and Public Funding*. Gilsum, N.H.: Avocus Publishing, 1995.
Examines the impact of censorship on artists; includes chapters by many who are active on censorship battlefields.

Walsh, Frank. *Sin and Censorship: The Catholic Church and the Motion Picture Industry*. New Haven, Conn.: Yale University Press, 1996.
An examination of the Catholic church and its relationship with the motion picture industry from the 1920s to the 1990s.

ENCYCLOPEDIAS AND DICTIONARIES

"Adams, John." *World Book Encyclopedia*. Vol. 1. Chicago: World Book, Inc., 1994.
Offers a brief look at the Alien and Sedition Acts in the context of Adams's administration.

"Alien and Sedition Acts." *Academic American Encyclopedia*. Vol. 1. Danbury, Conn.: Grolier, 1991, pp. 293–94.
Offers brief details.

"Alien and Sedition Acts." *Encyclopedia Americana*. Vol. 25. Danbury, Conn.: Grolier, 1991, pp. 579–80.
Short entry that covers legislative and political history.

Bullock, Alan and Oliver Stallybrass, eds. *The Harper Dictionary of Modern Thought*. New York: Harper & Row, 1977.
Includes entries relevant to intellectual freedom.

"Censorship." *Academic American Encyclopedia*. Vol. 4. Danbury, Conn.: Grolier, 1991, pp. 246–48.
Covers U.S. and British censorship, censorship in public schools and libraries, obscenity and pornography, and restraints on mass media.

"Censorship." *Collier's Encyclopedia*. Vol. 5. New York: Macmillan, 1990.
Examines history of censorship; includes censorship by church and state, as well as private censorship.

"Censorship." *Encyclopedia Americana*. Vol. 6. Danbury, Conn.: Grolier, 1991, pp. 161–67.
Many-faceted overview of censorship; includes U.S. Supreme Court decisions, mass media, libel, creative expression, postal censorship, and self-censorship.

"Censorship." *The New Britannica Macropaedia: Knowledge in Depth*. Vol. 1. 15th ed. Chicago: Encyclopedia Britannica, 1992, pp. 619–25.
In-depth coverage; includes requirements of self-government, origins of freedom of speech, global censorship, comment on Supreme Court cases.

"Censorship." *World Book Encyclopedia*. Vol. 3. Chicago: World Book, Inc., 1994, pp. 345–46.
Includes brief entries on political and religious censorship, as well as a description of methods of censorship.

"Constitution of the United States." *Encyclopedia Americana*. Vol. 7. Danbury, Conn.: Grolier, 1991, pp. 659–73
Discussion of the history of the U.S. Constitution; section on the Bill of Rights; gives full text of Constitution and amendments.

Foerstel, Herbert N. *Free Expression and Censorship in America: An Encyclopedia*. Westport, Conn.: Greenwood Press, 1997.

Includes a wide variety of topics; examines major censorship incidents and traces cases; offers interviews with frequently banned authors.

"Freedom of the Press." *Collier's Encyclopedia*. Vol. 10. New York: Macmillan, 1990, pp. 353–57.
Covers history of and controversy over U.S. and global censorship.

"Freedom of the Press." *Encyclopedia Americana*. Vol. 8. Danbury, Conn.: Grolier, 1991, pp. 296–97.
Covers history, defamation, national security, and global issues.

"Freedom of the Press." *World Book Encyclopedia*. Vol. 11. Chicago: World Book, Inc., 1994, pp. 507–08.
A brief reference.

"Freedom of Speech." *Encyclopedia Americana*. Vol. 8. Danbury, Conn.: Grolier, 1991, pp. 298–99.
Includes history, explanation of "clear and present danger" test; discusses global issues.

"Freedom of Speech." *World Book Encyclopedia*. Vol. 11. Chicago: World Book, Inc., 1994, pp. 506–07.
A brief reference.

Green, Johnathon. *The Encyclopedia of Censorship*. New York: Facts On File, 1990.
Includes a vast number of entries, including terms, people, laws, and historical references.

Hitzeroth, Deborah and Sharon Heerboth. *Movies: The World on Film*. San Diego, Calif.: Lucent Books, 1991.
Reviews many facets of the motion picture industry; discusses censorship and films.

Hurwitz, Leon. *Historical Dictionary of Censorship in the United States*. Westport, Conn.: Greenwood Press, 1985.
Entries relating to censorship and history.

"Journalism." *Academic American Encyclopedia*. Vol. 11. Danbury, Conn.: Grolier, 1991, pp. 454–56.
Covers history of journalism as well as issues in modern journalism. Includes censorship issues.

"Journalism." *Encyclopedia Americana*. Vol. 16. Danbury, Conn.: Grolier, 1991, pp. 183–87.
Examines journalism from early history to the present day; includes television and radio regulation.

"Obscenity." *Encyclopedia Americana*. Vol. 20. Danbury, Conn.: Grolier, 1991, p. 598.
Lists books deemed obscene; discusses history of obscenity; examines Constitutional limitations and briefly discusses the Commission on Obscenity and Pornography of the U.S. Congress.

"Obscenity and Pornography." *World Book Encyclopedia*. Vol. 14. Chicago: World Book, Inc., 1994, pp. 643–44.
Examines the law, mentions cases.
"Pornography." *Encyclopedia Americana*. Vol. 15. Danbury, Conn.: Grolier, 1991, pp. 441–42.
Brief explanation.
"Press, Freedom of the." *Encyclopedia Americana*. Vol. 22. Danbury, Conn.: Grolier, 1991, p. 570.
Looks at history and briefly examines representative Supreme Court cases.
"Speech, Freedom of." *Encyclopedia Americana*. Vol. 22. Danbury, Conn.: Grolier, 1991, p. 570.
Briefly examines Constitutional guarantees, judicial interpretation, and history.

PERIODICALS, REPORTS, BROCHURES, AND PAMPHLETS

Many of these publications, as well as others, are available through the organizations listed in chapter 7.
ACLU Briefing Paper on Artistic Freedom. New York: ACLU Arts Censorship Project.
Answers questions regarding obscenity and arts funding.
Popular Music Under Seige. New York: ACLU Arts Censorship Project.
Answers questions regarding music censorship.
Adler, Allan., ed. *Litigation Under the Federal Open Government Laws*, 18th ed. The Center for National Security Studies, ACLU, Washington, D.C.
Provides information regarding lawsuits pursuant to the FOIA.
Adler, Robert Allan. *Using the FOIA: A Step-by-Step Guide*. The Center for National Security Studies, ACLU, Washington, D.C.
A layperson's step-by-step guide to making requests under the Freedom of Information Act.
The American Civil Liberties Union Arts Censorship Project Newsletter. American Civil Liberties Union New York: ACLU (published semiannually).
American Library Association Policies on Intellectual Freedom: Interpretations of the Library Bill of Rights. Chicago: Office of Intellectual Freedom, American Library Association.
Series includes a wide variety of topics.
Attack on Freedom to Learn. People for the American Way, Washington, D.C.
A report documenting more than 300 attempts to remove or restrict book access across the country. Also details public education challenges related to sex education and other issues.

Annotated Bibliography

Censorship News. New York: National Coalition Against Censorship (published quarterly).
> Contains information and discussion about freedom of expression issues,
> including current school censorship controversies, threats to the free flow
> of information, and obscenity laws.

Censorship in the Schools. Chicago: Office of Intellectual Freedom, American
Library Association, Item no. 6604-7.
> Brochure—available in bulk.
> Covers student press, as well as library and curricular materials.

Coalition Building Resource Book. Chicago: Office of Intellectual Freedom,
American Library Association, Item no. 6600-4.
> Brochure—available in bulk.
> Provides information on organizing a coalition.

The Creative Spirit Must Be Free. New York: ACLU Arts Censorship Project.
> Pamphlet on the history of arts censorship and the work of the Arts
> Censorship Project.

Freedom of Expression Quarterly. Washington, D.C.: National Campaign For
Freedom of Expression.
> Presents news and analysis of current issues concerning freedom of artistic
> expression and First Amendment rights generally.

Freedom to Read Foundation News. Chicago: Freedom to Read Foundation,
American Library Association (published monthly).
> Updates Freedom to Read Foundation members regarding the organiza-
> tion's activities.

Gora, Joel M., Gary M. Stern and Morton H. Halperin. *The Basic Guide to
Free Expression*. Carbondale, Ill.: Southern Illinois Press, 1991. (Available
through ACLU, Washington, D.C.)
> This technical manual used by attorneys is updated annually. It provides
> comprehensive information regarding the Privacy Act, the Freedom of
> Information Act, and other "open government" laws.

Heins, Marjorie. *Media Violence and Free Speech*. ACLU Arts Censorship
Project, 1995.
> An analysis supporting the theory that violence in the media is not a major
> contributing factor to aggressive behavior.

Intellectual Freedom Action News. Chicago: Office of Intellectual Freedom,
American Library Association (published monthly).
> Reports on incidents of censorship.

Intellectual Freedom and Censorship Q & A. Chicago: Office of Intellectual
Freedom, American Library Association, 1995.
> Eight-page guide to intellectual freedom; includes defense of intellectual
> freedom in the library.

NCFE Bulletin. Seattle, Wash.: National Campaign for Freedom of Expression (published four times annually).
Reports on intellectual freedom issues.

National Campaign for Freedom of Expression Update. Seattle, Wash.: National Campaign for Freedom of Expression (published bimonthly).
Addresses specific freedom of expression issues as they arise.

Newsletter on Intellectual Freedom. Chicago: ALA Intellectual Freedom Committee, American Library Association (published bimonthly).
Examines freedom of expression issues.

The Right to Protest: The Basic ACLU Guide to Free Expression. Washington, D.C.: ACLU 1991. Item no. 1120.
Focuses on intellectual freedom and the right to protest.

ARTICLES

GENERAL

Alter, J. "Does Bloody Footage Lose Wars?" *Newsweek*, February 11, 1991, vol. 117, pp. 38–42.
Examines censorship during the Persian Gulf War.

Berry III, J. N. "War Is a Library Issue." *Library Journal*, March 1, 1991, vol. 116, p. 10.
Looks at the relationship between censorship and war.

Bishop, Don, and Rosette Sion Bishop. "Still Outspoken at 92." *Editor and Publisher*, July 1, 1995, vol. 128, pp. 42–45.
Details career of seventy-three-year-old journalist Robert St. John, including war correspondence during World War II.

Brewster, Todd. "First and Foremost." *Life*, Fall 1991, vol. 14, pp. 60–67.
Focuses on civil rights cases and freedom of speech.

Brislin, Tom. "Extra! The Comic Book Journalist Survives the Censors of 1995." *Journalism History*, Autumn 1995, vol. 21, pp. 123–32.
Focuses on censorship in the 1950s, particularly of comic books.

Campbell, Duncan, and Nigelan Townson. "University Press Blocks Gay Book." *New Statesman and Society*, August 12, 1988, vol. 1, p. 7.
Reports on censorship of gay literature.

"Chronicle of Censorship." *New Statesman and Society*. April 5, 1991, vol. 4, pp. 9–11.
Offers a chronology of censorship from 1455 to 1990.

"Cooler Heads Win Out." *Time*, October 30, 1989, vol. 134, p. 59.
Reports on the Senate's refusal to pass the anti–flag-burning statute after the measure passed in the House.

Annotated Bibliography

Darbishire, Helen. "Free Speech: Democracy's Watchdog." *UNESCO Courier*, March 1994, vol. 47, pp. 18–23.

Assesses the dangers of censorship when viewed in the framework of human rights; explores self-censorship's role in technology.

Dwyer, V. "Literary Firestorm." *Maclean's*, April 1, 1991, vol. 104, p. 55.

Reviews arguments regarding U.S. and Canadian censorship of Bret Easton Ellis's violent novel *American Psycho*.

Fields, Howard. "Coping with the Reagan Years: Battles Over Censorship." *Publishers Weekly*, January 5, 1990, vol. 236, pp. 30–32.

Profiles Reagan's role and influence regarding censorship.

Goldberg, Beverly. "On the Line for the First Amendment." *American Liberties*, September 1995, vol. 26, pp. 774–79.

Interview with Judith Krug, executive director of the Office for Intellectual Freedom. Offers analysis of the challenges to intellectual freedom.

"Hard Line on Porn." *The Economist*, August 10, 1996, vol. 340, p. 42.

Details the U.K. agreement to regulate Internet newsgroups for pornography.

Henthoff, Nat. "Free Speech: Are There Limits?" *Progressive*, May 1993, vol. 57, pp. 16–18.

Examines free speech; includes profiles of Supreme Court cases.

Hernandez, Debra Gersch. "Reprehensible Speech Protected." *Editor and Publisher*, September 21, 1996, vol. 129, pp. 18–21.

Profiles a District Court case against a publisher of manuals that provide murder instructions.

"The Highest Court Stands 5–4 on a Burning Issue." *U.S. News and World Report*, July 3, 1981, vol. 187, p. 8.

Deals with the Supreme Court's decision in flag-burning case.

Jacoby, Tamar. "Time to Outlaw Racial Slurs? New Questions About Protecting Hate Speech." *Newsweek*, June 6, 1988, vol. 111, p. 59.

Examines hate speech and the white supremacy movement.

Kiebowicz, Richard B. "The Telegraph, Censorship and Politics at the Outset of the Civil War." *Civil War History*, June 1994, vol. 40, pp. 95–119.

Reports on the role of the telegraph and its relation to censorship; also reports on censorship in general.

Kroll, Edwin. "Don't Print That!" *Progressive*, October 1992, vol. 56, pp. 4–7.

Examines three books and advocates the importance of printing all books in their entirety to assure First Amendment freedoms; includes reference to Mapplethorpe's art.

LaMarche, G. "Some Thoughts on the 'Chilling Effect'." *Art Journal*, Winter 1991, vol. 50, pp. 56–59.

Analyzes censorship and the courts, as well as the NEA. Includes discussion of the Scopes trial's legacy, music lyrics, Salman Rushdie, and the *Pentagon Papers.*

LaMarche, G., and W. B. Rubenstein. "The Love That Dare Not Speak." *Nation*, November 5, 1990, vol. 251, pp. 524–26.
Examines censorship in the context of gay and lesbian issues; advocates opposition to censorship in gay and lesbian movement.

Lincove, David A. "Propaganda and the American Public Library from the 1930s to the Eve of WWII." *RQ*, Summer 1994, vol. 33, pp. 510–24.
An examination of censorship stemming from political and social bias from the 1930s to World War II.

"Losing a Friend on the Court." *Advertising Age*, July 18, 1991, vol. 62, pp. 18–23.
Editorial praising Supreme Court Justice Thurgood Marshall's stance on First Amendment issues and looking at the impact of his retirement.

Lowe, Alexandra Dylan. "The Price of Speaking Out." *ABA Journal*, September 1, 1996. vol. 82, pp. 48–51.
Details the phenomenon of SLAPPs, also known as "strategic lawsuits against public participation."

Mallowe, Mike. "Don't Be So Quick to Censor." *U.S. Catholic*, August 1995, vol. 60, pp. 20–22.
An examination of the complexities of censorship arguments; details distinction between censorship and censure. Advocates that prosecution, not censorship, is the answer.

Manciaux, Michel. "The Right to Be Heard." *UNESCO Courier*, October 1991, pp. 13–16.
Focuses on children's rights, including freedom of speech.

McGinnis, John O. "The Left vs. Free Speech." *Commentary*, October 1994, vol. 98, pp. 59–61.
An analysis of antithetical viewpoints on censorship.

Plagens, P. "Censorship." *Newsweek*, December 31, 1990, vol. 116, pp. 38–40.
Examines censorship and the direction it is likely to take. Includes discussion of Mapplethorpe and other controversial artists.

Reid, Calvin, and Bridget Kinsella. "In Banned Books Week, Censorship Still Thrives." *Publishers Weekly*, September 23, 1996, vol. 243, pp. 12–16.
Discusses national and international book banning.

Reuther, Rosemary Radford. "Strategy to Stop Snappers at Speakers' Heels." *National Catholic Reporter*, December 11, 1987, vol. 24, p. 12.
Column dealing with freedom of speech in the Catholic church.

"Science, Technology, and the Constitution." *Environment*, March 1988, vol. 30, p. 22.

Reports on freedom of information and communication of technical information.

Stone, I. F. "When Free Speech Was First Condemned; the Trial of Socrates Reconsidered." *Harper's Magazine*, February 1988, vol. 276, pp. 60–66.
A philosophical analysis of freedom of speech issues.

Sussman, Leonard R. "'Pressticide' and Press Ethics." *Freedom Review*, January/February, 1995, vol. 26, pp. 64–69.
Profiles global press and politics.

Tesich, S. "A Government of Lies." *Nation*, January 6, 1992, vol. 254, pp. 12–15.
Reports on censorship and the Persian Gulf War from the perspective of the Nixon and Reagan administrations.

Turque, Bill. "SLAPPing the Opposition; How Developers and Officials Fight Critics." *Newsweek*, March 5, 1990, vol. 114, p. 22.
An examination of SLAPPs lawsuits, particularly in the areas of real estate and environment; examines moral and legal aspects.

Underwood, Nora. "Truth and Consequences." *Maclean's*, February 1, 1988, vol. 101, p. 45.
Details freedom of speech issues in the Ernst Zundel antisemitism case.

"Waving the Flag." *The New Republic*, January 23, 1989, vol. 200, pp. 7–9.
Editorial regarding flag desecration.

ARTS

"Axe That Axel." *The Economist*, May 21, 1988, vol. 307, p. 66.
Deals with music censorship.

Baldwin, Carl. "NEA Chairman Does Turnabout on AIDS Exhibition." *Art in America*, January 1990, vol. 78. pp. 31–33.
Reports on art exhibitions and federal funding.

Cembalest, Robin. "Fighting Back." *Art News*, December 1992, vol. 91, p. 30.
Profiles controversial art and commends civil rights organizations for working to combat censorship of art.

Crane, Philip M., and Claiborne Pell. "Should Congress Cease Funding the National Endowment for the Arts?" *The American Legion*, November 1996, vol. 141, p. 10.
Democratic and Republican senators air their opposing views on federal arts funding.

Czitrom, Daniel. "The Politics of Performance: From Theater Licensing to Movie Censorship in the Turn-of-the-Century." *American Quarterly*, December 1992, vol. 44, pp. 525–554.

Profiles theater regulation and censorship in 1890s New York.

DeRogatis, Jim. "Rock and Roll." *Rolling Stone Australia*, March 1996, issue no. 520, pp. 19–21.

Interview with former Nirvana band member Chris Novoselic; includes his views on censorship.

Doctorow, E. L. "Art vs. the Uniculture." *The Nation*, March 1, 1992, vol. 253, pp. 675–78.

Discussion of free speech, especially in relation to the arts.

Geier, Thom, and Jim Impoco. "Shame Isn't Fleeting." *U.S. News and World Report*, June 19, 1995, vol. 118, p. 57.

Examines the trend to replace censorship in Hollywood with "the bully pulpit of shame." Raises questions regarding Time-Warner's relationship with distributors of "gangsta" rap music.

Heard, Alex. "Mapplethorpe of My Eye." *The New Republic*, August 21, 1989, vol. 201, pp. 10–13.

Deals with Mapplethorpe's homoerotic photos, censorship, and NEA funding.

Hillerman, T. "The Enemy Within: Censorship in Rock Music in the 1950s." *South Atlantic Quarterly*, Fall 1991, vol. 90, pp. 675–708.

Compares censorship of rock musicians to censorship of films and books.

Hoffman, B. "The Thought Police Are Out There." *Art Journal*, Fall 1991, vol. 50, pp. 40–45.

Examines First Amendment application to contemporary visual arts and other intellectual freedom issues.

Hunter, S. "The Right to Rap." *Cobblestone*, September 1991, vol. 12, pp. 40–43.

Examines the pros and cons of warning labels on records; includes reference to rap group 2 Live Crew.

"Indecent Request." *The New Republic*, April 9, 1990, vol. 202, pp. 5–7.

An editorial dealing with obscenity, the NEA, and federal funding for the arts.

"In the Ayes of the Beholders." *Omni*, February 1991, vol. 13, p. 10.

Playwright Arthur Miller advocates that the U.S. government's attempt to legislate selective arts funding resembles 1960s Soviet censorship.

Jacobson, Daniel. "Freedom of Speech Acts? A Response to Layton." *Philosophy and Public Affairs*, Winter 1995, vol. 24, pp. 64–80.

Focuses on the arguments for and against censorship of pornography.

Light, Judy. "Jury Acquits Museum in Landmark Art Trial." *Dance Magazine*, December 1990, vol. 64, pp. 12–14.

Profiles the case of a Cincinnati, Ohio, art museum that displayed Mapplethorpe homoerotic art.

Lyons, B. "Artistic Freedom and the University." *Art Journal*, Winter 1991, vol. 50, pp. 77–84.
Explores academic freedom in relation to the visual arts.

Patton, Cindy. "White Racism/Black Signs: Censorship and Images of Race Relations." *Journal of Communications*, Spring 1995, vol. 45, pp. 67–78.
Focuses on U.S. film censorship between the world wars.

"The Piper's Tune: Abortion and Censorship." *The Economist*, November 16, 1991, vol. 321, pp. A31–33.
Discusses censorship and abortion during the Bush administration.

Rubenstein, William. "The Love That Dare Not Speak: Censoring Gay Expression." *The Nation*, November 5, 1990, vol. 251, pp. 254–56.
Deals with censorship in homosexual art and literature, including an examination of NEA funding.

"Siding with Rosie." *New Statesman*, September 20, 1996, vol. 125, p. 5.
Details the removal from a London gallery of a Mapplethorpe photo depicting bare buttocks of young girl.

Wallace, B. "Bush's Compromise: A Newer Form of Censorship?" *Art in America*, November 1990, vol. 78, pp. 57–62.
Profiles reauthorization plan for NEA agreed on by Bush administration and NEA chairman.

Serrill, Michael, and Angelo Bonnie. "Controversy Crashed the Party." *Time*, July 10, 1995, vol. 146, p. 42
Examines accusations of censorship regarding the UN's fiftieth anniversary commemorative book *A Vision of Hope*.

Simmons, Jerrold. "The Censoring of 'Rebel Without a Cause'." *Journal of Popular Film and Television*, Summer 1995, vol. 23, pp. 56–64.
An analysis of 1952 censorship focusing on the film *Rebel Without a Cause*.

"2 Live Crew Freed by Jury in Obscenity Trial." *Jet*, November 5, 1990, vol. 79, pp. 14–16.
Details the case of rap group 2 Live Crew, their arrest and removal from a Florida stage, and the progress of the criminal case.

Volz, E. J. "You Can't Play That." *School Library Journal*, July 1991, vol. 37, pp. 16–19.
A comparison of 1990s and 1950s music censorship.

Walker, Paulette W. "U.S. Appeals Court Rejects 'Decency' Standards for Grants from the Arts Endowment." *The Chronicle of Higher Education*, November 15, 1996, vol. 43, p. A43.
Reports on the rejection of a provision that would have prevented federal funding of projects that might be labeled "obscene."

Webb, Michael. "Art: Vintage Movie Posters." *Architectural Digest*, April 1994, vol. 51, pp. 256–63.

Examines the history of movie posters, including relevant censorship issues.

Williams, Alex, and Stephen J. Dubner. "Celluloid Zeros." *New York*, February 14, 1994, vol. 27, pp. 18–22.
Revisits Hollywood's Production Code and the resulting film censorship.

FOREIGN

Adelkhah, Fariba. "A Boom in the Marketplace of Ideas." *World Press Review*, April 1995, vol. 42, pp. 15–18.
Reports that Tehran magazines are finally debating political and social issues, though penalties still exist for publications that do not self-censor.

Alton, David. "Our Video Culture." *Contemporary Review*, April 1994, vol. 264, pp. 169–73.
Examines effects of video and television violence on British children.

Bell, David A. "Paristroika: Is Gorbo Another Louis XVI?" *The New Republic*, July 11, 1988, vol. 199, pp. 21–23.
Written by a doctoral candidate in history at Princeton University, this article compares Russian and French intellectual freedom principles and realities.

Boulton, L. "Not Quite the First Amendment." *World Press Review*, August 1990, vol. 37, pp. 68–72.
Discusses a Soviet law that abolished censorship.

Colm, Sara. "Cambodia's Muzzled Press." *Freedom Review*, November/December 1994, vol. 25, pp. 28–31.
Explores Cambodian censorship in the 1990s.

Cornwall, M. "News, Rumour and the Control of Information in Austria-Hungary, 1914–1982." *History*, February 1992, vol. 77, pp. 50–65.
Deals with censorship during the twentieth century.

Daniloff, Nicholas. "Mightier Than the Sword: The Role of Journalists in Russia." *Harvard International Review*, Spring 1995, vol. 17, pp. 36–41.
Profiles journalism in Russia.

David. "Genet, the Theater and the Algerian War." *Theater Research International*, Autumn 1994, vol. 19, pp. 226–238.
Examines the depiction of Algerians in the work of French playwrights.

Ehmeir, Walter. "Publishing South African Literature in English in the 1960s." *Research in African Literatures*, Spring 1995, vol. 26, pp. 111–32.
An analysis of South African government regulation and censorship of literature.

Francis, Diane. "A New Attack on Freedom of Speech." *Maclean's*, May 31, 1993, vol. 106, p. 9.

Advocates that Canadian criminal sanctions for contributing beyond legal limits to political campaigns are tantamount to censorship.

"Freedom of Speech, à la Française." *The Economist*, November 23, 1996, vol. 341, p. 55.
Reports on French rap duo jailed for song lyrics referring to "fascist" police.

Fruean, Christopher. "Crumbling Confidence." *Free China Review*, May 1995, vol. 45, pp. 52–58.
Discussion of Hong Kong's politics and history, including freedom of speech and press issues.

Gies, David T. "Glorious Invalid: Spanish Theater in the Nineteenth Century." *Hispanic Review*, Spring 1993, vol. 61, pp. 213–247.
Examines many aspects of Spanish theater in the 1900s, including censorship.

Halligan, Fionnuala. "Banned in China." *World Press Review*, November 1991, vol. 38, p. 58.
Focuses on the Chinese film industry; includes analysis of events surrounding the film *Raise the Red Flag*.

Hames, P. "Prague Sprung." *New Statesman and Society*, April 5, 1991, vol. 4, pp. 22–24.
Describes Czechoslovakian films banned in the 1960s.

Hashemi, S., and C. Cherigny. "Identity Crisis in Iran." *World Press Review*, February 1992, vol. 39, p. 53.
Reprint of *Le Monde* article focusing on censorship in Iranian films.

Henderson, C. "The Filtered War." *New Statesman and Society*, April 5, 1991, vol. 4, pp. 16–19.
Probes global censorship; focuses on Persian Gulf War censorship.

Hirst, Derek. "Locating the 1650s in England's Seventeenth Century." *History*, July 1996, vol. 81, pp. 359–84.
Examines politics and analyzes censorship in England from 1640 to 1660.

Jacobs, Karrie. "Germany Stomps Skinhead Music." *Rolling Stone*, November 11, 1993, p. 18.
Reports on freedom of speech issues and German music.

Jayasankaran, S. "The Unkindest Cut." *Far Eastern Economic Review*, June 11, 1995, vol. 158, p. 32.
Focuses on Malaysian film censorship.

Kelleher, John. "And the Banned Played On." *Times Higher Education Supplement*, April 29, 1994, issue no. 1121, pp. 18–22.
An examination of the British Journal Index on censorship and freedom of speech issues.

Kelly, C., and B. Shelby. "Counting the Hours in Cameroon." *World Press Review*, January 1992, vol. 39, p. 51.

Interview with an editor who discusses press censorship.

Klima, Ivan. "Freedom and Garbage." *World Press Review*, April 1995, vol. 42, pp. 51–53.

An examination of the free expression in the Czech Republic.

Laxman, R. K. "Freedom to Cartoon, Freedom to Speak." *Daedalus*, Fall 1989, vol. 118, pp. 68–92.

Examines freedom of press and political cartoons in India.

Loveman, Brian. "Protected Democracies and Military Guardianship: Political Transitions in Latin America." *Journal of Interamerican Studies and World Affairs*, 1994, vol. 36, p. 105.

Details the constitutions and censorship in Latin America.

Murray, Jay. "Report from Havana." *Art in America*, October 1992, vol. 80, pp. 65–69.

Profiles censorship of Cuban art and its impact on Cuban artists.

Nicholson, Steve. "Unnecessary Plays: European Drama and the British Censor in the 1920s." *Theater Research International*, Spring 1995, vol. 20, pp. 30–37.

O'Malley, Chris and Mariette DiChristina. "Reigning in the Net." *Popular Science*, vol. 249, p. 22.

China's strict Internet regulations and their impact on China's progress in cyberspace are examined.

"Privacy and Paedophilia." *Economist*, August 3, 1996, vol. 340, p. 146.

An examination of Sweden's child pornography laws.

Reeves, Nicholas. "The Power of Film Propaganda—Myth or Reality?" *Historical Journal of Film, Radio and Television*, 1993, vol. 13, pp. 181–202.

Reports on film propaganda in Great Britain during World War I.

"Regional Review: Singapore." *Asian Business Review*, September 1996, issue N, pp. 10–12.

Examines Internet censorship in Singapore.

"Seen But Not Heard." *Economist*, August 8, 1992, vol. 324, p. 17.

Advocates that "Britain should lift broadcasting ban on Northern Ireland's terrorist sympathisers."

Sims, Calvin. "Chileans Are Prosecuted for Criticizing Officials." *New York Times*, November 10, 1996, vol. 146, p. 6(n).

Reports on intellectual freedom issues in Chile.

"Solidarity and Freedom." *Current*, June 1990, pp. 37–41.

Transcript of Lech Walesa speech; focuses on solidarity and civil rights in Poland.

Tighe, Carl. "Polish Writers and the Transition from Socialist 'Unreality' to a Capitalist 'Reality'." *Journal of European Studies*, September 1994, vol. 24, pp. 205–42.

An examination of the writer as catalyst to social change, including an analysis of censorship under General Jaruzelski.

Tismaneau, Vladimir. "Homage to Goania: the Romanian Opposition Gets Bashed." *The New Republic*, July 30, 1990, vol. 203, pp. 16–19.

Reports on intellectual freedom issues in Romania.

Usher, Graham. "Palestinian Authority, Israeli Rule." *The Nation*, February 5, 1996, vol. 262, pp. 15–19.

Discusses Palestinian authority and free speech issues.

Verburg, Peter. "Struggle for Control of the Airwaves." *Alberta Report/Western Report*, November 21, 1994, vol. 21, p. 49.

An analysis of censorship of Canadian airwaves prompted by the banning of "Mighty Morphin Power Rangers" in Canada because of violence.

INTERNET

Bennahum, David S. "The Internet's Private Side." *New York Times*, March 2, 1996, vol. 145, p. 19.

Explores the need for alternatives to governmental regulation of cyberspace; examines the Communications Decency Act.

"Bill of Goods." *New Hampshire Business Review*, October 11, 1996, vol. 18, pp. 42–50.

Profiles ACLU's legal position and action against the Communications Decency Act.

Brody, Herb. "Of Bytes and Rights." *Technology Review*, November–December, 1992, vol. 95, pp. 22–30.

Details intellectual freedom issues as they relate to electronic communications.

"Child Safety Tips." *Multimedia Schools*, November/December, 1995, vol. 2, pp. 10–16.

Reference to specific websites dealing with censorship and child safety.

Cohen, Jodi B. "Germany Plans Online Law." *Editor and Publisher*, June 1, 1996, vol. 129, pp. 56–65.

Relates German justice minister's plan to introduce a law that would not hold online providers responsible for pornography or neo-Nazi propaganda.

Deloughry, Thomas J. "Colleges Oppose Proposed Ban on 'Indecent' Material on the Internet." *Chronicle of Higher Education*, December 15, 1995, vol. 42, pp. A24–29.

Examines proposed legislation and free speech limitations.

Dibbell, Julian, and John F. Dickerson. "Muzzling the Internet: Can This Congress Find a Way to Preserve Civil Liberties while Curbing Cyberporn? So Far, No." *Time*, December 18, 1995, vol. 146, pp. 75–78.
Discussion of telecommunications reform bill and its impact and shortcomings regarding child protection.

Eshoo, Anna. "Government Should Stay off the Backs of Superhighway Users." *Business Journal Serving San Jose & Silicon Valley*, vol. 13, pp. 39–41.
Examines the consequences of censorship and criticizes the Christian Coalition's position on censorship.

Frook, John Evan. "Ratings for Web Content in the Works." *Communications Week*, September 25, 1995, issue no. 576, pp. 69–71.
Discusses proposed PICS (platform for Internet content selection).

Garber, Joseph R. "Dirty Bits, Naughty Bites." *Forbes*, August 26, 1996, vol. 158, p. 82.
Editorial decrying legislative interference with Internet access. Focuses on sex on the Internet and alternative means of controlling access.

Harders, Julie. "Censorship in Cyberspace: Proposed On-line Decency Standards Tougher than Traditional Print, Broadcast Rules." *Quill*, October 1995, vol. 83, p. 25.
Examines proposed telecommunications legislation in light of First Amendment. Compares House and Senate packages.

Henthoff, Nat. "Indecent Proposal: With the Communications Decency Act, Washington Considers Controlling Cyberspace." *Entertainment Weekly*, March 31, 1995, n. 268, pp. 64–66.
A discussion of the Communications Decency Act and its impact.

Katt, Spencer F. "Public-Spirited Spence Strives to Clean Up the Net." *PC Week*, February 12, 1996, vol. 13, pp. 114–17.
Discusses censorship of the web subsequent to Telecommunications Bill passage.

Lange, Larry. "Big Brother Is Surfing the Net." *Electronic Engineering Times*, June 24, 1996, no. 907, pp. 1–3.
Discusses a variety of Internet issues, including censorship.

Lannon, Larry. "Censorship? No Way!" *Telephony*, June 26, 1994, vol. 228, p. 56
Examines the dichotomy and similarities between electronic communication and verbal communication; details libel suit against Prodigy.

Lappin, Ted. "Aux Armes, Netizens!" *Nation*, February 26, 1996, vol. 262, pp. 6–8.
Editorial examining the negative implications of the Telecommunications Reform Bill.

Levy, Steven. "The Senate's Bomb Scare." *Newsweek*, August 12, 1996, vol. 128, p. 48.

A critical attack on Internet regulation including excerpts from Senate hearings regarding the bomb construction information available on one website.

Lewis, Peter H. "An Internet Author of Sexually Violent Fiction Faces Charges." *New York Times*, February 11, 1995, vol. 144, p. 7(n).

Reports on the Jake Baker case in which a University of Michigan student published stories of sexual torture and murder on the Internet.

Paul, Lauren Gibbons. "CDA Bill: A Time to Kill? *PC Week*, August 19, 1996, vol. 13, pp. 1–2.

Examines business Internet policies for employees.

Rash Jr., Wayne. "CompuServe Flashes a Green Light on an Internet Censorship Mess." *Communications Week*, January 15, 1996, vol. 146, pp. 74–76.

Criticizes German censorship of the net and analyzes the impact of censorship on the international cyberspace community.

Reid, Calvin. "Publishers Protest Scope and Language of Anti-Cybersmut Bill." *Publishers Weekly*, April 10, 1995, vol. 242, p. 9.

Examines §312 of the Communications Decency Act, and its impact.

———. "Cyber Family Values." *Publishers Weekly*, March 4, 1996, vol. 243, p. 16.

Profiles FAIC (Families Against International Censorship) and the group's activities.

Wallich, Paul. "More Rules of the Road." *Scientific American*, February 1996, vol. 274, pp. 331–33.

Profiles laws regarding Internet censorship and reactions.

Wildstorm, Steve, and Toddi Gutner. "Cybersmut: How to Lock out the Kids." *Business Week*, February 12, 1996, no. 3462, pp. 98–100.

Profiles software for individual control of access to pornographic material on the Internet.

Wise, Jeff. "The Modem Is No Match for the Sword." *Time Australia*, August 19, 1996, no. 34, p. 96.

Explores Australian and international censorship in relation to advancing technology.

"Lawless: Too Many Loopholes in the Net." *Economist*, July 1, 1995, vol. 336, pp. 15–18.

Examines cyberspace, cyberporn, and freedom of speech; includes discussion of Congressional hearing regarding bomb-making instructions available on the Internet.

RADIO/TELEVISION BROADCASTING

Ahearne, J. F. "Commerce Committee Hears Alcohol Ad Labeling Arguments." *Broadcasting*, April 6, 1992, vol. 122, pp. 11–13.
Profiles debate over warnings on television and radio wine and beer advertisements.

Bayles, Martha. "Fake Blood." *Brookings Review*, Fall 1993, vol. 11, p. 20.
Examines violence in the media and explores censorship versus regulation.

Chapman, Steve. "Censorship Won't Eliminate Violent Crimes." *Human Events*, October 16, 1993, vol. 53, pp. 18–23.
Examines the government's role in censorship of television. Asserts that censorship cannot cure violent crime.

Fisher, Raymond L. "Hate Fills the Airwaves," *USA Today*, May 1996, vol. 124, pp. 46–49.
Reports on hate speech on radio and cable TV; examines the social and moral aspects of talk shows.

Forbes, Malcolm S. "Viewers, Not Politicians, Should Decide What They Can Watch." *Forbes*, February 14, 1993, vol. 153, pp. 26–29.
Deals with law and cable TV broadcasting.

Freedman, Morris, "Taming the Media-Violence Hysteria." *Education Week*, June 5, 1996, vol. 15, pp. 44–46.
Focuses on the influence of television violence on aggressive behavior; examines television news censorship.

Goldstein, Richard. "You Gotta' Have Friends." *Village Voice*, April 5, 1996, vol. 39, pp. 8–10.
Examines censorship of the U.S. mass media.

Lichtenstein, B. "The Censor Within." *Channels*, November 5, 1990, vol. 10, pp. 16–19.
Raises issues regarding self-censorship and its impact on diversity in programming and includes details of specific cases.

Mallory, Maria. "That's One Angry Camel." *Business Week*, 7 March, 1994, no. 3361, pp. 94–96. Analyzes the R. J. Reynolds Joe Camel advertisements and their impact.

Markey, Edward. "Markey Wins on V-Chip." *Broadcasting and Cable*, August 7, 1995, vol. 125, pp. 10–12.
Focuses on the v-chip, designed to offer control over programming.

Pexton, Patrick. "Can the Press and Services Be Allies?" *Air Force Times*, October 23, 1995, no. 12, p. 12.
Raises issues regarding mass media and national security.

"Radio Goes to War." *Brand Week*, September 4, 1995, vol. 35, pp. 16–20.
Deals with censorship of radio broadcasts during World War II.

"The (Red) Lion King." *Broadcasting & Cable*, July 4, 1994, vol. 124, pp. 58–60.
An editorial focusing on FCC and Supreme Court decisions regarding broadcasters and cable operators.

Rosen, Jeffrey. "The End of Obscenity." *New Republic*, July 15, 1996, vol. 215, pp. 6–8.
Distinguishes between indecency and obscenity in an examination of a Pennsylvania case that struck down portions of the Communications Decency Act.

Sheinfeld, Lois P. "FCC Doublespeak." *Film Comment*, September–October 1987, vol. 23, pp. 87–91.
Deals with the FCC Fairness Doctrine and obscenity in the mass media.

Smith, Laura C. "Way Too Hot to Handle." *Entertainment Weekly*, March 31, 1995, no. 268, p. 74.
An analysis of television regulation in the 1950s and 1960s; focuses on the "Smothers Brothers Comedy Hour."

Teinowitz, Ira. "Ad Groups Rally Against Phillip Morris." *Advertising Age*, June 30, 1996, vol. 67, pp. 54–59.
Deals with Phillip Morris' legal agreement to restrict its ads.

Wackerman, Daniel T. "Mind's Eye." *America*, March 2, 1996, vol. 174, p. 8.
Opposes governmental interference regarding programming; advocates parental control.

Wallach, Van, and George T. Chronis. "Florida Legislators Clamp Down on 'Excessively Violent' Video Games." *Video Store*, February 19, 1995, vol. 17, pp. 12–16
Profiles proposed Florida legislation that would prohibit sale to minors of excessively violent video games.

SCHOOL/LIBRARY/TEXTBOOK ISSUES

"ALA, Coalition Challenges New Internet Computer Law." *Computers in Libraries*, May 1996, vol. 16, pp. 50–52.
Examines potential impact if Communications Decency Act were to become law and details the possibility of criminal charges against libraries if the CDA were enacted.

Birnbach, Norman. "The Right to Hate." *Seventeen*, February 1993, vol. 52, p. 64.
Examines campus speech codes and hate speech.

Burke, S. "Banishing Books?" *U.S. News and World Report*, May 18, 1992, vol. 112, p. 76.
Details a survey's findings that many favor censorship in libraries.

Click, J. William. "Educating for the First Amendment." *Contemporary Education*, Winter 1995, vol. 66, pp. 77–82.

Profiles the First Amendment and its interpretation in conjunction with the rights of U.S. students.

"Death Knell for Speech Codes?" *Chronicle of Higher Education*, July 1, 1992, vol. 38, pp. A1–A4.

Analysis of Supreme Court decision against a city hate speech ordinance. Article postulates that case will not greatly impact campus speech codes.

Dentzinger, John. "School Daze." *Playboy*, June, 1988, vol. 35, p. 52.

Discussion focusing on *Hazelwood v. Kuhlemier* case and censorship of student newspapers. Brief examination of select constitutional amendments as they apply to students.

Dodge, S. "Students Fight Administrators and Each Other for Educational Control of Campus Newspapers." *Chronicle of Higher Education*, March 4, 1992, vol. 38, p. A35.

Examines free press and conflicts between students and administrators.

Dority, B. "The PC Speech Police." *Humanist*, March 1992, vol. 52, pp. 31–32.

Advocates that political correctness has led to academic censorship; includes specific campus codes and incidents.

Eveslage, Thomas S. "Stifling Student Expression: A Lesson Taught, a Lesson Learned." *Contemporary Education*, Winter 1995, vol. 66, pp. 86–89.

Explores free speech restrictions in U.S. high schools.

Finley, Paris, and Paul Huebner. "Debate: Should Schools Regulate Message T-Shirts?" *NEA Today*, September 15, 1994, vol. 13, p. 47.

Reports on students and intellectual freedom issues.

Fleming, Dan. "Ethical Issues in the Classroom." *The Clearing House*, October 1987, vol. 61, pp. 85–88.

Examines moral and religious aspects of education. Includes textbook censorship.

Garry, Patrick. "Censorship by the Free-Speech Generation." *National Forum*, Spring 1995, vol. 75, pp. 29–32.

Details free speech and censorship issues on college campuses; includes speech codes and a discussion of political correctness.

Greve, Michael S. "Forcing Free Speech." *Reason*, July 1995, vol. 27, pp. 56–59.

Profiles Stanford University's free speech code and its repeal.

Greve, Michael S. "Yes: Call It What It Is—Censorship." *ABA Journal*, February 1994, vol. 80, pp. 40–43.

States the author's position regarding a New Hampshire creative writing teacher who lost his tenure for creating a "hostile environment."

Henthoff, Nat. "The New Jacobins." *Reason*, November 1991, vol. 23, p. 30.
Analyzes freedom of speech in the context of political correctness; examines political facets of federal aid to higher education.

"High Court Backs Censorship of High School Newspapers." *Jet*, February 1, 1988, vol. 73, p. 38.
Reports on intellectual freedom issues in school publications.

"Censorship Nettles Students." *American Journalism Review*, November 1995, vol. 17, pp. 7–10.
Deals with students' rights and examines censorship of students' publications.

Lincove, David A. "Propaganda and the American Public Library from the 1930s to the Eve of WWII." *RQ*, Summer 1994, vol. 33, pp. 510–24.
Profiles U.S. censorship caused by political and social bias.

Manos, Keith T. "The Censor's Dilemma." *School Library Journal*, April 1993, vol. 39, p. 52.
Details censorship of student publications; examines specific legal cases.

Meyer, Nancy J. "Free Speech for College Students: How Much Is Enough?" *Communications and the Law*, March 1991, vol. 13, pp. 69–87.
Examines the balance between individual student liberty and the accomplishment of objectives in the academic environment.

"OIF Says Gay Titles Top 'Most Challenged' List." *American Libraries*, April 1994, vol. 25, pp. 372–74.
A report by the American Library Association Office of Intellectual Freedom that homosexuality was the number one reason for challenge of library materials during the survey period. Article synopsizes specific titles.

Olson, Todd. "The Case of the Disappearing Books." *Scholastic Update*, November 3, 1995, vol. 128, pp. 8–10.
An examination of book banning focuses on the firing of a New Hampshire teacher who assigned books featuring gay characters.

Powell, Monica. "Campus Tongue-Leashing Expands." *Insight*, January 15, 1990, vol. 6, pp. 52–54.
Examines campus speech codes.

Robbins, Louise S. "Anti-Communism, Racism, and Censorship in the McCarthy Era." *Journal of Education for Library and Information Sciences*, Fall 1994, vol. 35, pp. 331–36.
Examines the firing of a librarian in the 1950s for offering "subversive material" in the classroom.

Stempel III, Guido H. "Living the First Amendment." *Contemporary Education*, Winter 1995, vol. 66, pp. 96–98.
Emphasizes the role of schools in familiarizing students with the First Amendment.

Stevens, Mark. "The New Telecommunications Law—What Does It Mean for Education?" *The Journal*, March 1996, vol. 23, pp. 28–31.

Looks at the implications of the act for education; includes discussion of Internet censorship.

Strossen, Nadine. "Legal Scholars Who Would Limit Free Speech." *Chronicle of Higher Education*, July 7, 1993, vol. 39, pp. B1–B3.

Deals with censorship of hate speech and sexual expression; advocates the responsibility of educators to defuse arguments against free speech.

Stuart, Reginald. "First Amendment: Friend and Sometimes Foe." *Emerge*, February 1994, vol. 5, pp. 94–97.

Reports on speech codes on campus; argues for censorship in instances of racial or other denigrating song lyrics.

Weiner, Jon. "Words That Wound: Free Speech for Campus Bigots?" *The Nation*, February 26, 1990, vol. 250, pp. 272–77.

Examines hate speech, racism, and campus speech codes.

GOVERNMENT DOCUMENTS AND CONGRESSIONAL QUARTERLY PUBLICATIONS

Arons, Stephen. *Value Conflict Between American Families and American Schools.* Amherst, Mass.: University of Massachusetts at Amherst and National Institute of Education, 1981, GPO item no. 0466-A-03.

The final report to the National Institute of Education in regard to grant no. NIE-G-79-0161: addresses censorship issues and educational accountability.

"Breyer Gets Warm Reception from Senate Judiciary." *Congressional Quarterly Weekly Report*, July 16, 1994, vol. 52, pp. 1958–67.

Excerpts from Senate Judiciary Committee hearing regarding Supreme Court nominee Judge Stephen Breyer. Freedom of speech is among the many topics covered.

Clark, Charles S. "School Censorship." *Congressional Quarterly Researcher*, February 19, 1993, vol. 3, p. 145.

Examines a variety of topics, including activism, court cases, and parents' role in school book selection.

"Complaints about Broadcast Journalism." Washington, D.C.: U.S. Federal Communications Commission. Office of Public Affairs, Public Services Division. Mass Media Bureau, 1996, publication no. 8310-80.

Sets out the broadcaster's freedoms and obligations, as well as explaining that the FCC is not the arbiter of truth in news; includes new children's TV Rules, effective January 2, 1997.

Dumas, K. "Backers of Porn-Victims Bill Fight for Panel Approval." *Congressional Weekly Report*, June 18, 1992, vol. 50, pp. 1711–17.

An analysis of arguments regarding a controversial victims' rights bill and its relationship to pornography.

"The FCC and Broadcasting." Washington, D.C.: U.S. Federal Communications Commission. Office of Public Affairs, Public Services Division. Mass Media Bureau, 1996, publication no. 8310-100.

Describes the role of the FCC in broadcasting; details laws relating to broadcasting and FCC powers; includes section on advertising.

"The FCC and Freedom of Speech." Washington, D.C.: U.S. Federal Communications Commission. Office of Public Affairs, Public Services Division. Mass Media Bureau, 1996, publication no. 8310-75.

Set out FCC enforcement of prohibition against obscene and indecent broadcasts.

Ferber, Martin M. *Management and Censorship Issues of Stars and Stripes: Statement of Martin M. Ferber, Director, Manpower and Logistics Issues, National Security and International Affairs Division, before the Subcommittee on Readiness, Committee on Armed Services, United States House of Representatives.* Washington, D.C.: U.S. General Accounting Office, 1989, GPO item no. 0546-D-01.

A report on newspaper censorship in the United States.

Gottleib, Stephen S. *The Right to Read: Censorship in the School Library.* Bloomington, Ind.: ERIC Clearinghouse on Reading and Communication Skills, Indiana University; Washington, D.C.: U.S. Department of Education, Office of Educational Research and Improvement, Educational Resources Information Center, 1990, GPO item no. 0466-A-03 (MF).

A report on library censorship in the United States.

"Indecency Provision Attacked as Clinton Signs Bill." *Congressional Weekly Report*, February 10, 1996, vol. 54, p. 359.

Details the reactions to §652, the telecommunications bill.

"Internet 'Indecent' Ban Blocked by Judges." *Congressional Quarterly Weekly Report*, June 15, 1996, vol. 54, pp. 1673–77.

Report on a portion of the telecommunications law.

Mills, Mike. "TV Violence: Hill May Not Wait for More Industry Action." *Congressional Quarterly Weekly Report*, September 4, 1993, vol. 51, pp. 2338–42.

Reviews a variety of bills, including v-chip proposal and Senator Paul Simon's "action against TV violence."

Newell, Gregory J. *Freedom of the Press: the Need for Vigilance: October 30, 1984.* Washington, D.C., U.S. Department of State, Bureau of Public Affairs, Office of Public Communication, Editorial Division, 1984, GPO item no. 0877-C.
An examination of political aspects of journalism.

U.S. Attorney General's Commission on Pornography. *Attorney General's Commission on Pornography, Final Report.* Washington, D.C.: U.S. Department of Justice, 1986, GPO item no. 0717.
A report on pornography by the attorney general and the department of Justice.

U.S. Congress, House, Committee on Energy and Commerce, Subcommittee on Commerce, Consumer Protection, and Competitiveness. *Music Lyrics and Commerce: Hearings Before the Subcommittee on Commerce, Consumer Protection, and Competitiveness of the Committee on Energy and Commerce.* House of Representatives, 103rd Congress, 2nd sess., February 11 and May 5, 1994. Washington, D.C.: GPO, 1994, GPO item nos. 1019-A, 1019-B (MF) Hearing focusing on rap music, obscenity, music and youth, and violence in mass media.

U.S. Congress, House, Committee on Energy and Commerce. Subcommittee on Telecommunications and Finance. *Telephone Decency Act of 1987: Hearing Before the Subcommittee on Telecommunications and Finance of the Committee on Energy and Commerce.* House of Representatives, 100th Congress, 1st sess., on H.R. 1786 . . . September 30, 1987. Washington, D.C.: GPO, 1988, GPO item nos. 1019-A, 1019-B.
Hearings regarding telephone laws, obscenity, and commercial policy.

U.S. Congress, House, Committee on Government Operations. *The Administration's Initiatives to Expand Polygraph Use and Impose Lifelong Censorship on Thousands of Government Employees: Twenty-fifth Report.* House of Representatives, 98th Congress, 1st sess., November 22, 1983. Washington, D.C.: U.S. GPO, 1983, GPO item nos. 1008-C, 1008-D.
A report dealing with U.S. officials and employees, their security classifications, and censorship.

U.S. Congress, House, Committee on Government Operations, Legislation and National Security Subcommittee. *Congress and the Administration's Secrecy Pledges: Hearing before a Subcommittee of the Committee on Government Operations.* House of Representatives, 100th Congress, 2nd sess., August 10, 1988. Washington, D.C.: GPO, 1988, GPO item nos. 1016-A, 1016-B.
Report on executive privilege and security classification of government documents.

U.S. Congress, House, Committee on Interstate and Foreign Commerce, Subcommittee on Communications. *Sex and Violence on TV: Hearings Before the Subcommittee on Communications of the Committee on Interstate and*

Foreign Commerce. House of Representatives, 95th, 1st sess., March 2, 1977. Washington, D.C.: 1978, GPO, GPO item no. 1019.

Hearings on sex in mass media.

U.S. Congress, House, Committee on the Judiciary, Subcommittee on Crime. *Child Protection and Obscenity Enforcement Act of 1988. Hearings before the Subcommittee on Crime of the Committee on the Judiciary.* House of Representatives, 100th Congress, 2nd Session, on H.R. 1213, H.R. 1438, H.R. 2605, H.R. 3889, and H.R. 4257, April 28, June 16, and August 11, 1988. Washington, D.C.: GPO, 1989, GPO item nos. 1020-A, 1020-B.

Hearings on legislation and its effectiveness in fighting child abuse as related to pornography.

U.S. Congress, House, Committee on Post Office and Civil Service. Subcommittee on Postal Personnel and Modernization. *Prevent Mailing Unsolicited Sexually Oriented Ads. Hearing Before the Subcommittee on Postal Personnel and Modernization of the Committee on Post Office and Civil Service.* House of Representatives, 101st Congress, 1st sess., on H.R. 1210. Washington, D.C.: GPO, 1990, GPO item nos. 1022-B, 1022-C (MF)

Hearings on unordered merchandise and unsolicited mailing, including direct mailing of obscene material.

U.S. Congress, House, Committee on Science, Subcommittee on Basic Research and U.S. Congress, House, Committee on Science, Subcommittee on Technology. *Cyberporn, Protecting Our Children from the Back Alleys of the Internet: Joint Hearing Before the Subcommittee on Basic Research and the Subcommittee on Technology of the Committee on Science.* U.S. House of Representatives, 104th Congress, 1st sess., July 26, 1995. Washington, D.C.: GPO, GPO item nos. 1025-A-01, 1025-A-02.

Hearing regarding Internet, Internet access control, and online information services.

U.S. Congress, Senate, Committee on the Judiciary. *Child Protection and Obscenity Enforcement Act and Obscenity Enforcement Act: Hearing Before the Committee on the Judiciary.* United States Senate, 100th Congress, 2nd sess., on §703 and 2033, June 8, 1988, Washington, D.C.: GPO, 1990, GPO item nos. 1042-A, 1042B (MF)

Hearing on reparation to crime victims in obscenity cases.

U.S. Congress, Senate, Committee on the Judiciary. *Cyberporn and Children: The Scope of the Problem, the State of the Technology, and the Need for Congressional Action: Hearing Before the Committee on the Judiciary.* U.S. Senate, 104th Congress, 1st sess. on §92, July 24, 1995. Washington, D.C.: GPO, GPO item nos. 1042-A, 1042-B (MF).

Hearings regarding the Internet, pornography, children, and online information.

U.S. Congress, Senate, Committee on the Judiciary. *Pornography Victims Compensation Act of 1992: Report Together with Additional and Minority Views (to Accompany* §1521.) Washington, D.C.: GPO, 1992, GPO item nos. 1008-C, 1008-D (MF).

U.S. Congress, Senate, Committee on the Judiciary, Subcommittee on Criminal Law. *Cable-Porn and Dial-a-Porn Control Act: Hearing Before the Subcommittee on Criminal Law of the Committee on the Judiciary.* U.S. Senate, 99th Congress, 1st sess., on §1090, July 31, 1985. Washington, D.C.: GPO, 1986, GPO item nos. 1042-A, 1042-B.
Hearing on pornography and communication.

U.S. Congress, Senate, Committee on the Judiciary, Subcommittee on Juvenile Justice. *Effect of Pornography on Women and Children: Hearings Before the Subcommittee on Juvenile Justice of the Committee on the Judiciary, United States Senate.* United States Senate, 98th Congress, 2nd sess. on Oversight on Pornography, Child Abuse, Child Molestation, and Problems of Conduct Against Women, Washington, D.C., August 8, September 12 and 25, and October 30, 1984; Pittsburgh, Penn., October 18, 1984. Washington, D.C.: GPO, 1985, GPO item nos. 1042-A, 1042-B.
Hearings on pornography, including social aspects of pornography and sexual abuse of children.

U.S. Congress, Senate, Committee on the Judiciary, Subcommittee on Security and Terrorism. *The Use of Computers to Transmit Material Inciting Crime: Hearing Before the Subcommittee on Security and Terrorism of the Committee on the Judiciary.* U.S. Senate, 99th Congress, 1st sess, on the Use of Computers to Transmit Material that Incites Crime and Constitutes Interstate Transmission of Implicit Obscene Matter, June 11, 1985. Washington, D.C.: 1985, GPO, GPO item nos. 1042-A, 1042-B.
Hearing regarding pornography, sex crimes, children, and computer crimes.

U.S. Department of the Army. *Civil Censorship.* Washington, D.C.: Departments of the Army, the Navy, and the Air Force, 1981, GPO item no. 0324.
An indexed handbook for the armed services.

U.S. Department of Justice, U.S. Dept. of Justice, Criminal Division and National Obscenity Enforcement Unit. *Beyond the Pornography Commission: The Federal Response.* Washington, D.C.: National Obscenity Enforcement Unit, Criminal Division, U.S. Department of Justice: 1988, GPO item no. 0717.
Reports on the federal government's responses to the recommendations made by the attorney general's Commission on Pornography; summary of the commission's findings is included.

U.S. Department of Justice, Criminal Division, National Obscenity Enforcement Unit. *Obscenity Enforcement Reporter: A Publication of the National*

Obscenity Enforcement Unit. Washington, D.C.: U.S. Department of Justice, 1988, GPO item no. 0716-C-01.

Deals with obscenity in periodicals.

U.S. Department of Justice. *The National Obscenity Enforcement Unit.* Washington, D.C.: Office of the Attorney General, 1988, GPO item no. 0717.

Deals with obscenity and law enforcement.

U.S. General Accounting Office. *Stars and Stripes: Inherent Conflicts Lead to Allegations of Military Censorship: Report to the Congress.* The Office of General Accounting, December, 1988. Washington, D.C.: GAO, 1988, GAO/NSIAD Report no. 89–60, GPO item no. 0546-D (MF).

U.S. Library of Congress. *Japanese Government Documents and Censored Publications: a Checklist of the Microfilm Collection.* Washington, D.C.: Library of Congress, 1992, GPO item no. 0806-G-01.

Available in English and Japanese, this bibliography of a microfilm catalogue lists censored Japanese publications.

U.S. President, 1981–1989: Reagan, and U.S. Congress, House Committee on the Judiciary, U.S. Congress, House Committee on Ways and Means and U.S. Congress, House Committee on Energy and Commerce. *Proposed Legislation—Child Protection and Obscenity Enforcement Act of 1987: Message from the President of the United States Transmitting for Immediate Consideration and Enactment the Child Protection and Obscenity Enforcement Act of 1987.* Washington, D.C.: GPO, 1987, GPO item no. 0996-A.

Recommendations regarding children in pornography, sex in mass media, and obscenity.

AUDIOVISUAL MATERIALS

This listing includes a variety of films, as well as transcripts available through Journal Graphics in Boulder, Colorado, (800) 255-6397. In addition to transcripts listed, Journal Graphics has videos available for some listings. Because the law and the cultural and political climate can change so rapidly on the censorship front, news programs are particularly valuable for capturing the mood of the country at any given time.

Researchers can access audiotapes of arguments before the Supreme Court of the United States through Supreme Court archives in Washington, D.C. Additionally, audio and transcripts of oral arguments are offered on the Internet and may be accessed through the URL *http://oyez.at.nwu.edu/oyez.html.*

Censorship

VIDEOS

Books Under Fire. Films, Inc. 1983, 58 min.
Debate between parents, teachers, and clergy regarding values and concepts and their relationship to censorship.

Censored. Direct Cinema, 1987, 30 min.
Fictional account of student who submits article to school newspaper stating why she wants to stay in school while pregnant.

Censorship and Selection: Choosing Books for Public Schools. PBS, 1982, 58 min.
Includes subjects covered at the 1982 Conference of the National School Board Association; reports on selection, use, and removal of school library books.

Constitutional Issues and Liability: Part 3. Phoenix, 1984, 18 min.
Focuses on the constitutional rights of students, teachers, and administrators; covers a variety of constitutional issues, including censorship, corporal punishment, due process, and search and seizure.

Damned in the U.S.A. New York: Gabriel Films.
Looks at U.S. censorship.

The Day They Came to Arrest the Book. Film Fair, 1988, 47 min.
Depicts a student reaction when *Huckleberry Finn* is removed from the school library; focuses on First Amendment issues.

The First Amendment and Hate Speech. PBS 1992, 58 min. Offensive speech and conduct examined through a panel discussion; includes protection of symbolic speech.

Freedom and Its Allies: Part 3. Takoma Public Library (no year), 16 min.
Deals with public relations and bias selection.

For Freedom's Sake. Townson, Md.: Library Video Network, 1996, 22 min.
Briefly covers the history of intellectual freedom; reports on case studies and explores the manner in which libraries have handled censorship issues.

Freedom in Reading: Part I. Takoma Public Library (no year), 7 min.
Very basic introduction to the First Amendment and intellectual freedom; includes challenged book titles.

Going Too Far. Ambrose, 1990, 47 min.
Dan Rather appears as host for discussion on obscenity and pornography in the United States.

Mary Kate's War. National Geographic, 1975, 25 min.
Portrays Mary Katherine Goddart, who published a Maryland journal suggesting that the colonies accept British rule. When Whigs demanded the name of the author, she refused the information. Focuses on freedom of the press.

National Security and Freedom of the Press. MacArthur, 1984, 60 min.

Panelists discuss whether the Constitution gives the American public the "right to know."

Patently Offensive: Born Under Seige. Filmmakers, 1992, 58 min.

An examination of pornography in a social and historical context; explores individual rights in the framework of artistic freedom and family values.

We Are Hablando. Latino Midwest, 1991, 14 min.

An experimental documentary focusing on personal, artistic, and global censorship.

Revolution in Print. Chicago: ALA Video, 1989, 19 min.

Profiles France's rise to freedom of expression in the eighteenth century; describes how the printing press of the time worked.

T. J.'s Rights. Film Ideas, 1990, 18 min.

After a book is pulled from the shelves, students begin to investigate their rights under the Bill of Rights.

The Speaker: A Film about Freedom. Chicago: American Library Association, 1977, 42 min.

Focuses on intellectual freedom.

TRANSCRIPTS AVAILABLE THROUGH JOURNAL GRAPHICS

ACLU President Calls Obscenity Provision Inappropriate. CNN: "Business Day," February 9, 1996, item no. 6028-2, video available.

Discusses the Telecommunications Act.

Alexander in the Spotlight as the New Head of the NEA. NPR: "All Things Considered," October 19, 1993, item no. 1275-4.

Explores the National Endowment for the Arts and the debate over federal funding for obscene or pornographic works.

British News Ban Allows Sight, But Not Sound, of Adams. NPR: "All Things Considered," February 2, 1994, item no. 1381-9.

Reports on the ban in Britain and Northern Ireland on broadcasts of those accused of terrorism; the ban is enforceable under to a 1988 law.

Censorship and Children's Literature. CNN: "Global View," October 1, 1994, item no. 26.

Compares censorship of children's literature in America to more liberal policies in other coutries.

China Restricts Economic News Reporting. CNN: "World View," January 17, 1996, item no. 75-4, video available.

Focuses on new media controls in China.

CompuServe Censors German Services. NPR: "All Things Considered," January 4, 1996, item no. 2082-12.

Discusses CompuServe's censoring of specific newsgroups, as directed by the German government; examines implications.

Congress Hears Debate on "Gangsta" Rap. CNN: "World News Tonight," February 11, 1994, item no. 627-7.

Reports on congressional hearings regarding hate language and violent language in music and their effects. Free speech activists comment.

Cyberporn. CNN: "Crossfire," December 5, 1995, item no. 1518, video available.

Focuses on children's access to pornography on the Internet; free speech and procensorship advocates debate.

Free Speech Issues Crop Up in Cyberspace. CNN: "Prime News," January 10, 1996, item no. 1391-4.

Discussion of First Amendment rights in cyberspace.

Free Speech Movement Celebrates 30th Anniversary. NPR: "All Things Considered," December 3, 1994, item no. 1685-3.

Interviews with former University of California-Berkeley students who were active in the 1964 rallies that began the Free Speech Movement.

Hong Kong Worries They Will Lose Freedom of Press. CNN: "World View," December 22, 1995, item no. 57-4, video available.

Newspaper publisher from Hong Kong voices concern about censorship by the government and the resulting self-censorship.

Impact of Violence in Movies Debated. CNN: "Talk Back Live," November 30, 1995, item no. 285, video available.

An assessment of the influence of film violence details a violent act that may have found its roots in the film *The Money Train.*

Indecency Provision in Telecom Bill Sparks Controversy. NPR: "All Things Considered," February 7, 1996, item no. 2116-6.

Proponents and opponents of the Communications Decency Act comment.

Internet Blocking Offers Alternative to Censorship. CNN: "News Night," December 9, 1995, item no. 37-3.

Reviews software designed to block children from accessing certain portions of the Internet.

Killer Book: The Controversy Over Hit Man. CNN: "Larry King Live," February 1, 1996, item no. 1659-2, video available.

First Amendment discussion of a how-to murder book on which a multiple murder is said to be based.

Michigan Student in Trouble for Electronic Stalking. CNN: "The World Today." February 10, 1995, item no. 867-6.

Raises questions regarding a student who wrote and placed on the Internet a fictional story of horrific sexual torture; the student used the name of a real person for the tortured character in his story.

Proposed Ban on Indecent Speech on the Internet. ABC: "World News Tonight," February 8, 1996, item no. 6028-2.

ACLU members and others comment on censorship of cyberspace.

Regulating Cyberspace: A Complicated International Issue. CNN: "World View," December 29, 1995, item no. 62-8, video available.

A communications law expert assesses international Internet censorship.

Sex in Literature. PBS: "Charlie Rose," May 9, 1994, item no. 1112-1, video available.

Authors discuss "the place of pornography in literature."

Students Rally Behind Porn-Producing Teacher. CNN: "Newsnight," January 19, 1996, item no. 249-8, video available.

Examines students' protest after their English teacher, who was associated with X-rated films as an actor and producer, was fired.

Television Industry Agrees to Adopt Rating System. CNN: "Business Day," February 16, 1996, item no. 1287-2.

Focuses on the ratings system, comments by network executive.

Television Turmoil. CNN: "Crossfire," March 3, 1996, item no. 1593, video available.

A discussion of the television industry's proposed ratings system.

University of Massachusetts Installs Stiff Speech Code. NPR: "Morning Edition," December 5, 1995, item no. 1752-14.

Examines new speech code at the University of Massachusetts at Amherst.

V-Chip in Use in Canada. ABC: "ABC World News Tonight," February 8, 1996, item no. 6028-3.

Explores Canadian use of the v-chip, which allows control over violent or sexually explicit television shows.

Variety of Groups Try to Censor Materials for Schools. NPR: "Morning Edition," September 1, 1994, item no. 1424-3.

A profile of a report that details 462 attempts in the past year to ban virtually every art form, as well as lesson plans, in American schools.

Violent U.S. Films Could Be Censored in Euro-Countries. CNN: "The International Hour," November 4, 1994, item no. 710-4.

Film journalist discusses violent American films such as *Natural Born Killers* and *Reservoir Dogs* and their reception in other countries.

Violent Video Games Spur Push for Ratings System. CNN: "Newsnight," January 9, 1994, item no. 592-4.

Explores the future of voluntary ratings system by video game industry to circumvent federal regulation.

Yevgeni Kiselyov Talks About Russia. PBS: "Charlie Rose," December 5, 1995, item no. 1523-1.

Russian journalist reports on Russian press.

CHAPTER 7

ORGANIZATIONS AND ASSOCIATIONS

Thousands of organizations exist to serve those interested in censorship. Many specialize in a specific area such as the visual arts or music. Others are more generalized and are active in all aspects of censorship. This chapter lists and briefly describes national organizations. Annotations are not provided for the state and local organizations, as their missions and areas of interest tend to change more frequently.

The organizations listed here participate in a wide variety of activities. Some exist only for educational purposes. Others offer a wider range of services, including legal representation and advocacy before the United States Congress. Many offer informative publications.

In order to facilitate research, e-mail addresses and URLs are listed in addition to telephone numbers and addresses. E-mail addresses are used to access online services, and can send or receive electronic mail. URLs are Internet addresses for web sites that contain information. Often, sites will offer links to other sites with further information on specific topics.

E-mail and URL addresses can change. Should this happen, it is sometimes possible to locate an organization by entering its name in the appropriate field on a search screen.

NATIONAL

Alliance for Community Media
666 Eleventh Street Northwest
Suite 806
Washington, DC 20001-4542
(202) 393-2650
e-mail: AllianceCM@aol.com
URL: http://www.eff.org/
pub/Groups/AllianceCM

Works to ensure access to electronic media; advocates education.

American Arts Alliance
1319 F Street Northwest
Suite 500
Washington, DC 20004
(202) 289-1776
e-mail: aaa@artswire.org

An advocate for arts institutions throughout the country; works with Congress and a variety of agencies to advance arts interests.

American Association of University Professors
1012 14th Street Northwest
Suite 500
Washington, DC 20005
(202) 737-5526
e-mail:aaup@igc.apc.org
URL: http://www.igc.apc.org/aaup/

Aids members of the book community to uphold freedom of expression.

American Booksellers Foundation for Free Expression
828 South Broadway
Tarrytown, NY 10591
(914) 591-2665 ext. 267
e-mail:info@bookweb.org
URL: http://www.ambook.org/aba/

Mission is to aid booksellers and others in the book community in support of free expression.

American Civil Liberties Union
125 Broad Street
New York, NY 10004
(212) 549-2500
e-mail: infoaclu@aclu.org
URL: http://www.aclu.org/

A public interest organization dedicated to protecting civil liberties of all Americans; active in legal matters.

American Library Association (see Office of Intellectual Freedom)
The Cato Institute
1000 Massachusetts Avenue Northwest
Washington, DC 20001
(202)842-0200
e-mail: cato@cato.org
URL: http://www.cato.org/

Nonpartisan association that undertakes research on a variety of government-related issues; offers many studies and other publications.

Association of American University Presses
584 Broadway
Suite 400
New York, NY 10012
(212) 941-6610
e-mail: www-team@press.uchicago.edu.
URL: http://aaup.pupress.princeton.edu/

Supports university presses.

Association of Independent Video and Filmmakers
304 Hudson Street
Sixth Floor
New York, NY 10013
(212) 807-1400
e-mail: AIV FFIV@aol.com
URL: http://www.virtualfilm.com/AIVF/

Advocate for access by independents to public television and cable systems, theaters, museums, galleries, and community centers.

Authors Guild
330 West 42nd Street
9th Floor
New York, NY 10036
(212) 563-5904

Professional society of published authors; lobbies for freedom of expression and other issues important to authors.

Benton Foundation– Communications Policy Project
1634 Eye Street Northwest
12th Floor
Washington, DC 20006
(202) 638-5770

Encourages the use of techniques and technologies of communications to advocate on behalf of the democratic process.

Center for Democracy and Technology
1001 G Street Northwest
Suite 700 East
Washington, DC 20001
(202) 637-9800
e-mail: djw@cdt.org
URL: http://www.cdt.org/

A public interest group that researches policy and provides public education and coalition structure support to advance constitutional civil liberties and democratic values.

The Center for Media Education
1511 K Street Northwest
Suite 518
Washington, DC 20005
(202) 628-2620

A public policy and research organization that educates the public about media issues and policies and encourages debate about these issues.

Citizens Internet Empowerment Coalition
1001 G Street Northwest
Suite 700 East
(202) 637-9800
e-mail: ciec@cdt.org
URL: http://www.ciec.org/

Examines Internet censorship issues and encourages public awareness and participation in regard to such issues.

College Art Association
275 Seventh Avenue
New York, NY 10001
(212) 691-1051
e-mail: caa@pipeline.com

Members are teachers, scholars, critics, museum professionals, scholars, art dealers, art librarians, collectors; focuses on scholarship and teaching history and criticism of visual arts.

Comic Book Legal Defense Fund
P.O. Box 693
Northampton, MA 01061
(800) 992-2533
e-mail: cbldf@codexx.com.
URL: http://www.edgeglobal.com/cbldf/

Advocates for freedom of expression.

Committee Against Censorship National Council of Teachers of English
1111 W. Kenyon
Urbana, IL 61801
(715) 328-3870
e-mail: nctechsuh@vmd.cso.uiuc.edu

Supports English teachers and others and advocates for freedom of expression.

Computer Professionals for Social Responsibility
P.O. Box 717
Palo Alto, CA 94302
(415) 322-3778
e-mail: cpsr@csli.stanford.edu
URL:
http://www.cs.virginia.edu/~hwh6k/public/cyber-rights.html

Goal is to protect privacy and civil liberties.

Consortium for School Networking
P.O. Box 6519
Washington, DC 20035-5913
(202) 466-6296
e-mail: membership@cosn.org
URL: gopher://digital.cosn.org/

Assists educators and students in accessing information and communications resources; strives to reach those involved in every aspect of network technology and its application to K-12 education.

Censorship

The Creative Coalition
1100 Avenue of the Americas
12th Floor
New York, NY 10036
(212) 512-5515

An organization made up of those from the arts and entertainment communities; goal is to educate members and public in general on social and political issues.

Electronic Frontier Foundation (EFF)
1550 Bryant Street
San Francisco, CA 94103
(415) 436-9333
e-mail: info@eff.org
URL: http://www.eff.org/

Works to protect individual rights; "supports legal and legislative action to protect the civil liberties of online users." Large Internet presence.

Electronic Privacy Information Center
666 Pennsylvania Avenue
Washington, DC 20003
(202) 544-9240
e-mail: info@epic.org
URL: http://epic.digicash.com/epic

Sponsored by the Fund for Constitutional Government, this public interest center works to direct attention to emerging privacy arenas relating to the national information infrastructure.

Feminists for Free Expression
2525 Times Square Station
New York, NY 10108
(212) 702-6292
e-mail: freedom@well.com
URL: www.well.com/user/freedom/

Works through legal, legislative, and educational conduits to assure the security of First Amendment rights.

First Amendment Foundation
1313 West 8th Street

Los Angeles, CA 90017
(213) 484-0266
e-mail:NCARL@aolcom

Acts as an advocate for First Amendment rights.

Freedom of Information Committee
c/o American Society of Newspaper Editors
11600 Sunrise Valley Drive
Reston, VA 22091
(703) 648-1145
e-mail: flandon@infi.net

Supports journalists and others in intellectual freedom issues.

Freedom to Read Committee
Association of American Publishers
1718 Connecticut Avenue Northwest
Seventh Floor
Washington, DC 20009
(202) 232-3335

Works to promote intellectual freedom, literacy, and legislation; active in litigation.

Freedom to Read Foundation
American Library Association
50 East Huron Street
Chicago, IL 60611
(312) 944-6780
(800) 545-2433
e-mail: U35907@UICVM.UIC.EDU
URL: http://www.ala.org/

Supports intellectual freedom.

Global SchoolNet Foundation
P.O. Box 243
Bonita, CA 91908-0243
(619) 475-4852
e-mail: info@gsn.org
URL: http://www.gsn.org/

Offers educational information to students, educators, business, government, and the community.

Hollywood Policy Center
3679 Motor Avenue
Suite 300
Los Angeles, CA 90034
(310) 287-2803

Serves as bridge between the entertainment industry and policy advocates.

Human Rights Watch Fund for Free Expression
485 Fifth Avenue
New York, NY 10017-6104
(212) 972-8400
e-mail: hrwync@hrw.org

Focuses on the connection between freedom of expression and global social problems by illustrating the impact of censorship and information policies on important issues.

Individual Rights Foundation
Box 67398
Los Angeles, CA 90006-9507
(310) 843-3699
e-mail: 76042.3271@compuserv.com

Focuses on individual liberties.

The Internet Users Consortium
7031 East Camelback
Suite 102-515
Scottsdale, AZ 85251
(602) 874-1492
e-mail: molsen@indirect.com
URL: http://www.indirect.com/
www/molsen/index.html

Works to develop the Internet.

Lambda Legal Defense and Education Fund
120 Wall Street
Suite 1500
New York, NY 10005
(212) 809-8585
e-mail: lldef@ael.com
URL: http://www.thebody.com/
lambda/lambda.html

Goal is to achieve recognition of civil rights of lesbians, gay men and people with HIV/AIDS through public policy endeavors, education, and litigation.

Libraries for the Future
521 Fifth Avenue
Suite 1612
New York, NY 10175-1699
(212) 682-7446
e-mail: lff@incl.com
URL: http://www.lff.org/

Supports librarians and others in a variety of areas. Works to enhance the relationship between libraries and communities.

The Media Coalition, Incorporated
139 Fulton Street
Suite 302
New York, NY 10038
e-mail: 73770.3472@compuserv.com

Active in representing First Amendment rights of film producers and distributors; active in litigation.

MeDIA Consortium (Media Democracy in Action)
4302 Halfe Street
Alexandria, VA 22309
(703) 780-1160

Promotes freedom of expression and focuses on equity and access in telecommunications and media arts policy.

Motion Picture Association of America
1600 I Street Northwest
Washington, DC 20006
(202) 293-1966
e-mail: pegge@mpaa.org
URL: http://www.mpaa.org

Active in a variety of areas; advocates before governmental agencies; fights censorship of motion picture, television, and home video producers.

National Association of Artists'
 Organizations
918 F Street Northwest
Suite 611
Washington, DC 20004
(202) 347-6350
e-mail: naao@artswire.org

Promotes civil liberties of artist-run organizations.

National Association of Recording
 Merchandisers
9 Eves Drive
Marlton, NJ 08053
(609) 596-2221

Advocates on behalf of merchandisers of home entertainment products, with a focus on music.

National Coalition Against
 Censorship
275 Seventh Avenue
New York, NY 10001
(212) 807-6222
e-mail: ncac@netcom.com
URL: http://www.ncac.org/

Coalition of national nonprofit organizations; goal is to fight censorship.

National Campaign for Freedom of
 Expression
918 F Street Northwest
#609
Washington, DC 20004
(800) 477-6233
e-mail: ncfe@nwlink.com
URL: http://www.tmn.com/
Artswire/www/ncfe/ncfe.html

An advocacy and education network of artists, arts organizations, and the public; goal is to fight censorship and advocate freedom of expression.

National Federation of Community
 Broadcasters
Fort Mason Center
Building D

San Francisco, CA 94123
(415) 771-1160
e-mail: NFCB@aolcom

Advocates on behalf of radio stations to agencies such as the FCC.

National Freedom of Information
 Coalition
c/o Freedom of Information
 Foundation of Texas
400 South Record Street
6th Floor
Dallas, TX 75202
(214) 977-6658
e-mail: foift@airmail.net
URL: http://www.reporters.net/
nfoic/

Focuses on freedom of information issues.

National Humanities Alliance
21 Dupont Circle
Suite 800
Washington, DC 20036
(202) 296-4994
e-mail: jhammer@cni.org

Works to bring public interest entities together on behalf of federal programs in the humanities.

Office for Intellectual Freedom
American Library Association (ALA)
50 East Huron Street
Chicago, IL 60611
(312) 280-4223
(800) 545-2433
e-mail: u24803@uicvm.uic.edu
URL: http://www.ala.org/

Educates librarians and the public in general about free access to ideas and information; offers support to librarians and others challenged by censorship issues.

PEN American Center Freedom to
 Write Committee
568 Broadway

New York, NY 10012
(212) 334-2181
e-mail: pen@echonyc.com
URL: http://www.pen.org/

Defends the right to freedom of expression; holds consultative status with United Nations; defends writers and journalists.

People for the American Way
2000 M Street Northwest
Suite 400
Washington, DC 20036
(202) 467-4999
e-mail: pfaw@pfaw.org
URL: http://www.pfaw.org/

Works to further fundamental rights such as freedom of expression; offers legal and technical aid to educators and parents challenged by censorship issues.

Reporters Committee for Freedom of the Press
1101 Wilson Boulevard
Suite 1910
Arlington, VA 22209-2248
(703) 897-2100
e-mail: rcfp@cais.com
URL: http://www.rcfp.org/rcfp/

Advocates First Amendment freedom.

Rock Out Censorship
P.O. Box 147
Jewett, OH 43986
(614) 946-6535
e-mail: roc@clover.net
URL: http://www.xnet.com/
~paigeone/noevil/roc.html

Advocates for First Amendment freedom.

Rock the Vote
1460 Fourth Street
Suite 200
Santa Monica, CA 90401
(310) 656-2464

e-mail: rocthevote@aol.com
URL: http://www.rockthevote.org/

Works to educate youth and encourage youth to vote; works to protect freedom of speech.

Theater Communications Group
355 Lexington Avenue
New York, NY 10017
(212) 697-5230

Provides forum addressing needs of non-profit professional theater, including needs and interests of artists and management.

Thomas Jefferson Center for the Protection of Free Expression
400 Peter Jefferson Place
Charlottesville, VA 22901
(804) 295-4784
e-mail: jwheeler@igc.apc.org
URL: http://tjcenter.org/

Dedicated to free expression in all of its forms; focuses on education and public policy.

Volunteer Lawyers for the Arts
1 East 53rd Street
New York, NY 10002
(212) 319-2787

Provides legal advice and representation.

Voters Telecommunications Watch
233 Court Street #2
Brooklyn, NY 11201
(718) 596-2851
e-mail: shabbir@panix.com
URL: http://www.vtw.org/

Monitors federal legislation relating to telecommunications and civil liberties.

STATE AND LOCAL

ALABAMA

ACLU of Alabama
P.O. Box 447
Montgomery, AL 36101
(334) 262-0304

Alabama Library Association
400 South Union Street
Suite 255
Montgomery, AL 36104
(334) 262-5210

ALASKA

ACLU of Alaska
P.O. Box 201844
Anchorage, AK 99520
(907) 276-2258

Alaska Library Association
436 Main #30
Ketchikan, AK 99901
(907) 225-9815
e-mail: charg@muskox.alaska.edu

ARIZONA

ACLU of Arizona
P.O. Box 17148
Phoenix, AZ 85011
(602) 650-1967

Arizona Library Association
14449 North 73rd Street
Scottsdale, AZ 85260
(602) 998-1954
e-mail: meeting@enet.net

ARKANSAS

ACLU of Arkansas
103 Capitol #1120
Little Rock, AR 72201
(501) 374-2660

Arkansas Library Association
Coleman Management Resources,
  Incorporated
Three Financial Centre, Suite 409
900 South Shackelford
Little Rock, AR 72211
(501) 661-1127

CALIFORNIA

ACLU of California
Northern California
1663 Mission Street
Suite 460
San Francisco, CA 94103
(415) 621-2488

ACLU of California
Southern California
1616 Beverly Boulevard
Los Angeles, CA 90026
(213) 977-9500

Cal-ACT (Californians Against
  Censorship Together)
1800 Market Street #1000
San Francisco, CA 94102
e-mail: calact@netcom.com

California First Amendment
  Coalition
926 P Street
Suite 1406
Sacramento, CA 95814
(916) 447-2322
URL:
http:www.ccnet.com/csne/cfac.html

California Library Association
717 K Street Suite 300
Sacramento, CA 95814-3477
(916) 447-8541
e-mail: cmember@netcom.com

Coalition for the Right to Know
464 19th Street
Oakland, CA 94612

First Amendment Congress
University of Denver
2301 South Gaylord
Denver, CO 80208
(303) 871-4430
e-mail: jlucas@du.edu

International Society for Individual
  Liberty
1800 Market Street
San Francisco, CA 94102

Media Watch
P.O. Box 618
Santa Cruz, CA 95061

No More Censorship Defense Fund
P.O. Box 419092
San Francisco, CA 94141-9092

Project Censored
Sonoma State University
Rohnert Park, CA 94928

Right to Rock Network
c/o RRC
Box 341305
Los Angeles, CA 90034

Sacramento Citizens Against
  Censorship
7902 Gerver Road #202
Sacramento, CA 95828-4300

Southern California Coalition for
  Intellectual Freedom
University of California Library
Riverside, CA 93517

COLORADO

ACLU of Colorado
400 Corona Street
Denver, CO 80218
(303) 777-5482

First Amendment Congress
2301 South Gaylord Street
Denver, CO 80210-5201

Colorado Library Association
P.O. Box 700
Pinecliffe, CO 80471
(303) 582-5777

CONNECTICUT

ACLU of Connecticut
32 Grand Street
Hartford, CT 06106
(203) 247-9823

Connecticut Coalition for Academic
  Freedom
786 South Main Street
Middletown, CT 06457

Connecticut Council for Social
  Studies
Lyme-Old Lyme High School
Old Lyme, CT 06371

Connecticut Council of Teachers of
  English
Central Connecticut State
  University English Department
New Britain, CT 06050

Connecticut Education Association
Capitol Place
#500/21 Oak Street.
Hartford, CT 06106-8001
(860) 525-5641

Connecticut Library Association
Box 1046
Norwich, CT 06360
(203) 885-2760

Connecticut State Federation of
  Teachers
35 Marshall, Rd.
Rocky Hill, CT 06067-1400

New England Anti-Censorship
  Coalition
P.O. Box 330814
West Hartford, CT 06133-0813

DELAWARE

ACLU of Delaware
702 King Street #600A
Wilmington, DE 19801
(302) 654-3966

Delaware Library Association
P.O. Box 816
Wilmington, DE 19903-0816

DISTRICT OF COLUMBIA

District of Columbia Library
  Association
P.O. Box 14177
Benjamin Franklin Station
Washington, DC 20044

FLORIDA

ACLU of Florida
225 Northeast 34th Street
Suite 102
Miami, FL 33137
(305) 576-2336

Brechner Center for Freedom of
  Information
University of Florida
  College of Journalism and
  Communications
3208 Weimer Hall
Gainesville, FL 32611
(352) 392-2273
URL:
http://www.jou.ufl.ed/brechner/
brochure.htm

Central Floridians Against
  Censorship
620 Cranes Way #201
Altamonte Springs, FL 32701-7782

First Freedom, Incorporated
1202 North Franklin Street
Tampa, FL 33602

Florida Coalition Against Censorship
310 Michigan Avenue
Lynn Haven, FL 32444-1428
(904) 271-3136
e-mail: pipking@mail.firn.edu
URL: http://www.afn.org/ht-free/
fcac.thml

Floridians for Freedom
P.O. Box 10873
St. Petersburg, FL 33733-0873

Florida Library Association
1144 West Morse Boulevard
Suite 201
Winter Park, FL 32789-3788
(407) 647-8839

The Freedom Forum First
  Amendment Center
Vanderbilt University
1207 18th Avenue South
Nashville, TN 37212
e-mail: web@fac.org
URL: http://www.fac.org/

GEORGIA

ACLU of Georgia
142 Mitchell Street Southwest
Suite 301
Atlanta, GA 30303
(404) 523-5398

Cobb Citizens Coalition
P.O. Box 965336
Marietta, GA 30066

Georgia First Amendment
  Foundation
990 Edgewood Avenue Northeast
Atlanta, GA 30307
(404) 577-7103
e-mail: gfaf@mindspring.com
URL:
http://www.mindspring.com/~gfaf/

Georgia Library Association
c/o Bob Richardson

Young Harris College
P.O. Box 39
Young Harris, GA 30582
(706) 379-3526 ext. 5142
e-mail: bobrich@yhc.edu

HAWAII

ACLU of Hawaii
P.O. Box 3410
Honolulu, HI 96801
(808) 522-5900

Hawaii Library Association
P.O. Box 4441
Honolulu, HI 96814-4441

IDAHO

ACLU of Idaho
P.O. Box 1897
Boise, ID 83701
(208) 344-5243

Idaho Library Association
Timothy A. Brown
Boise State University
Boise, ID 83725
(208) 385-1234
e-mail: alibrown@idbsu.idbsu.edu

ILLINOIS

ACLU of Illinois
203 North LaSalle Street #1405
Chicago, IL 60601-1210
(312) 201-9740

Greater Chicago Citizens for the
  Arts
1150 North Lake Shore Drive #13D
Chicago, IL 60611-1024

Illinois Education Association
Rt. 1 Box 292
Coben, IL 62920

Illinois Library Association
33 West Grand Avenue #301
Chicago, IL 60610
(312) 644-1896

Parents for Rock and Rap
P.O. Box 53
Libertyville, IL 60048

INDIANA

ACLU of Indiana
1031 East Washington Street
Indianapolis, IN 46202
(317) 635-4056

Ft. Wayne Citizens Against
  Censorship
P.O. Box 10623
Forty Wayne, IN 48853

Indianapolis Library Federation
6408 Carrollton Avenue
Indianapolis, IN 46220-1615

IOWA

ACLU of Iowa
446 Insurance Exchange Building
Des Moines, IA 50309
(515) 243-3576

Iowa Freedom Foundation
550 11th Street
Des Moines, IA 50309

Iowa Library Association
823 Insurance Exchange Building
Des Moines, IA 50309
(515) 243-2172

KANSAS

ACLU of Kansas & Western
  Missouri
706 West 42nd Street
Suite 108

Kansas City, MO 64111
(816) 756-3113

Kansas Library Association
Leroy Gattin
South Central Kansas Library
  System
901 North Main
Hutchinson, KS 67501-4401
(316) 663-5441
e-mail: lgattin@databank.com

KENTUCKY

ACLU of Kentucky
425 West Muhammad Ali Boulevard
Suite 230
Louisville, KY 40202
(502) 581-1181

Kentucky Library Association
1501 Twilight Trail
Frankfort, KY 40601
(502) 223-5322

LOUISIANA

ACLU of Louisiana
P.O. Box 70496
New Orleans, LA 70172
(504) 522-0617

Louisiana Library Association
P.O. Box 3058
Baton Rouge, LA 70821
(504) 342-4928
e-mail: lla@pelican.state.lib.la.us

MAINE

ACLU of Maine
97 A Exchange Street
Portland, ME 04101
(207) 774-5444

Maine Library Association
Maine Municipal Association

Community Drive
Augusta, ME 04330

MARYLAND

ACLU of Maryland
2219 Saint Paul Street
Baltimore, MD 12128
(410) 889-8555

Maryland Library Association
400 Cathedral Street
Baltimore, MD 21201
(410) 727-7422
e-mail: mla@epfl1.epflbalto.org

MASSACHUSETTS

ACLU of Massachusetts
99 Chauncey Street
Suite 310 Boston, MA 02111
(617) 482-3170

Boston Coalition for Freedom of
  Expression
c/o Mobius
354 Congress Street
Boston, MA 02210
(617) 497-7193
e-mail: mobius1@world.std.com

Massachusetts Library Association
Countryside Offices
707 Turnpike Street
North Andover, MA 01845
(508) 686-8543

MICHIGAN

ACLU of Michigan
1249 Washington Boulevard
Suite 2910
Detroit, MI 48226-1822
(313) 961-4662

Michigan Library Association
6810 South Cedar Street
Suite 6

Lansing, MI 48911
(517) 694-6615
e-mail: mla@mlc.lib.mi.us

MINNESOTA

ACLU of Minnesota
1021 Broadway
Minneapolis, MN 55411
(612) 522-2423

Freethinker Forum
P.O. Box 14447
St. Louis, MO 63178

Minnesota Coalition Against
 Censorship
c/o MFT
168 Aurora Avenue
St. Paul, MN 55103

Minnesota Library Association
North Regional Library System
1315 Lowry Avenue North
Minneapolis, MN 55411-1398
e-mail: mnla@augsburg.edu

MISSISSIPPI

ACLU of Mississippi
P.O. Box 2242
Jackson, MS 39225
(601) 355-6464

Mississippi Library Association
P.O. Box 20448
Jackson, MS 9289-1448
(601) 352-3917

MISSOURI

ACLU of Eastern Missouri
 (see also ACLU Kansas and
 Western Missouri)
4557 Laclede Avenue
St. Louis, MO 63108
(314) 361-2111

Mississippi Library Association
1306 Business 63 South
Suite B
Columbia, MO 65201
(314) 449-4655
e-mail: jmccartn@mail.more.net

Greater Kansas City Coalition
 Against Censorship
706 West 42nd Street #108
Kansas City, MO 64111-3199

Missouri Coalition Against
 Censorship
4557 Laclede Avenue
St. Louis, MO 63108-2103

MONTANA

ACLU of Montana
P.O. Box 3012
Billings, MT 59103
(406) 248-1086

Montana Library Association
P.O. Box 505
Helena, MT 59624
(406) 447-4343
e-mail: jthomas@saints.carroll.edu

Montanans Against Censorship
P.O. Box 8372
Missoula, MT 59807

NEBRASKA

Academic Freedom Coalition of
 Nebraska
515 North Thomas Avenue
Oakland, NE 68045

ACLU of Nebraska
P.O. Box 81455
Lincoln, NE 68501
(402) 476-8091

Nebraska Library Association
Washoe Country Library
301 South 30th Street

Lincoln, NE 68510-1424
(402) 476-6111
e-mail: bdavis@neon.nlc.state.ne.us

NEVADA

ACLU of Nevada
325 South Third Street
Suite 25
Las Vegas, NV 89101
(702) 366-1226

Nevada Library Association
301 South Center Street
P.O. Box 2151
Reno, NV 89505
(712) 785-4190

NEW HAMPSHIRE

ACLU of New Hampshire
18 Low Avenue
Concord, NH 03301
(603) 225-3080

New Hampshire Library Association
Wolfeboro Public Library
P.O. Box 710
Wolfeboro, NH 03894
(603) 569-2428

NEW JERSEY

ACLU of New Jersey
2 Washington, Place
Newark, NJ 03301
(201) 642-2084

New Jersey Library Association
4 West Lafayette
Trenton, NJ 08608

NEW MEXICO

ACLU of New Mexico
120 Alvarado Drive Northeast
Suite 200

Albuquerque, NM 87108
(505) 266-5915

New Mexico Library Association
11200 Montgomery Northeast
Eldorado Square
Suite 8
Albuquerque, NM 87111
(505) 292-9883
e-mail: curntevent@aol.com

NEW YORK

ACLU of New York
132 West 43rd Street
2nd Floor
New York, NY 10036
(212) 382-0557

Media Against Censorship
c/o DCTV
87 Lafayette Street
New York, NY 10013

New York Civil Rights Coalition
3 West 35th Street
New York, NY 10001

New York Library Association
252 Hudson Avenue
Albany, NY 12210
(518) 432-6925
e-mail: skeitel@transit.nyser.net

The Society for Electronic Access
P.O. Box 7081
New York, NY 10116-7081
(212) 592-3801
e-mail: sea@sea.org

Students Organizing Students
22 Prince Street
New York, NY 10012-3505

NORTH CAROLINA

ACLU of North Carolina
P.O. Box 28004

Raleigh, NC 27611
(919) 834-3390

Citizens Against Censorship
4809 Kenview Street
Greensboro, NC 27410

**Internet Association of the
Carolinas (IAC)**
160 Wind Chime Ct.
Raleigh, NC 27615-6459
(919) 870-6498
e-mail: info@iac.org
URL: http://www.iac.org/iac/

Many Voices, One Community
1002 Tallyhoe Trail
Chapel Hill, NC 27516

North Carolina Library Association
c/o State Library of New York
109 East Jones Street, Room 27
Raleigh, NC 27601-1023
(919) 839-6252
e-mail: slla.clt@ncdcr.dcr.state.nc.us

NORTH DAKOTA

North Dakota Library Association
Chester Fritz Library
University of North Dakota
P.O. Box 9000
Grand Forks, NE 58202-90000

OHIO

ACLU of Ohio
1223 West 6th Street
2nd Floor
Cleveland, OH 44113
(216) 781-6276

**Coalition Against Censorship
in the Arts**
1600 Thompson Heights Drive #511
Cincinnati, OH 45223-1666

Ohio Library Council
35 East Gay Street

Columbus, OH 43215
(614) 221-9057

OKLAHOMA

ACLU of Oklahoma
600 Northwest 23rd Street
Suite 104
Oklahoma City, OK 73106
(405) 524-8511

Oklahoma Library Association
300 Hardy Drive
Edmond, OK 73013
(405) 348-0506

OREGON

ACLU of Oregon
P.O. Box 40585
Portland, OR 97240-0585
(503) 227-6928
e-mail: info@aclu-or.org/aclu

**Oregon Coalition for Free
Expression**
P.O. Box 40407
Portland, OR 97240

Oregon Education Association
6900 South Haines Road
Tigard, OR 97223

Oregon Intellectual Clearinghouse
State Library Building
Salem, OR 97310-0640

Oregon Library Association
P.O. Box 2042
Salem, OR 97308-2042
(503) 370-7019

PENNSYLVANIA

ACLU of Pennsylvania
P.O. Box 1161
Philadelphia, PA 19105
(215) 923-4357

ACLU-Pittsburgh Chapter
237 Oakland Avenue
Pittsburgh, PA 15213
(412) 681-7736

Apollo Ridge School Board
818 Moore Avenue
Box 487
North Apollo, PA 15673

Armstrong County Citizens Against
  Censorship
Box 278
Freeport, PA 16229

First Amendment Coalition of
  Pennsylvania
Courier Times
8400 Route 13
Levittown, PA 19068

Freedom to Learn Network
2020 Downyflake Lane #301A
Allentown, PA 18103-4776

RHODE ISLAND

ACLU of Rhode Island
212 Union Street
Room 211
Providence, RI 02903
(401) 831-7171

Center for Public Information
428 Smith Street
Providence, RI 02908

Rhode Island Library Association
300 Richmond Street
Providence, RI 02903

SOUTH CAROLINA

ACLU of South Carolina
1338 Main Street
Suite 800
Columbia, SC 29201
(803) 799-5151

South Carolina Library Association
P.O. Box 219
Goose Creek, SC 29445
(803) 761-8600 ext. 31

Oconee Citizens Against Censorship
104 University Drive
Seneca, SC 29678

SOUTH DAKOTA

South Dakota Library Association
Mikkelsen Library
Augustana College
Sioux Falls, SD 57297
(605) 336-4921
e-mail: asmith@inst.augie.edu

TENNESSEE

ACLU of Tennessee
P.O. Box 120160
Nashville, TN 37212
(615) 320-7142

Tennessee Library Association
P.O. Box 15814
Nashville, TN 37215-8417
(615) 297-8316

TEXAS

ACLU of Texas
P.O. Box 3629
Austin, TX 78764
(512) 441-0077

Center for Critical Thinking
2243 34th Street
Lubbock, TX 79411-1735

Citizens Against Censorship
P.O. Box 2781
San Angelo, TX 76902

Electronic Freedom Fighters
P.O. Box 18957
Austin, TX 78760

First Amendment Coalition of Texas
1104 West Avenue #101
Austin, TX 78701

Politechs, Inc.
1104 West Avenue #101
Austin, TX 78701

Texas Freedom Alliance
P.O. Box 1624
Austin, TX 78767

Texas Library Association
3355 Bee Cave Road #401
Austin, TX 78746
(512) 328-1518
e-mail: phs@tenet.edu

UTAH

ACLU of Utah
Boston Building
9 Exchange Place
Suite 715
Salt Lake City, UT 84111
(801) 521-9289

Organization for Protection of
  First Amendment
209 East 5th Street
Salt Lake City, UT 84111

Utah Library Association
P.O. Box 711789
Salt Lake City, UT 84171-8789
(801) 581-3691
e-mail: cranders@u.cc.utah.edu

VERMONT

ACLU of Vermont
110 East State Street
Montpelier, VT 05602
(802) 223-6304

Vermont Library Association
Box 803
Burlington, VT 05402-0803

VIRGINIA

ACLU of Virginia
6 North Sixth Street
Suite 400
Richmond, VA 23219
(804) 644-8022

Virginia Library Association
669 South Washington Street
Alexandria, VA 22314-4109
(703) 519-7732

Virginians Against Censorship
P.O. Box 64608
Virginia Beach, VA 23467

WASHINGTON

ACLU of Washington
705 Second Avenue
Suite 300
Seattle, WA 98104
(206) 624-2180

Northwest Feminists
  Anti-Censorship Taskforce
NW/FACT #275
12345 Lake City Way Northeast
Seattle, WA 98125
(206) 292-1159
e-mail: nw-fact@aa.net

Washington Coalition Against
  Censorship
6548 Jones Avenue Northwest
Seattle, WA 98117

Washington Education Association
33434 8th Avenue South
Federal Way, WA 98003

Washington Library Association
4016-1st Avenue NE
Seattle, WA 98105
(206) 545-1529

Washington Music Industry
  Coalition

300 Lenora Street #P120
Seattle, WA 98121

WEST VIRGINIA

ACLU of West Virginia
P.O. Box 3952
Charleston, WV 25339
(304) 345-9246

West Virginia Library Association
c/o Frederic Glazer, Executive
  Director
West Virginia Library Commission
Science & Cultural Center
Charleston, WV 25305
(304) 558-2041
e-mail: glaserf@wvlc.wvnet.edu

WISCONSIN

ACLU of Wisconsin
207 East Buffalo Street
Suite 325
Milwaukee, WI 53202-5712

(414) 272-4032
e-mail: acluwisc@mail.execpc.com

Wisconsin Intellectual Freedom
  Coalition
4800 Ivywood Trail
McFarland, WI 53558

Wisconsin Library Association
4785 Hayes Road
Madison, WI 53704
(608) 242-2040
e-mail:
martin@milkyway.wils.wisc.edu

WYOMING

ACLU of Wyoming
P.O. Box A
Laramie, WY 82070
(307) 745-4515

Wyoming Library Association
P.O. Box 1387
Cheyenne, WY 82003
(307) 632-7622

PART III

APPENDICES

APPENDIX A

ACRONYMS AND INITIALS

ABA   American Bar Association
ACLU   American Civil Liberties Union
ALA   American Library Association
BBC   British Broadcasting Commission
CIS   Congressional Information Index Service
CIA   Central Intelligence Agency
CQ   Congressional Quarterly
DOE   Department of Energy
EFF   Electronic Frontier Foundation
EFOIA   Electronic Freedom of Information Act
FAIC   Families Against International Censorship
FACT   Feminist Anti-Censorship Task Force
FCC   Federal Communications Commission
FOIA   Freedom of Information Act
GDCS   Government Documents Catalog Service
GPO   Government Publications Office
HUAC   House Un-American Activities Committee
IFIDA   International Film Importers and Distributors of America
MPAA   Motion Picture Association of America
MPPA   Motion Picture Producers and Distributors of America
NAACP   National Association for the Advancement of Colored People
NAAO   National Association of Artists' Organization
NATO   National Association of Theater Owners
NCAC   National Coalition Against Censorship
NCFE   National Committee for Freedom of Expression
NEA   National Endowment for the Arts
NOW   National Organization for Women
OIF   Office for Intellectual Freedom
PICS   Platform for International Content Selection

PMRC   Parents' Music Resource Center
RIAA   Recording Industry Association of America
SLAPPs   Strategic Lawsuits Against Public Participation
TVK   Television Kampuchea
UNESCO   United Nations Educational, Scientific, and Cultural Organization
WWW   World Wide Web

APPENDIX B

GLOSSARY

Alien and Sedition Acts Laws that were enacted to prohibit expression against the government and the armed services.

American Civil Liberties Union (ACLU) An organization formed in 1925 to protect civil liberties, such as freedom of expression and freedom of religion. The ACLU has been active in civil rights litigation.

Areopagitica Full title—"Areopagitica: a speech of Mr. John Milton in 1644 for the library of the unlicenc'd printing, to the Parliament of England." John Milton's famous work in which he attacked Parliament for censorship and advocated that laws of suppression be abandoned.

Bill of Rights The first ten amendments to the United States Constitution. The First Amendment grants the rights to freedom of speech, freedom of the press, freedom of religion, freedom of assembly, and freedom to petition the government.

blasphemy A statement that contradicts the truth of Christianity and its teachings or the existence of God.

clear and present danger test A criterion to determine whether speech is protected under the First Amendment. First enunciated by Justice Oliver Wendell Holmes in the U.S. Supreme Court case *Schenck v. United States*, these words have been frequently used when discussing First Amendment issues.

cold war The tension between the United States and Russia after World War II. The cold war caused a red scare, which severely suppressed expression and led to unwarranted charges of disloyalty against thousands.

fiduciary duty A duty of utmost trust.

flag desecration The intentional mutilation or destruction of a flag.

Freedom of Information Act (FOIA) Enacted in 1966, this act granted the right to access information that had been classified as secret by the government; however, the act did not grant the right to access all government information.

167

gag law A statute requiring prior approval before information may be printed or broadcast.

hate speech Spoken expression that denigrates another. Hate speech is generally expression against a minority.

House Committee on Un-American Activities (HUAC) A government committee that investigated people for Communist ties or other activities it deemed disloyal.

jammed broadcasts Radio transmissions barred from reception; a common practice in the Soviet Union prior to *glasnost*.

libel Written or pictorial communication that injures a person by damaging the person's character or exposing the person to ridicule.

Magna Carta A charter enacted to limit the power of the king of England and grant rights to citizens. Signed into law in 1215 by King John of England, the Magna Carta signaled the beginning of the end of despotic rule.

Motion Picture Producers and Distributors of America (MPPA) The regulatory organization formed by the motion picture industry in 1922. Recognizing that federal regulation was imminent, the motion picture industry formed its own organization. It put into place the Productions Code and later, a rating system.

obscenity Sexual representations that are not permitted by law because of their lewd or disgusting nature. Each state has its own obscenity laws, and obscenity is judged by local community standards.

Parliament The British legislative body; includes the House of Lords and the House of Commons.

Pentagon Papers, The A seven-thousand-page document detailing deception that lead to the Vietnam War. The document was prepared at the direction of Robert McNamara, President Johnson's secretary of defense. Contents of the *Pentagon Papers*, a classified document, were leaked to the press by Daniel Ellsberg.

pornography Sexual representations that are erotic or lewd. Not all pornography is punishable by law. *Pornography* is a broader term than *obscenity*.

speech code Regulation that specifies rules regarding prohibited speech on campus. Universities enact speech codes in an attempt to quell hate speech.

Star Chamber An early English tribunal where members appointed by the king sat in judgment on accused individuals who were not allowed to have attorneys or trials. Punishment was generally swift and severe. The Star Chamber was abolished in 1641.

symbolic speech Nonverbal expression; symbolic speech is generally afforded the same First Amendment protections as verbal or written expression. Flag-burning and the wearing of armbands are examples of symbolic speech.

Appendix B

v-chip   also known as the anti-violence chip, this device offers the technology to control material received by television.

yellow journalism   Sensational reporting, often without regard to truth or accuracy.

APPENDIX C

FIRST AMENDMENT TO THE UNITED STATES CONSTITUTION

Congress shall make no law respecting an establishment of religion, or prohibiting the free exercise thereof; or abridging the freedom of speech, or of the press; or the right of the people peaceably to assemble, and to petition the Government for a redress of grievances.

APPENDIX D

FLAG DESECRATION
STATUTES AND BILLS

Throughout history, a variety of flag desecration bills have graced the floors of the United States House of Representatives and Senate. The bills and laws included here are considered some of the most important.

FLAG PROTECTION ACT OF 1989
(18 USC SEC. 700)

The Flag Protection Act of 1989 is comprised of that portion of the following United States Code section which appears under "AMENDMENTS". The portion of the code section prior to "AMENDMENTS" was passed in 1968. In the 1990 case *U.S. v. Eichman*, the United States Supreme Court struck down the Flag Protection Act of 1989.
-CITE-
 18 USC Sec. 700
-EXPCITE-
 TITLE 18 - CRIMES AND CRIMINAL PROCEDURE
 PART I - CRIMES
 CHAPTER 33 - EMBLEMS, INSIGNIA, AND NAMES
-HEAD-
 Sec. 700. Desecration of the flag of the United States; penalties
-STATUTE-
 (a) (1) Whoever knowingly mutilates, defaces, physically defiles, burns, maintains on the floor or ground, or tramples upon any flag of the United States shall be fined under this title or imprisoned for not more than one year, or both.

(2) This subsection does not prohibit any conduct consisting of the disposal of a flag when it has became worn or soiled.

(3) As used in this section, the term "flag of the United States" means any flag of the United States, or any part thereof, made of any substance, of any size, in a form that is commonly displayed.

(c) Nothing in this section shall be construed as indicating an intent on the part of Congress to deprive any State, territory, possession, or the Commonwealth of Puerto Rico of jurisdiction over any offense over which it would have jurisdiction in the absence of this section.

(d) (1) An appeal may be taken directly to the Supreme Court of the United States from any interlocutory or final judgment, decree, or order issued by a United States district court ruling upon the constitutionality of subsection (a).

(2) The Supreme Court shall, if it has not previously ruled on the question, accept jurisdiction over the appeal and advance on the docket and expedite to the greatest extent possible.
-SOURCE-
(Added Pub. L. 90–381, Sec. 1, July 5, 1968, 82 Stat. 291; amended Pub. L. 101–131, Sec. 2, 3, Oct. 28, 1989, 103 Stat. 777.)
-MISC1-

AMENDMENTS

1989 - Subsec. (a). Pub. L. 101–131, Sec. 2(a), amended subsec. (a) generally. Prior to amendment, subsec. (a) read as follows: "Whoever knowingly casts contempt upon any flag of the United States by publicly mutilating, defacing, defiling, burning, or trampling upon it shall be fined not more than $1,000 or imprisoned for not more than one year, or both."

Subsec. (b). Pub. L. 101–131, Sec. 2(b), amended subsec. (b) generally. Prior to amendment, subsec. (b) read as follows: "The term 'flag of the United States' as used in this section, shall include any flag, standard colors, ensign, or any picture or representation of either, or of any part or parts of either, made of any substance or represented on any substance, of any size evidently purporting to be either of said flag, standard, color, or ensign of the United States of America, or a picture or a representation of either, upon which shall be shown the colors, the stars and the stripes, in any number of either thereof, or of any part or parts of either, by which the average person seeing the same without deliberation may believe the same to represent the flag, standards, colors, or ensign of the United States of America."

Subsec. (d). Pub. L. 101–131. Sec. 3, added subsec. (d).

Censorship

Mr. CALLAHAN, Mr. CALVERT, Mr. CAMP, Mr. CANADY of Florida, Mr. CHABOT, Mr. CHAMBLISS, Mrs. CHENOWETH, Mr. CHRISTENSEN, Mr. CHRYSLER, Mrs. CLAYTON, Mr. CLEMENT, Mr. COBLE, Mr. COBURN, Mr. COLLINS of Georgia, Mr. COMBEST, Mr. COOLEY, Mr. COSTELLO, Mr. COX of California, Mr. CRAMER, Mr. CRANE, Mr. CRAPO, Mr. CREMEANS, Mrs. CUBIN, Mr. CUNNINGHAM, Ms. DANNER, Mr. DAVIS, Mr. DE LA GARZA, Mr. DEAL of Georgia, Mr. DELAY, Mr. DIAZ-BALART, Mr. DICKEY, Mr. DOOLITTLE, Mr. DORNAN, Mr. DOYLE, Mr. DREIER, Mr. DUNCAN, Ms. DUNN of Washington, Mr. EHRLICH, Mr. EMERSON, Mr. ENGLISH of Pennsylvania, Mr. ENSIGN, Mr. EVERETT, Mr. FAWELL, Mr. FIELDS of Texas, Mr. FLANAGAN, Mr. FOLEY, Mr. FORBES, Mrs. FOWLER, Mr. FOX of Pennsylvania, Mr. FRANKS of Connecticut, Mr. FRANKS of New Jersey, Mr. FRELINGHUYSEN, Mr. FRISA, Mr. FUNDERBURK, Mr. GALLEGLY, Mr. GANSKE, Mr. PETE GEREN of Texas, Mr. GILMAN, Mr. GOODLATTE, Mr. GOODLING, Mr. GOSS, Mr. GRAHAM, Mr. GENE GREEN of Texas, Mr. GUNDERSON, Mr. GUTKNECHT, Mr. HALL of Texas, Mr. HANCOCK, Mr. HANSEN, Mr. HASTERT, Mr. HASTINGS of Washington, Mr. HAYWORTH, Mr. HEFLEY, Mr. HEFNER, Mr. HEINEMAN, Mr. HERGER, Mr. HILLEARY, Mr. HOBSON, Mr. HOLDEN, Mr. HORN, Mr. HOSTETTLER, Mr. HUNTER, Mr. HUTCHINSON, Mr. HYDE, Mr. ISTOOK, Mr. JACOBS, Mr. JEFFERSON, Mr. JOHNSON of South Dakota, Mr. SAM JOHNSON of Texas, Mr. JONES, Mr. KASICH, Mrs. KELLY, Mr. KING, Mr. KINGSTON, Mr. KNOLLENBERG, Mr. LaHOOD, Mr. LARGENT, Mr. LATHAM, Mr. LaTOURETTE, Mr. LAUGHLIN, Mr. LAZIO of New York, Mr. LEWIS of Kentucky, Mr. LIGHTFOOT, Mr. LINDER, Mr. LIPINSKI, Mr. LIVINGSTON, Mr. LoBIONDO, Mr. LONGLEY, Mr. LUCAS, Mr. MANTON, Mr. MANZULLO, Mr. MARTINEZ, Mr. MARTINI, Mr. MASCARA, Mr. McCOLLUM, Mr. McCRERY, Mr. McDADE, Mr. McHUGH, Mr. McINNIS, Mr. McINTOSH, Mr. McKEON, Mr. McNULTY, Mr. MENENDEZ, Mr. METCALF, Mrs. MEYERS of Kansas, Mr. MICA, Ms. MOLINARI, Mr. MOORHEAD, Mr. MURTHA, Mr. MYERS of Indiana, Mrs. MYRICK, Mr. NETHERCUTT, Mr. NEUMANN, Mr. NEY, Mr. NORWOOD, Mr. NUSSLE, Mr. ORTIZ, Mr. OXLEY, Mr. PACKARD, Mr. PALLONE, Mr. PARKER, Mr. PAXON, Mr. PAYNE of Virginia, Mr. PETERSON of Minnesota, Mr. PICKETT, Mr. POMBO, Mr. POMEROY, Mr. QUILLEN, Mr. QUINN, Mr. RADANOVICH, Mr. RAHALL, Mr. RAMSTAD, Mr. RIGGS, Mr. ROBERTS, Mr. ROGERS, Mr. ROSE, Mr. ROTH, Mrs. ROUKEMA, Mr. ROYCE, Mr. SALMON, Mr. SAXTON, Mr. SCARBOROUGH, Mr. SCHAEFER, Mrs. SEASTRAND, Mr. SENSENBRENNER, Mr. SCHIFF, Mr. SHUSTER, Mr. SISISKY, Mr. SKEEN, Mr. SKELTON, Mr. SMITH of New Jersey, Mrs. SMITH of Washington, Mr. SOUDER, Mr. SPENCE, Mr. STEARNS, Mr. STOCKMAN, Mr. STUMP,

Mr. STUPAK, Mr. TALENT, Mr. TATE, Mr. TAUZIN, Mr. TAYLOR of Mississippi, Mr. TAYLOR of North Carolina, Mr. TEJEDA, Mr. THOMAS, Mr. THORNBERRY, Mrs. THURMAN, Mr. TIAHRT, Mr. TORKILDSEN, Mr. TOWNS, Mr. TRAFICANT, Mr. TUCKER, Mr. UPTON, Mr. VOLK-MER, Mrs. VUCANOVICH, Mrs. WALDHULTZ, Mr. WALSH, Mr. WAMP, Mr. WATTS of Oklahoma, Mr. WELDON of Florida, Mr. WELDON of Pennsylvania, Mr. WELLER, Mr. WHITFIELD, Mr. WICKER, Mr. WIL-SON, Mr. WISE, Mr. WOLF, Mr. YOUNG of Alaska, Mr. YOUNG of Florida, Mr. ZELIFF, and Mr. ZIMMER) introduced the following joint resolution; which was referred to Committee on the Judiciary.

JOINT RESOLUTION

Proposing an amendment to the Constitution of the United States authorizing the Congress and the States to prohibit the physical desecration of the flag of the United States.

Resolved by the Senate and House of Representatives of the United States of America in Congress assembled, (two-thirds of each House concurring therein), That the following article is proposed as an amendment to the Constitution of the United States, which shall be valid to all intents and purposes as part of the Constitution when ratified by the legislatures of three-fourths of the several States within seven years after the date of its submission for ratification:

"ARTICLE—

"The Congress and the States shall have power to prohibit the physical desecration of the flag of the United States.".

HOUSE JOINT RESOLUTION 54 (1997)

By 1997, the House had introduced another flag desecration bill.

105TH CONGRESS
1ST SESSION

H. J. RES. 54

Proposing an amendment to the Constitution of the United States authorizing the Congress to prohibit the physical desecration of the flag of the United States.

Censorship

IN THE HOUSE OF REPRESENTATIVES

FEBRUARY 13, 1997

Mr. SOLOMON (for himself, Mr. LIPINSKI, Mr. ANDREWS, Mr. ARCHER, Mr. BACHUS, Mr. BAKER, Mr. BALDACCI, Mr. BALLENGER, Mr. BARCIA, Mr. BARR of Georgia, Mr. BARRETT of Nebraska, Mr. BARTLETT of Maryland, Mr. BARTON of Texas, Mr. BASS, Mr. BATEMAN, Mr. BEREUTER, Mr. BILBRAY, Mr. BILIRAKIS, Mr. BISHOP, Mr. BLILEY, Mr. BLUNT, Mr. BOEHLERT, Mr. BOEHNER, Mr. BONO, Mr. BOSWELL, Mr. BRYANT, Mr. BUNNING, Mr. BURR of North Carolina, Mr. BURTON of Indiana, Mr. BUYER, Mr. CALLAHAN, Mr. CAMP, Mr. CANADY of Florida, Mr. CANNON, Mr. CHABOT, Mr. CHRISTENSEN, Mr. COBLE, Mr. COBURN, Mr. COLLINS, Mr. COMBEST, Mr. COX of California, Mr. CRAMER, Mr. CRANE, Mr. CRAPO, Mrs. CUBIN, Mr. CUNNINGHAM, Ms. DANNER, Mr. DAVIS of Virginia, Mr. DEAL of Georgia, Mr. DELAY, Mr. DIAZ-BALART, Mr. DICKEY, Mr. DOOLEY of California, Mr. DOYLE, Mr. DUNCAN, Mr. EDWARDS, Mrs. EMERSON, Mr. ENGLISH of Pennsylvania, Mr. ENSIGN, Mr. EHRLICH, Mr. EVERETT, Mr. EWING, Mr. FOLEY, Mr. FORBES, Mrs. FOWLER, Mr. FOX of Pennsylvania, Mr. FRANKS of New Jersey, Mr. FRELINGHUYSEN, Mr. FROST, Mr. GALLEGLY, Mr. GANSKE, Mr. GIBBONS, Mr. GILLMOR, Mr. GOODE, Mr. GOODLATTE, Mr. GOSS, Mr. GRAHAM, Ms. GRANGER, Mr. GREEN, Mr. GUTKNECHT, Mr. HALL of Texas, Mr. HAMILTON, Mr. HANSEN, Mr. HASTERT, Mr. HASTINGS of Washington, Mr. HAYWORTH, Mr. HEFLEY, Mr. HERGER, Mr. HILL, Mr. HILLEARY, Mr. HINOJOSA, Mr. HOLDEN, Mr. HORN, Mr. HOSTETTLER, Mr. HULSHOF, Mr. HUNTER, Mr. HUTCHINSON, Mr. HYDE, Mr. JEFFERSON, Mr. JENKINS, Mr. JOHN, Mr. SAM JOHNSON of Texas, Mrs. KELLY, Mrs. KENNELLY of Connecticut, Mr. KIM, Mr. KING, Mr. KINGSTON, Mr. KNOLLENBERG, Mr. LAHOOD, Mr. LARGENT, Mr. LATHAM, Mr. LATOURETTE, Mr. LINDER, Mr. LIVINGSTON, Mr. LOBIONDO, Mr. LUCAS of Oklahoma, Mr. MALONEY of Connecticut, Mr. MANTON, Mr. MANZULLO, Mr. MARTINEZ, Mr. MASCARA, Mr. MCCOLLUM, Mr. MCCRERY, Mr. MCDADE, Mr. MCHUGH, Mr. MCINNIS, Mr. MCINTOSH, Mr. MCKEON, Mr. MCNULTY, Mr. MENENDEZ, Mr. METCALF, Ms. MOLINARI, Mr. MURTHA, Mrs. MYRICK, Mr. NETHERCUTT, Mr. NEUMANN, Mr. NEY, Mr. NORWOOD, Mr. NUSSLE, Mr. ORTIZ, Mr. OXLEY, Mr. PACKARD, Mr. PALLONE, Mr. PAPPAS, Mr. PARKER, Mr. PAXON, Mr. PETERSON of Minnesota, Mr. PICKERING, Mr. PICKETT, Mr. PITTS, Mr. QUINN, Mr. RADANOVICH, Mr. RAHALL, Mr. RAMSTAD, Mr. REYES, Mr. RIGGS, Mr. RILEY, Mr. ROEMER, Mr. ROGAN,

Mr. ROGERS, Mr. ROYCE, Mr. ROTHMAN, Mr. SANDLIN, Mr. SAXTON, Mr. DAN SCHAEFER of Colorado, Mr. BOB SCHAFFER of Colorado, Mr. SCHIFF, Mr. SENSEN-BRENNER, Mr. SHIMKUS, Mr. SHUSTER, Mr. SISISKY, Mr. SKEEN, Mr. SKELTON, Mr. SMITH of New Jersey, Mr. SMITH of Oregon, Mrs. SMITH of Washington, Mr. SOUDER, Mr. SPENCE, Mr. STEARNS, Mr. STENHOLM, Mr. STUMP, Mr. TALENT, Mr. TAYLOR of North Carolina, Mr. THOMAS, Mrs. THURMAN, Mr. TIAHRT, Mr. TOWNS, Mr. TRAFICANT, Mr. TURNER, Mr. WALSH, Mr. WAMP, Mr. WATKINS, Mr. WATTS of Oklahoma, Mr. WELDON of Florida, Mr. WELDON of Pennsylvania, Mr. WELLER, Mr. WHITFIELD, Mr. WISE, Mr. WOLF, Mr. WYNN, Mr. YOUNG of Alaska, and Mr. YOUNG of Florida) introduced the following joint resolution; which was referred to the Committee on the Judiciary

JOINT RESOLUTION

Proposing an amendment to the Constitution of the United States authorizing the Congress to prohibit the physical desecration of the flag of the United States.

Resolved by the Senate and House of Representatives of the United States of America in Congress assembled (two-thirds of each House concurring therein), That the following article is proposed as an amendment to the Constitution of the United States, which shall be valid to all intents and purposes as part of the Constitution when ratified by the legislatures of three-fourths of the several States within seven years after the date of its submission for ratification:

"ARTICLE—

"The Congress shall have power to prohibit the physical desecration of the flag of the United States.".

APPENDIX E

COMMUNICATIONS DECENCY ACT

TITLE V - BROADCAST OBSCENITY AND VIOLENCE

Subtitle A - Obscene, Harassing, and Wrongful Utilization of Telecommunications Facilities

SEC. 501. SHORT TITLE.

This title may be cited as the "Communications Decency Act of 1995".

SEC. 502. OBSCENE OR HARASSING USE OF TELECOMMUNICATIONS FACILITIES UNDER THE COMMUNICATIONS ACT OF 1934.

Section 223 (47 U.S.C. 223) is amended–

(1) by striking subsection (a) and inserting in lieu thereof:

"(a) Whoever–

"(1) in interstate or foreign communications–

"(A) by means of a telecommunications device knowingly–

"(i) makes, creates, or solicits, and

"(ii) initiates the transmission of, any comment, request, suggestion, proposal, image, or other communication which is obscene, lewd, lascivious, filthy, or indecent, with intent to annoy, abuse, threaten, or harass another person;

"(B) by means of a telecommunications device knowingly–

"(i) makes, creates, or solicits, and

178

"(ii) initiates the transmission of, any comment, request, suggestion, proposal, image, or other communication which is obscene or indecent knowing that the recipient of the communication is under 18 years of age regardless of whether the maker of such communication placed the call or initiated the communication;

"(C) makes a telephone call or utilizes a telecommunications device, whether or not conversation or communication ensues, without disclosing his identity and with intent to annoy, abuse, threaten, or harass any person at the called number or who receives the communication;

"(D) makes or causes the telephone of another repeatedly or continuously to ring, with intent to harass a person at the called number; or

"(E) makes repeated telephone calls or repeatedly initiates communication with a telecommunications device, during which conversation or communication ensues, solely to harass any person at the called number or who receives the communication;

"(2) knowingly permits a telecommunications facility under his control to be used for any activity prohibited by paragraph (1) with the intent that it be used for such activity,

shall be fined under title 18, United States Code, or imprisoned not more than two years, or both."; and

(2) by adding at the end the following new sub sections:

"(d) Whoever—

"(1) in interstate or foreign communications knowingly–

"(A) uses an interactive computer service to send to a specific person or persons under 18 years of age, or

"(B) uses any interactive computer service to display in a manner available to a person under 18 years of age,

any comment, request suggestion, proposal, image, or other communication that, in context, depicts or describes, in terms patently offensive as measured by contemporary community standards, sexual or excretory activities or organs, regardless of whether the user of such service placed the call or initiated the communication; or

"(2) knowingly permits any telecommunications facility under such person's control to be used for an activity prohibited by paragraph (1) with the intent that it be used for such activity,

shall be fined under title 18, United States Code, or imprisoned not more than two years, or both.

"(e) In addition to any other defenses available by

"(1) No person shall be held to have violated subsection (a) or (d) solely for providing access or connection to or from a facility, system, or network not under that person's control, including transmission, downloading, intermediate storage, access software, or other related capabilities that are incidental to providing such access or connection that does not include the creation of the content of the communication.

"(2) The defenses provided by paragraph (1) of this subsection shall not be applicable to a person who is a conspirator with an entity actively involved in the creation or knowing distribution of communications that violate this section, or who knowingly advertises the availability of such communications.

"(3) The defenses provided in paragraph (1) of this subsection shall not be applicable to a person who provides access or connection to a facility, system, or network engaged in the violation of this section that is owned or controlled by such person.

"(4) No employer shall be held liable under this section for the actions of an employee or agent unless the employee's or agent's conduct is within the scope of his employment or agency and the employer (A) having knowledge of such conduct, authorizes or ratifies such conduct, or (B) recklessly disregards such conduct.

"(5) It is a defense to a prosecution under sub section (a) or (d) that a person–

"(A) has taken in good faith, reasonable, effective, and appropriate actions under the circumstances to restrict or prevent access by minors to a communication specified in such subsections, which may involve any appropriate measures to restrict minors from such communications, including any method which is feasible under available technology; or

"(B) has restricted access to such communication by requiring use of a verified credit card, debit account, adult access code, or adult personal identification number.

"(6) The Commission may describe measures which are reasonable, effective, and appropriate to restrict access to prohibited communications under subsection (d). Nothing in this section authorizes the Commission to enforce, or is intended to provide the Commission with the authority to approve, sanction, or permit, the use of such measures. The Commission has no enforcement authority over the failure to utilize such measures. The Commission shall not endorse specific products relating to such measures. The use of such measures shall be admitted as evidence of good faith efforts for purposes of this paragraph in any action arising under subsection (d). Nothing in this section shall be construed to treat interactive computer services as common carriers or telecommunications carriers.

"(f) (1) No cause of action may be brought in any court or administrative agency against any person on account of any activity that is not in violation of any law punishable by criminal or civil penalty, and that the person has taken in good faith to implement a defense authorized under this section or otherwise to restrict or prevent the transmission of, or access to, a communication specified in this section.

Appendix E

"(2) No State or local government may impose any liability for commercial activities or actions by commercial entities, nonprofit libraries, or institutions of higher education in connection with an activity or action described in subsection (a) (2) or (d) that is inconsistent with the treatment of those activities or actions under this section: Provided, however, That nothing herein shall preclude any State or local government from enacting and enforcing complementary oversight, liability, and regulatory systems, procedures, and requirements, so long as such systems, procedures, and requirements govern only intrastate services and do not result in the imposition of inconsistent rights, duties or obligations on the provision of interstate services, nothing in this subsection shall preclude any State or local government from governing conduct not covered by this section.

"(g) nothing in subsection (a), (d), (e), or (f) or in the defenses to prosecution under (a) or (d) shall be construed to affect or limit the application or enforcement of any other Federal law.

"(h) For purposes of this section–

"(1) The use of the term 'telecommunications device' in this section–

"(A) shall not impose new obligations on broadcasting station licensees and cable operators covered by obscenity and indecency provisions elsewhere in this Act; and

"(B) does not include the use of an inter active computer service.

"(2) The term 'interactive computer service' has the meaning provided in section 230(f) (2)

"(3) The term 'access software' means software (including client or server software) or enabling tools that do not create or provide the content of the communication but that allow a user to do any one or more of the following:

"(A) filter, screen, allow, or disallow content;

"(B) pick, choose, analyze, or digest content; or

"(C) transmit, receive, display, forward, cache, search, subset, organize, reorganize, or translate content.

"(4) The term 'institution of higher education' has the meaning provided in section 1201 of the Higher Education Act of 1965 (20 U.S.C. 1141).

"(5) The term 'library' means a library eligible for participation in State-based plans for funds under title III of the Library Services and Construction Act (20 U.S.C. 355e et seq.).".

SEC. 503. OBSCENE PROGRAMMING ON CABLE TELEVISION,

Secion 639 (47 U.S.C. 559) is amended by striking "not more than $10,000" and inserting "under title 18, United States Code,".

SEC. 504. SCRAMBLING OF CABLE CHANNELS FOR NONSUBSCRIBERS.

Part IV of title VI (47 U.S.C. 551 et seq.) is amended by adding at the end the following:

SEC. 640. SCRAMBLING OF, CABLE CHANNELS FOR NONSUB-SCRIBERS.

"(a) SUBSCRIBER REQUEST.–Upon request by a cable service subscriber, a cable operator shall, without charge, fully-scramble or otherwise fully block the audio and video portion of each channel carrying such programming so that one not a subscriber does not receive it.

"(b) DEFINITION.–As used in this section, the term 'scramble' means to rearrange the content of the signal of the programming so that the program cannot be viewed or heard in an understandable manner.".

SEC. 505. SCRAMBLING OF SEXUALLY EXPLICIT ADULT VIDEO SERVICE PROGRAMMING.

(a) REQUIREMENT.–Part IV of title I (47 U.S.C. 551 et seq.), as amended by this Act, is further amended by adding at the end the following:

"SEC. 641. SCRAMBLING OF SEXUALLY EXPLICIT ADULT VIDEO SERVICE PROGRAMMING.

"(a) REQUIREMENT.–In providing sexually explicit adult programming or other programming that is indecent on any channel of its service primarily dedicated to sexually-oriented programming, a multichannel video programming distributor shall fully scramble or otherwise fully block the video and audio portion of such channel so that one not a subscriber to such channel or programming does not receive it.

"(b) IMPLEMENTATION.–Until a multichannel video programming distributor complies with the requirement set forth in subsection (a), the distributor shall limit the access of children to the programming referred to in that subsection by not providing such program during the hours of the day (as determined by the Commission) when a significant number of children are likely to view it.

"(c) DEFINITION.–As used in this section, the term 'scramble' means to rearrange the content of the signal of the programming so that the programming cannot be viewed or heard in an understandable manner.".

"(b) EFFECTIVE DATE.–The amendment made by subsection (a) shall take effect 30 days after the date of the enactment of this Act.

SEC. 606. CABLE OPERATOR REFUSAL TO CARRY CERTAIN PROGRAMS.

(a) PUBLIC, EDUCATION, AND GOVERNMENTAL CHANNELS.–Section 611(e) (47 U.S.C. 531(e)) is amended by inserting before the period the following: ", except a cable operator may refuse to transmit any public access program or portion of a public access program which contains obscenity, indecency, or nudity".

(b) CABLE CHANNELS FOR COMMERCIAL USE.–Section 612(c) (2) (47 U.S.C. 532(c) (2)) is amended by striking "an operator" and inserting "a cable operator may refuse to transmit any leased access program or portion of a leased access program which contains obscenity, indecency, or nudity and".

SEC. 507. CLARIFICATION OF CURRENT LAWS REGARDING COMMUNICATION OF OBSCENE MATERIALS THROUGH THE USE OF COMPUTERS.

(a) IMPORTATION OR TRANSPORTATION.–Section 1462 of title 18, United States Code, is amended–

(1) in the first undesignated paragraph, by inserting "or interactive computer service (as defined in section 230(f) (2) of the Communications Act of 1934)" after "carrier"; and

(2) in the second undesignated paragraph–

(A) by inserting "or receives," after "takes";

(B) by inserting "or interactive computer service (as defined in section 230(f)(2) of the Communications Act of 1934)" after "common carrier"; and

(C) by inserting "or importation" after "carriage".

(b) TRANSPORTATION FOR PURPOSES OF SALE OR DISTRI-BUTION.–The first undesignated paragraph of section 1465 of title 18, United States Code, is amended–

(1) by striking "transports in" and inserting "transports or travels in, or uses a facility or means of,";

(2) by inserting "or an interactive computer service (as defined in section 230(f) (2) of the Communications Act of 1934) in or affecting such commerce" after "foreign commerce" the first place it appears;

(3) by striking ", or knowingly travels in" and all that follows through "obscene material in inter state or foreign commerce," and inserting "of".

(c) INTERPRETATION.–The amendments made by this section are clarifying and shall not be interpreted to limit or repeal any prohibition contained in sections 1462 and 1465 of title 18, United States Code, before such amendment, under the rule established in United States v. Alpers, 338 U.S. 680 (1950).

SEC. 508. COERCION AND ENTICEMENT OF MINORS.

Section 2422 of title 18, United States Code, is amended–

(1) by inserting "(a)" before "Whoever knowingly"; and

(2) by adding at the end the following:

"(b) Whoever, using any facility or means of inter state or foreign commerce, including the mail, or within the special maritime and territorial jurisdiction of the United States, knowingly persuades, induces, entices, or coerces any individual who has not attained the age of 18 years to engage in prostitution or any sexual act for which person may be criminally prosecuted, or attempts to do so shall be fined under this title or imprisoned not more than 10 years, or both."

SEC. 509. ONLINE FAMILY EMPOWERMENT.

Title II of the Communications Act of 1934 (47 U.S.C. 201 et seq.) is amended by adding at the end the following new section:

"SEC. 230. PROTECTION FOR PRIVATE BLOCKING AND SCREENING OF OFFENSIVE MATERIAL

"(a) FINDINGS.–The Congress finds the following:

"(1) The rapidly developing array of Internet and other interactive computer services available to individual Americans represent an extraordinary advance in the availability of educational and informational resources to our citizens.

"(2) These services offer users a great degree of control over the information that they receive, as well as the potential for even greater control in the future as technology develops.

"(3) The Internet and other interactive computer services offer a forum for a true diversity of political discourse, unique opportunities for cultural development, and myriad avenues for intellectual activity.

"(4) The Internet and other interactive computer services have flourished, to the benefit of all Americans with a minimum of government regulation.

"(5) Increasingly Americans are relying on interactive media for a variety of political, educational, cultural, and entertainment services.

"(b) POLICY.–It is the policy of the United States–

"(1) to promote the continued development of the Internet and other interactive computer services and other interactive media;

"(2) to preserve the vibrant and competitive free market that presently exists for the Internet and other interactive computer services, unfettered by Federal or State regulation;

"(3) to encourage the development of technologies which maximize user control over what information is received by individuals, families, and schools who use the Internet and other interactive computer services;

"(4) to remove disincentives for the development and utilization of blocking and filtering technologies that empower parents to restrict their children's access to objectionable or inappropriate online material; and

"(5) to ensure vigorous enforcement of Federal criminal laws to deter and punish trafficking in obscenity, stalking, and harassment by-means of computer.

"(c) PROTECTION FOR GOOD SAMARITAN BLOCKING AND SCREENING OF OFFENSIVE MATERIAL.–

"(1) TREATMENT OF PUBLISHER OR SPEAKER.–No provider or user of an interactive computer service shall be treated as the publisher or speaker of any information provided by another information content provider.

"(2) CIVIL LIABILITY.–No provider or user of an interactive computer service shall be held liable on account of–

"(A) any action voluntarily taken in good faith to restrict access to or availability of material that the provider or user considers to be obscene, lewd, lascivious, filthy, excessively violent, harassing, or otherwise objectionable, whether or not such material is constitutionally protected; or

"(B) any action taken to enable or make available to information content providers or others the technical means to restrict access to material described in paragraph (1).

"(d) EFFECT ON OTHER LAWS.–

"(1) NO EFFECT ON CRIMINAL LAW.–Nothing in this section shall be construed to impair the enforcement of section 223 of this Act, chapter 71 (relating to obscenity) or 110 (relating to exploitation of children) of title 18, United States Code, or any other Federal criminal statute.

"(2) NO EFFECT ON INTELLECTUAL PROPERTY LAW.–Nothing in this section shall be construed to limit or expand any law pertaining to intellectual property.

"(3) STATE LAW.–Nothing in this section shall be construed to prevent any State from enforcing any State law that is consistent with this section. No cause of action may be brought and no liability may be imposed under any State or local law that is inconsistent with this section.

"(4) NO EFFECT ON COMMUNICATIONS PRIVACY LAW.–Nothing in this section shall be construed to limit the application of the Electronic Communications Privacy Act of 1986 or any of the amendments made by such Act, or any similar State law.

"(f) DEFINITIONS.–As used in this section:

"(1) INTERNET.–The term 'Internet' means the international computer network of both Federal and non-Federal interoperable packet switched data networks.

"(2) INTERACTIVE COMPUTER SERVICE.–The term 'interactive computer service' means an information service, system, or access software provider that provides or enables computer access by multiple users to a computer server, including specifically a service or system that provides access to the Internet and such systems operated or services offered by libraries or educational institutions.

"(3) INFORMATION CONTENT PROVIDER.–The term 'information content provider' means any person or entity that is responsible, in whole or in part, for the creation or development of information provided through the Internet or any other interactive computer service.

"(4) ACCESS SOFTWARE PROVIDER.–The term 'access software provider' means a provider of software (including client or server software), or enabling tools that do any one or more of the following:

"(A) filter, screen, allow, or disallow content;

"(B) pick, choose, analyze, or digest content; or

"(C) transmit, receive, display, forward, cache, search, subset, organize, reorganize, or translate content."

APPENDIX F

Electronic Freedom of Information Act Amendments of 1996 (EFOIA)

SECTION 1. SHORT TITLE.

This Act may be cited as the 'Electronic Freedom of Information Act Amendments of 1996'.

SEC. 2. FINDINGS AND PURPOSES.

(a) FINDINGS–The Congress finds that–

(1) the purpose of section 552 of title 5, United States Code, popularly known as the Freedom of Information Act, is to require agencies of the Federal Government to make certain agency information available for public inspection and copying and to establish and enable enforcement of the right of any person to obtain access to the records of such agencies, subject to statutory exemptions, for any public or private purpose;

(2) since the enactment of the Freedom of Information Act in 1966, and the amendments enacted in 1974 and 1986, the Freedom of Information Act has been a valuable means through which any person can learn how the Federal Government operates;

(3) the Freedom of Information Act has led to the disclosure of waste, fraud, abuse, and wrongdoing in the Federal Government;

(4) the Freedom of Information Act has led to the identification of unsafe consumer products, harmful drugs, and serious health hazards;

(5) Government agencies increasingly use computers to conduct agency business and to store publicly valuable agency records and information; and

(6) Government agencies should use new technology to enhance public access to agency records and information.

(b) PURPOSES–The purpose of this Act are to–

(1) foster democracy by ensuring public access to agency records and information;

(2) improve public access to agency records and information;

(3) ensure agency compliance with statutory time limits; and

(4) maximize the usefulness of agency records and information collected, maintained, used, retained, and disseminated by the Federal Government.

SEC. 3. APPLICATION OF REQUIREMENTS TO ELECTRONIC FORMAT

Section 552(f) of title 5, United States Code, is amended to read as follows:

'(f) For purposes of this section, the term–

'(1) 'agency' as defined in section 551(1) of this title includes any executive department, military department, Government corporation, Government controlled corporation, or other establishment in the executive branch of the Government (including the Executive Office of the President), or any independent regulatory agency; and

'(2) 'record' and any other term used in this section in reference to information includes any information that would be an agency record subject to the requirements of this section when maintained by an agency in any format, including an electronic format.'.

SEC. 4. INFORMATION MADE AVAILABLE IN ELECTRONIC FORMAT AND INDEXATION OF RECORDS.

Section 552(a)(2) of title 5, United States Code, is amended–

(1) in the second sentence, by striking 'or staff manual or instruction' and inserting 'staff manual, instruction, or copies of records referred to in subparagraph (D)';

(2) by inserting before the period at the end of the third sentence the following: ', and the extent of such deletion shall be indicated on the portion of the record which is made available or published, unless including that indication would harm an interest protected by the exemption in subsection (b) under which the deletion is made';

(3) by inserting after the third sentence the following: 'If technically feasible, the extent of the deletion shall be indicated at the place in the record where the deletion was made.';

(4) in subparagraph (B), by striking 'and' after the semicolon;

(5) by inserting after subparagraph (C) the following:

'(D) copies of all records, regardless of form or format, which have been released to any person under paragraph (3) and which, because of the nature of their subject matter, the agency determines have become or are likely to become the subject of subsequent requests for substantially the same records; and

'(E) a general index of the records referred to under subparagraph (D);';

(6) by inserting after the fifth sentence the following: 'Each agency shall make the index referred to in subparagraph (E) available by computer telecommunications by December 31, 1999.'; and

(7) by inserting after the first sentence the following: 'For records created on or after November 1, 1996, within one year after such date, each agency shall make such records available, including by computer telecommunications or, if computer telecommunications means have not been established by the agency, by other electronic means.'.

SEC. 5. HONORING FORM OR FORMAT REQUESTS.

Section 552(a)(3) of title 5, United States Code, is amended–

(1) by inserting '(A)' after '(3)';

(2) by striking '(A)' the second place it appears and inserting '(i)';

(3) by striking '(B)' and inserting '(ii)'; and

(4) by adding at the end the following new subparagraphs:

'(B) In making any record available to a person under this paragraph, an agency shall provide the record in any form or format requested by the person if the record is readily reproducible by the agency in that form or format. Each agency shall make reasonable efforts to maintain its records in forms or formats that are reproducible for purposes of this section.

'(C) In responding under this paragraph to a request for records, an agency shall make reasonable efforts to search for the records in electronic form or format, except when such efforts would significantly interfere with the operation of the agency's automated information system.

'(D) For purposes of this paragraph, the term 'search' means to review, manually or by automated means, agency records for the purpose of locating those records which are responsive to a request.'.

SEC. 6. STANDARD FOR JUDICIAL REVIEW.

Section 552(a)(4)(B) of title 5, United States Code, is amended by adding at the end the following new sentence: 'In addition to any other matters to which a court accords substantial weight, a court shall accord substantial weight to an affidavit of an agency concerning the agency's determination as to technical feasibility under paragraph (2)(C) and subsection (b) and reproducibility under paragraph (3)(B).'.

SEC. 7. ENSURING TIMELY RESPONSE TO REQUESTS.

(a) MULTITRACK PROCESSING–Section 552(a)(6) of title 5, United States Code, is amended by adding at the end the following new subparagraph:

'(D)(i) Each agency may promulgate regulations, pursuant to notice and receipt of public comment, providing for multitrack processing of requests for records based on the amount of work or time (or both) involved in processing requests.

'(ii) Regulations under this subparagraph may provide a person making a request that does not qualify for the fastest multitrack processing an opportunity to limit the scope of the request in order to qualify for faster processing.

'(iii) This subparagraph shall not be considered to affect the requirement under subparagraph (C) to exercise due diligence.'.

(b) UNUSUAL CIRCUMSTANCES–Section 552(a)(6)(B) of title 5, United States Code, is amended to read as follows:

'(B)(i) In unusual circumstances as specified in this subparagraph, the time limits prescribed in either clause (i) or clause (ii) of subparagraph (A) may be extended by written notice to the person making such request setting forth the unusual circumstances for such extension and the date on which a determination is expected to be dispatched. No such notice shall specify a date that would result in an extension for more than ten working days, except as provided in clause (ii) of this subparagraph.

'(ii) With respect to a request for which a written notice under clause (i) extends the time limits prescribed under clause (i) of subparagraph (A), the agency shall notify the person making the request if the request cannot be processed within the time limit specified in that clause and shall provide the person an opportunity to limit the scope of the request so that it may be processed within that time limit or an opportunity to arrange with the agency an alternative time frame for processing the request or a modified request. Refusal by the person to reasonably modify the request or arrange such an alternative time frame shall be considered as a factor in determining whether exceptional circumstances exist for purposes of subparagraph (C).

'(iii) As used in this subparagraph, 'unusual circumstances' means, but only to the extent reasonably necessary to the proper processing of the particular requests—

'(I) the need to search for and collect the requested records from field facilities or other establishments that are separate from the office processing the request;

'(II) the need to search for, collect, and appropriately examine a voluminous amount of separate and distinct records which are demanded in a single request; or

'(III) the need for consultation, which shall be conducted with all practicable speed, with another agency having a substantial interest in the determination of the request or among two or more components of the agency having substantial subject-matter interest therein.

'(iv) Each agency may promulgate regulations, pursuant to notice and receipt of public comment, providing for the aggregation of certain requests by the same requestor, or by a group of requestors acting in concert, if the agency reasonably believes that such requests actually constitute a single request, which would otherwise satisfy the unusual circumstances specified in this subparagraph, and the requests involve clearly related matters. Multiple requests involving unrelated matters shall not be aggregated.'.

(c) EXCEPTIONAL CIRCUMSTANCES–Section 552(a)(6)(C) of title 5, United States Code, is amended by inserting '(i)' after '(C)', and by adding at the end the following new clauses:

'(ii) For purposes of this subparagraph, the term 'exceptional circumstances' does not include a delay that results from a predictable agency workload of requests under this section, unless the agency demonstrates reasonable progress in reducing its backlog of pending requests.

SEC. 8. TIME PERIOD FOR AGENCY CONSIDERATION OF REQUESTS.

(a) EXPEDITED PROCESSING–Section 552(a)(6) of title 5, United States Code (as amended by section 7(a) of this Act), is further amended by adding at the end the following new subparagraph:

'(E)(i) Each agency shall promulgate regulations, pursuant to notice and receipts of public comment, providing for expedited processing of requests for records—

'(I) in cases in which the person requesting the records demonstrates a compelling need; and

'(II) in other cases determined by the agency.

'(ii) Notwithstanding clause (i), regulations under this subparagraph must ensure—

'(I) that a determination of whether to provide expedited processing shall be made, and notice of the determination shall be provided to the person making the request, within 10 days after the date of the request; and

'(II) expeditious consideration of administrative appeals of such determinations of whether to provide expedited processing.

'(iii) An agency shall process as soon as practicable any request for records to which the agency has granted expedited processing under this subparagraph. Agency action to deny or affirm denial of a request for expedited processing pursuant to this subparagraph, and failure by an agency to respond in a timely manner to such a request shall be subject to judicial review under paragraph (4), except that the judicial review shall be based on the record before the agency at the time of the determination.

'(iv) A district court of the United States shall not have jurisdiction to review an agency denial of expedited processing of a request for records after the agency has provided a complete response to the request.

'(v) For purposes of this subparagraph, the term 'compelling need' means—

'(I) that a failure to obtain requested records on an expedited basis under this paragraph could reasonably be expected to pose an imminent threat to the life or physical safety of an individual; or

'(II) with respect to a request made by a person primarily engaged in disseminating information, urgency to inform the public concerning actual or alleged Federal Government activity.

'(vi) A demonstration of a compelling need by a person making a request for expedited processing shall be made by a statement certified by such person to be true and correct to the best of such person's knowledge and belief.'.

(b) EXTENSION OF GENERAL PERIOD FOR DETERMINING WHETHER TO COMPLY WITH A REQUEST–Section 552 (a)(6)(A)(i) of title 5, United States Code, is amended by striking 'ten days' and inserting '20 days'.

(c) ESTIMATION OF MATTER DENIED–Section 552(a)(6) of title 5, United States Code (as amended by section 7 of this Act and subsection (a) of this section), is further amended by adding at the end the following new subparagraph:

'(F) In denying a request for records, in whole or in part, an agency shall make a reasonable effort to estimate the volume of any requested matter the provision of which is denied, and shall provide any such estimate to the person making the request, unless providing such estimate would harm an interest protected by the exemption in subsection (b) pursuant to which the denial is made.'.

SEC. 9. COMPUTER REDACTION.

Section 552(b) of title 5, United States Code, is amended in the matter following paragraph (9) by inserting after the period the following: 'The amount of information deleted shall be indicated on the released portion of the record, unless including that indication would harm an interest protected by the exemption in this subsection under which the deletion is made. If technically feasible, the amount of the information deleted shall be indicated at the place in the record where such deletion is made.'.

SEC. 10. REPORT TO THE CONGRESS.

Section 552(e) of title 5, United States Code, is amended to read as follows:

'(e)(1) On or before February 1 of each year, each agency shall submit to the Attorney General of the United States a report which shall cover the preceding fiscal year and which shall include—

'(A) the number of determinations made by the agency not to comply with requests for records made to such agency under subsection (a) and the reasons for each such determination;

'(B)(i) the number of appeals made by persons under subsection '(a)(6), the result of such appeals, and the reason for the action upon each appeal that results in a denial of information; and

'(ii) a complete list of all statutes that the agency relies upon to authorize the agency to withhold information under subsection (b)(3), a description of whether a court has upheld the decision of the agency to withhold information under each such statute, and a concise description of the scope of any information withheld;

'(C) the number of requests for records pending before the agency as of September 30 of the preceding year, and the median number of days that such requests had been pending before the agency as of that date;

'(D) the number of requests for records received by the agency and the number of requests which the agency processed;

'(E) the median number of days taken by the agency to process different types of requests;

'(F) the total amount of fees collected by the agency for processing requests; and

'(G) the number of full-time staff of the agency devoted to processing requests for records under this section, and the total amount expended by the agency for processing such requests.

'(2) Each agency shall make each such report available to the public including by computer telecommunications, or if computer telecommunications means have not been established by the agency, by other electronic means.

'(3) The Attorney General of the United States shall make each report which has been made available by electronic means available at a single electronic access point. The Attorney General of the United States shall notify the Chairman and ranking minority member of the Committee on Government Reform and Oversight of the House of Representatives and the Chairman and ranking.

'(4) The Attorney General of the United States, in consultation with the Director of the Office of Management and Budget, shall develop reporting and performance guidelines in connection with reports required by this subsection by October 1, 1997, and may establish additional requirements for such reports as the Attorney General determines may be useful.

'(5) The Attorney General of the United States shall submit an annual report on or before April 1 of each calendar year which shall include for the prior calendar year a listing of the number of cases arising under this section, the exemption involved in each case, the disposition of such case, and the cost, fees, and penalties assessed under subparagraphs (E), (F), and (G) of subsection (a)(4). Such report shall also include a description of the efforts undertaken by the Department of Justice to encourage agency compliance with this section.'.

SEC. 11. REFERENCE MATERIALS AND GUIDES.

Section 552 of title 5, United States Code, is amended by adding after subsection (f) the following new subsection:

'(g) The head of each agency shall prepare and make publicly available upon request, reference material or a guide for requesting records or information from the agency, subject to the exemptions in subsection (b), including—

'(1) an index of all major information systems of the agency;

'(2) a description of major information and record locator systems maintained by the agency; and

'(3) a handbook for obtaining various types and categories of public information from the agency pursuant to chapter 35 of title 44, and under this section.'.

SEC. 12. EFFECTIVE DATE.

(a) IN GENERAL–Except as provided in subsection (b), this Act shall take effect 180 days after the date of the enactment of this Act.

(b) PROVISIONS EFFECTIVE ON ENACTMENT–Sections 7 and 8 shall take effect one year after the date of the enactment of this Act.

INDEX

195

Index

Denmark 34, 77
Department of Energy (DOE) 29, 165
Dialogue Concerning the Two Chief World Systems (book) 83
Dinant, David de 69
District of Columbia 154
DOE *see* Department of Energy
draft 12–13, 22–23
draft card mutilation *see* symbolic speech
Du Contrat social (book) 72
Dworkin, Andrea 18–19
Dworkin-MacKinnon laws 18–19

E

EBSCO (automated research system) 94
EFF *see* Electronic Frontier Foundation
EFOIA *See* Electronic Freedom of Information Act
Egypt 35
Electric Library (automated research system) 95
Electronic Freedom of Information Act (EFOIA) 28, 39, 165, 187–194
Electronic Frontier Foundation (EFF) 96, 148, 165
Electronic Privacy Information Center 148
Elizabeth I (queen of England) 6, 70
Ellsberg, Daniel 26, 57, 59, 83, 168
Emigrant, The 35

England 5–8, 70–73, 86–87
English Bill of Rights 71
Enlightenment 8
Erasmus, Desiderius 83
Espionage Act of 1917 12, 26, 37, 46–47, 87
Ethiopia 78
executions 45
Exon, James Jr. 31, 83
explosives 30, 32, 40

F

FACT *see* Feminist Anti-Censorship Task Force
Fairness Doctrine 38
Falwell, Jerry 78, 83
Families Against International Censorship 165
Family Shakespeare, The (book) 82
FBI *see* Federal Bureau of Investigation
FCC *see* Federal Communications Commission
FCC Act of 1934 *see* Fairness Doctrine
FCC v. Pacifica 15–16
Federal Anti-Pornography Act of 1873 *see* Comstock Act
Federal Bureau of Investigation (FBI) 28
Federal Communications Commission 15–16, 38, 40–41, 60–61, 75, 77, 78, 82, 96, 165
Federal Communications Commission Regulations on Indecency and Censorship 40–41
Federalists 9–10
feminism 18–20

Feminist Anti-Censorship Task Force (FACT) 88, 165
Feminists for Free Expression 148
fiduciary duty 27, 62, 167
Fifth Amendment (U.S. Constitution) 7
"fighting words" 14, 51
film 16–17, 55–56, 73, 74, 77–78, 93, 146, 149
film ratings 16–17
Filthy Words (monologue) 15, 77, 82
Finley et al. v. National Endowment for the Arts 18, 65–66
First Amendment (U. S. Constitution) 4, 9–11, 14, 18, 21, 24, 26, 35, 39, 46–47, 54–57, 68, 93, 148, 151–154, 160–161, 170
First Amendment Foundation 148
Fitterman, Marilyn 19
Flag Protection Act 23, 171–177
flag desecration *see* symbolic speech
Florida 3, 43, 154
FOIA *see* Freedom of Information Act
"Four Scenes in a Harsh Life" (play) 17
Fox's Libel Act 72
France 9–10, 69–70, 72–73, 84, 87, 97
Frank W. Snepp, III v. United States (1980) 61–62
Franklin, Benjamin 8
Franklin, James 7–8
Freedman v. Maryland (1965) 55–56

197

Index

201